Grimmelshausen the Storyteller

Studies in German Literature, Linguistics, and Culture

General editor James Hardin
(South Carolina)

Alan Menhennet

Grimmelshausen the Storyteller

A Study of the "Simplician" Novels

CAMDEN HOUSE

Copyright © 1997 by
CAMDEN HOUSE, INC.

Published by Camden House, Inc.
Drawer 2025
Columbia, SC 29202 USA

Printed on acid-free paper.
Binding materials are chosen for strength and
durability.

All rights reserved, including the right of reproduction
in electronic or any other form. All rights to this publication
will be vigorously defended.

Printed in the United States of America
First Edition

ISBN: 1–57113–102–7

Library of Congress Cataloging-in-Publication Data

Menhennet, Alan.
    Grimmelshausen the storyteller: a study of the "Simplician"
novels / Alan Menhennet.
      p.   cm. (Studies in German literature, linguistics, and
culture)
    Includes bibliographical references.
    ISBN 1–57113–102–7 (alk. paper)
    1. Grimmelshausen, Hans Jakob Christoph von, 1625–1676—Criticism
and interpretation. I. Title. II. Series: Studies in German
literature, linguistics, and culture (Unnumbered)
PT1732.M43   1997
833' .5—dc21   96–52520
                                                                                   CIP

Contents

Preface	vii
Acknowledgements	ix
References to Grimmelshausen's Works	x
Part One: The Writer's World	1
1: Grimmelshausen and His Age	3
2: Grimmelshausen and Baroque Dualism	28
Part Two: The Simplician Cycle	63
3: *Der abentheurliche Simplicissimus Teutsch*	65
4: Reaction: The *Continuatio*	96
5: Vice and Vitality: The *Ertzbetrügerin Courasche*	119
6: The Soldier's Tale: *Der seltzame Springinsfeld*	141
7: Peace and War: *Das wunderbarliche Vogelnest*	160
8: Squaring the Circle: Simplician Structure	179
Works Consulted	197
Index	205

Preface

THE PURPOSE OF this book is twofold. Firstly, my aim is to provide for English-speaking readers an introduction to a German novelist who deserves to be better known, not least because he repays their expenditure of time and effort by entertaining as well as enlightening them. To that end, I have translated all significant quotations and devoted more space to a general portrait of seventeenth-century Germany and its literary life than might otherwise have been appropriate.

At the same time, I hope to make a contribution to critical debate about Grimmelshausen—one that has some measure of originality. Without wishing to undermine the imposing edifice which has been erected by Grimmelshausen scholarship on the foundations laid by Günther Weydt, to which I am indeed deeply indebted, I would argue that some adjustment of emphasis is necessary if we are not to obscure behind a magnificent baroque structure the quality of vitality and immediacy as a storyteller that makes Grimmelshausen (without any loss of profundity) one of the great German comic novelists. My second major theme, which becomes more prominent as the survey of the Simplician corpus proceeds, is that of the so-called Simplician cycle. I cannot claim to have answered all the questions raised by this issue, but hope to have made some progress towards establishing a sense of coherence within the context of flexibility and mobility that is the essential precondition of the "Simplician manner."

Alan Menhennet
Jesmond, Newcastle upon Tyne
March 1997

Acknowledgements

MY THANKS ARE due to the University of Newcastle upon Tyne for granting me a sabbatical semester to complete the work on this book. I am particularly grateful to Professor Philip Yarrow for his encouragement, and for many helpful suggestions.

A. M.

References to Grimmelshausen's Works

Grimmelshausen's works are cited from the edition *Werke in Einzelausgaben*, R. Tarot, W. Bender, and F. G. Sieveke, eds. (Tübingen: Niemeyer, 1967-). References are given in parentheses, with the relevant abbreviation or short title where appropriate, at the end of the quotation in the text.

The individual works, with their editors, and the abbreviations used to refer to them in the text, are as follows:

Bart-Krieg: see *Kleinere Schriften*

Das wunderbarliche Vogelnest (ed. Tarot, 1970) (=*VN*)

Der abentheurliche Simplicissimus Teutsch nebst Continuatio desselben (ed. Tarot, 1967) (= respectively *ST; Continuatio*)

Der erste Beernhäuter: see *Kleinere Schriften*

Der seltzame Springinsfeld (ed. Sieveke, 1969) (=*Springinsfeld*)

Deß weltberuffenen Simplicissimi Pralerey und Gepräng mit seinem Teutschen Michel (ed. Tarot, 1976) (=*TM*)

Die Verkehrte Welt (ed. Sieveke, 1973)

Dietwalts und Amelinden anmuthige Liebs- und Leids-Beschreibung (ed. Tarot, 1967) (=*DA*)

Galgen Männlin: see Kleinere Schriften

Gauckel-Tasche: see *Kleinere Schriften*

Keuscher Joseph (ed. Bender, 1968) (=*KJ*)

Kleinere Schriften (ed. Tarot, 1973) (=*KS*)

Lebensbeschreibung der Ertzbetrügerin und Landstörtzerin Courasche (ed. Bender, 1967) (=*Courasche*)

Proximus und Lympida (ed. Sieveke, 1967) (=*PL*)

Rathstübel Plutonis (ed. Bender, 1975) (=*RP*)

Satyrischer Pilgram (ed. Bender 1970) (=*SP*)

Simplicianischer Zweyköpffiger Ratio Status (ed. Tarot, 1968) (=*RS*)

Ewigwährender Kalender (ed. K. Haberkamm), Konstanz 1967 (=*EWK*)

Part One:
The Writer's World

1: Grimmelshausen and His Age

Grimmelshausen's Life

THERE IS CONSIDERABLE irony in the fact that a standard life of Grimmelshausen, a writer who not only contemplates life but celebrates its inherent vitality to an extent that is rare in German literature, can probably never be written. Documentary evidence for a biography of Grimmelshausen is often scanty and for a substantial period of his life, practically non-existent.[1] It is clear from what is known or can be reasonably surmised that the general *shape* of his life is reflected in his works, but they form no reliable basis for speculation as to specific detail. As always when dealing with the culture and thought of seventeenth-century Germany, we have to come to terms with the fact that reality is an elusive and ambivalent concept.

The birthplace (Gelnhausen in Hesse, in the vicinity of Hanau and the Spessart) is known; the date of birth is less certain. Johann Jacob Christoph (or Christoffel) *von* Grimmelshausen, as he was later to style himself, was born in either 1621 or 1622. His mother, who had remarried after his father's death, moved away in 1627, while he stayed in Gelnhausen and was presumably brought up by his grandfather Melchior Christoph, who earned his living as a baker and had dropped the aristocratic "von" which the family had once borne. Gelnhausen had a grammar school (*Lateinschule*), which the boy presumably attended and at which he no doubt received a respectable basic education, but in 1634, disaster struck. Gelnhausen, a Protestant town, was sacked and plundered by Imperial soldiers, who had just defeated the Protestants at the battle of Nördlingen, one of the great encounters of the Thirty Years' War, and a battle which features significantly in the novels which we are to examine in the second part of this book.

The next fourteen years or so are shrouded in the dust and smoke of the war, with only occasional glimpses of a shadowy figure who might be our hero. It is likely that he was among the many survivors of the sack of Gelnhausen who took refuge in the nearest fortified Protestant stronghold, Hanau. The garrison there was headed by a Colonel Ramsay, who also appears in *Simplicissimus*. The young Grimmelshausen was in all probability kidnapped, as his Simplicissimus is, by marauding soldiers from an Imperial Croat regiment and forced to act as a groom and to steal food for them. This probably did not last long, and we assume that he was captured by Hessian troops and taken to Kassel some time in 1635. Our next glimpse shows him among the Catholics again, at the siege of Magdeburg in 1636, though in view of his age, presumably not yet participating in the actual fighting. He possibly witnessed the Battle of Wittstock in the same year. From now on, there was at least one element of stability in his life, in that he remained on the Catholic side until the end of the war in 1648 and indeed, became a Catholic himself, though we do not know exactly when. In 1638, we find him in the regiment of dragoons led by Graf Johann Wenzel von Götz, who operated first in Westphalia (where Simplicissimus has many adventures) and then on the Upper Rhine, whither he was sent to defend the fortress of Breisach, in which enterprise he was unsuccessful.

After the defeat of Götz's army, Grimmelshausen entered the service of Hans Reinhard von Schauenburg, who was organising the defence of the important fortress of Offenburg, a town on the River Kinzig a few miles to the southeast of Strasbourg. Grimmelshausen served first as a musketeer, but managed to attract the notice of his superiors and achieved the status of *Schreiber* (clerk) in the Regimental Chancellery under Johannes Witsch, who will have played an important part in helping him to develop his abilities and recover the educational ground he had lost. From this point on, he must have been a voracious reader;[2] at what stage he became a writer must remain a matter of conjecture, but the phenomenal speed at which his oeuvre appeared in the last decade of his life, when he was by no means a man of leisure, suggests that some work, at least, must have been done beforehand.

Grimmelshausen remained in Schauenburg's regiment until the end of the war, apart from a brief period as secretary to the regiment of Schauenburg's relative, Johann Burkhard von Elter, in Bavaria. At the end of the war, he returned to the Upper Rhine area, where he married in 1649 and settled down in the small town of Gaisbach, in the Rench Valley near Strasbourg, as a steward in the employ of von Schauenburg and of the latter's cousin Carl Bernhard. In the entry in the church register that records his marriage to Catharina Henniger, he is referred to as "von Grimmelshausen." Clearly, he had resolved to climb back up the social, as well as the intellectual ladder. There can be no doubt that he grasped the opportunities for self-education offered by his contacts with the educated and well-to-do strata of society. But there is no question of his having been on an equal social footing with these people. He existed between them and the common people, above all the peasants, whose work he had to oversee and whose taxes he had to collect. He was not in any way rich in the period during which he worked for the Schauenburgs, from 1649 to 1660: for two years (1657 and 1658) he tried setting up also as an innkeeper in Gaisbach.

After a period (1662–65) as steward of the estate of a Strasbourg doctor named Kueffer (where again, he would have had access to a good library), and two more years as an innkeeper at the Silver Star in Gaisbach, Grimmelshausen applied for and got the job of *Schultheiß* (village mayor or magistrate) in the village of Renchen, where he remained from 1667 until his death in 1676. Once again, he was an official in the employ of an aristocrat (in this case the Bishop of Strasbourg) in a kind of buffer position between the nobility and the peasantry, with responsibility for the collection of the Bishop's dues and the maintenance of law and order. His last years were darkened, once more, by war, when Louis XIV mounted his campaigns of expansion and became embroiled with the Holy Roman Empire, with the inevitable consequence of what is a frequent theme in Grimmelshausen's work, the tension between soldiers and peasants, as the area became occupied and heavy *Contributionen* (levies), against which Grimmelshausen more than once protested, were demanded of the common people.

During this hectic last decade of his life, Grimmelshausen brought out a stream of publications, all but three of them under anagrammatic pseudonyms. The date of composition is by no means certain in every case, and it is safest to go by date of publication.[3] They range from calendars, most notably the *Ewig-Währender Kalender* (Perpetual Calendar) of 1670, to satirical and moral pamphlets on a variety of topics, among which the *Satyrischer Pilgram* (1666); *Teutscher Michel*, a discourse on language (1672); and *Rathstübel Plutonis* (Council-Chamber of Pluto, 1672), a consideration of the theme of wealth, stand out. There is also a biblical novel, the *Keuscher Joseph* (Chaste Joseph, 1666), and two short novels, *Dietwalt und Amelinde* (1670) and *Proximus und Lympida* (1672) deal with both morally and socially noble characters and are written in a fairly conventional style. Finally, there is a series of works that are much harder to fit into the conventional categories of the seventeenth century, and which, despite their immense popularity, failed to gain recognition by the literary authorities of the period. It is these latter, a group of novels that the author himself characterised by the adjective "simplicianisch," and which it has become customary to call the "Simplician Cycle," that form the principal subject-matter of this study. Grimmelshausen himself, in the last of them, defined the group as an integral unity, comprising ten "books":

Books 1-5: *Der abentheurliche Simplicissimus Teutsch* (1668)
Book 6: *Continuatio des abentheurlichen Simplicissimi oder der Schluß desselben* (1669)
Book 7: *Lebensbeschreibung der Ertzbetrügerin und Landstörtzerin Courasche* (1670)
Book 8: *Der seltzame Springinsfeld* (1670)
Book 9: *Das wunderbarliche Vogelnest. Erster Teil* (1672)
Book 10: *Das wunderbarliche Vogelnest. Zweiter Teil* (1675)

The figure of Simplicissimus dominates the first six books and appears also in the next three, but it is not that fact to which Grimmelshausen refers when he calls them "simplicianisch," but their *Manier* or *Stylus*, that is, the manner of their narration. This will form the principal connecting thread of our examination of the novels as individual entities and it is of course an important source of unity. But it is not in itself capable of providing the kind of framework that is essential if we are truly to have the sense of inter-relation and interdependence that, as we shall see in due course, Grimmelshausen retrospectively claims for the Simplician corpus. It is on a discussion of the "Zyklusfrage" that we shall conclude, but the appropriate starting point would seem to be Grimmelshausen's position within his own baroque age, a position both representative and exceptional.

War and Peace: The Seventeenth-Century Background

War features prominently both in Grimmelshausen's personal life and in his creative work: in particular the Thirty Years' War (1618–48). What had begun as an attempt to restore order in the Holy Roman Empire had developed into a tug-of-war between forces both in and outside the Empire who welcomed or feared the idea of a Catholic Hapsburg hegemony in Germany. It was an international conflict, certainly, but it was also in a real sense (as Grimmelshausen among others called it) a "German war"; a traumatic experience, that is, for the German people of the time. And it is in that sense, as a German experience reflected in German literature, that it concerns us. Grimmelshausen was more directly caught up in the process than most writers of the time, who were generally shielded from the necessity of doing chores and stealing food for marauding cavalrymen, or of carrying a musket, by their status as educated members of the intelligentsia. Even so, the death, devastation, cruelty, hunger, fire, pestilence, and perhaps most of all the sense of instability that accompanied the war on its peripatetic course up and down and across the German lands, all had at the very least a significant psychological impact on the writers of the age.

The Thirty Years' War is very much a present reality in *Simplicissimus*, *Courasche*, and *Springinsfeld*. Battles and skirmishes form a large part of the ostensible "action" of these works; towns and cities are taken and lost (sometimes with bewildering rapidity) and there are many deaths (one thinks especially of Courage's string of husbands). But only rarely does the war itself come to stand at the thematic centre. It is a constant movement, a flow of events in which the goddess of fortune is queen and in which the hero or heroine manages as best he or she can. It partakes of the duality which we shall be studying in detail in the next chapter: dark as it is as a physical reality, it has the vitality that is one pole of the Simplician quality that unites the cycle. At the allegorical level of interpretation, which had such an appeal for the baroque culture of the seventeenth century, it could be said to provide the backdrop for the much more important battle for the soul of the central character. Its inconstancy throws into relief the central issue of *constantia*, to which we shall also come in the next chapter.

Seventeenth-century Germans were not entirely devoid of a sense of national identity, or of love for their *Vaterland*. The politics of the Holy Roman Empire did not allow of an assertion of patriotism in a practical form, such as war can usually call forth. Even when we do sense a resentment of the intervention of foreigners in German affairs, as for example in Rist's *Das friedewünschende Teutschland*, the dominant mood is one of passivity. Learned and unlearned alike viewed the war as a disaster, the cause of immense suffering that could be lamented, but had to be borne, and from which only God could release them. In the seventh part of his *Frauenzimmer Gesprächspiele* (Conversational Games for Ladies, 1647), Georg Philipp Harsdörffer, an intellectual much more cosily cushioned from the effects of the war than Grimmelshausen had been, prints an allegorical picture of it. The image is in fact a conceit: a "rhinoceros" made up of weapons and other military accoutrements, standing against a symbolic background of burning buildings. The appended explanation identifies this behemoth as War, and ends with the plea: "Ach komm! o güldner Fried / das Eisen werd ein Pflug! aus unsrem Leid ein Lied / der Segen aus dem Fluch." (O come, Golden Peace! Let the iron be beaten into a ploughshare, our suffering become song, the curse give way to blessing.)[4]

The basic conceit underlying this image of war and the style in which it is executed — for example the internal rhyme and the use of *Letternwechsel*, or the changing of a word, here *Leid*, by a simple transposition of letters into more or less its opposite — is characteristic of the general trend of the baroque style toward intellectualism, which we shall be examining in the next section. War is a terrible reality, of course, and its physical effects are duly registered, but it is experienced, so to speak, at one remove from reality, both here and in the intensely emotional sonnet "Threnen des Vatterlandes" (1636) of Andreas Gryphius. It is mind rather than matter that dominates in Harsdörffer's work. The nature of the *Gesprächspiele* is partly to inform, but primarily to entertain, tease and train the mind: "zu Fragen und Aufgaben zu veranlassen" (to occasion questions and mental exercises: 63). Gryphius too fragments reality into representative images in order to present a chilling catalogue of destruction, which in turn is meant to prepare the way — via the dual meaning of *Schatz* (treasure) — for a complaint at the destruction of religious freedom. This degree of intellectuality does not mean, however, that we should not take such an approach to the war seriously.

Harsdörffer's message, that only God can lift the curse, is typical of the time; it was God, after all, who had imposed it. God, says Heinrich Schütz in the dedication of his *Musikalische Exequien* (1636), has used the war as a rod to punish the Germans "um unsre schwere Sünd und große Missetat" (for our great sins and grievous misdoings).[5] The war, says Martin Opitz in his *Trostgedichte in Widerwärtigkeit des Krieges* (Consolations in the Adversity of War, 1620–21), is God's instrument ("Gottes Zeug") for the punishment of the German nation for having fallen away from the high moral standards of its ancient past, for its susceptibility to foreign influences, and its disunity.[6] In the material world, man is at the mercy of the "long arm" of Fortune.[7] War, for the seventeenth-century thinker, belonged (whether ancient or modern) to the realm of "history"; that is, the events by which man is caught up and propelled, whether with or against his will. They cannot be controlled and acquire meaning only when apparently wilful Fortune is seen to be the executive arm of a Fate (*Verhängnis*) that is closely related to the idea of Providence. At one level of perception, then, war is the province of Fortune. As Georg Greflinger puts it in his rhymed chronicle *Der Deutschen Dreyßig-Jähriger Krieg* (1657):

> Wann aber sich das Glück bey einem widrig stället /
> So hilfft es nicht / wie sehr daß man sich rund umwället
> und voll von Weisheit weis.[8]

[But when Fortune turns its hostile face to you, it matters not how many ramparts you build round yourself, or how wise you know yourself to be.]

To the observer devoid of religious insight (for example an unenlightened common soldier like Grimmelshausen's Springinsfeld), the result is a crude fatalism: mere luck decides his "Fatum," that is, what happens to him. In the *Simplicissimus*, the hero himself (the character at the time of the action, not the retrospective narrator) often feels this way; the more enlightened Herzbruder sees — as indeed does Greflinger[9] — that God is the ultimate authority, as He is the only source of salvation, in war as in peace (*ST 4*, chapter 26). The man who, like Herzbruder's antagonist Olivier, trusts to magic, remains Fortune's slave, a point which we shall see made in graphic form in part 2 of *Das wunderbarliche Vogelnest*. Opitz, considering the war from a more conventionally philosophical viewpoint, sees the only hope as lying in an essentially passive and inward attitude: repentance and the quest for the inner freedom and constancy of the Christian-Stoic sage who has learned that man is in himself merely "Fortune's plaything ... an image of inconstancy."[10]

Grimmelshausen does not disagree in any essential regard from the general drift. The polished intellectuality of Renaissance/baroque humanism is not, as we shall see, his forte, nor is the heroic mode. An approach through the concept of *Verhängnis* in history, which is illustrated particularly well by the dramas of Daniel Casper von Lohenstein, would be inappropriate in the

Simplician novels, since they are played out in a social context that, as Gerhard Spellerberg says, is not historically significant.[11] But through a character who has withdrawn from the world, his "Einsiedel" (hermit), he very early on establishes constancy as the defence against the attacks of Fortune. His attitude to the war itself is essentially a passive one: it is an unalterable and uncontrollable fact of life. The idea that it is a punishment from God, decided by what Grimmelshausen calls in his *Keuscher Joseph* "der himmlische Schluß" (heaven's decree), is enunciated in part 2 of *Das wunderbarliche Vogelnest* (*VN* 280, 283)[12] and echoed also in the conversation between Simplicius's "Meuder" (Ma) and Springinsfeld. The latter, as a soldier, will go to hell, she says, because God, like a true father, will cast the rod upon the fire after he has sufficiently chastised his errant child. (*Springinsfeld*, 72)

The social and cultural climate in which seventeenth-century German literature was produced shows radical differences from that which underlies the work of prominent German writers of the sixteenth century, such as Hans Sachs or Jörg Wickram, who used everyday middle-class settings and wrote in a corresponding spirit and style. The new manner, to which we generally give the name "baroque," is one of sophistication and is often designated as aristocratic in an extended sense, even when the practitioner himself is neither of noble birth, nor connected in any direct way with a court. In spite — perhaps even because — of a heightened sense of man's instability and susceptibility to the whims of Fortune, a rigid and hierarchical social order willed by Divine Providence was the perceived ideal, and it conditioned patterns of literary thinking as well. Corresponding hierarchies of genre and style apply in theory and practice: high, middle, or low, according to the status of the *res*, the matter in hand, which, in the rhetorical system that was standard for the time, preceded and predetermined the form taken by the words (*verba*).

The lynchpin of the social system was the doctrine of absolutism: the supreme authority under God of a prince or other ruling body. Rebellions there were in the period, but rebellion, except under religious sanction, was generally rejected,[13] most notably in one of the great masterpieces of seventeenth-century literature, Jost van den Vondel's *Lucifer* (1654). And while Vondel treats his theme at a universal level, his reference, in the dedication (to Emperor Ferdinand III) to ancient and modern history ("oude en jonge historien")[14] makes it likely that he had the example of Cromwell, and perhaps also that of Wallenstein in mind, among others. The absolutist principle was accepted by such men as Andreas Gryphius, the Syndic of the Estates of Glogau, who presents Charles I as a religious and political martyr in his *Carolus Stuardus*, and the Protestant clergyman Johann Rist. The latter's rebuking of a critic who had indulged in "slanderous" attacks on him is an illustration of the way in which the man of letters felt himself to be part of the absolutist hierarchy. Authority will be avenged: "denn der gerechter (*sic*) Gott hält fäst uber seinen Gesalbeten und lasset die Verächter der Obrigkeiten auch anderer unschuldiger Leute nicht ungestraffet." (. . . for God, who is just, watches steadfastly over His Anointed Ones, nor will He allow those who fail to respect the authorities of other innocent people to go unpunished.)[15]

The baroque age saw the construction of great palaces, such as Versailles, and the Winter Palace and the Belvedere in Vienna, both built for Prince Eugene, and this was entirely in accord with the spirit of the time, for magnificence, so enthusiastically hymned, for example, by Bossuet, was part of what it meant to be a king or a great nobleman;[16] part of the representative posture that was the most important part of his being. The private individual disappeared behind the public role he played. Grandeur, heroic and ornate, was the admired style . . . in the right place, of course. If the low-born or incompetent aspired to it, the result would be merely laughable: an infringement of the proper order, comparable to the attempt (as in Gryphius's *Herr Peter Squentz*) of a man who lacks the requisite learning and mastery of the craft to indulge in poetic composition. So that when, in Gryphius's *Horribilicribrifax*, the title "hero" comically mangles the forms of polite discourse, this is anything but a rejection of sophisticated *Courtoisie*, but rather an indirect endorsement of it.

It is certainly true that the baroque spirit achieved full bloom only after the Thirty Years' War, but it was already implicit much earlier. In literary terms, it can be stated as the full acceptance of Renaissance humanism into the German — as opposed to a merely Latin — context, under the conditions of the seventeenth century, when stable prosperity was harder to achieve, when cities such as Nuremberg, where a relatively self-confident middle-class merchant ethos could flourish, were losing ground to the influence of the courts. Even if it did not express itself in a specifically social form, there was a kind of cultural aristocratism built into the humanistic ethos. Opitz, whose seminal *Buch von der Deutschen Poeterey* was published in 1624, had already achieved a secure German humanism and left Hans Sachs far behind him. Much earlier, in the *Schönes Blumenfeld* (Pretty Field of Flowers, 1601) of Theobald Höck (1573–1619), we can see the baroque ethos struggling to free itself from sixteenth-century attitudes and habits. Höck had risen, through his native intelligence and noble patronage, to the socially elevated rank of what might be called the intellectual aristocracy, and while his literary talent was modest, his position made the publication of this collection of poems (with its characteristically baroque title) entirely appropriate. Without having mastered the principles of German prosody — first formulated in a satisfactory form by Opitz — he is aware of their existence and of the need to observe them. He castigates the Meistersinger for their ignorance of the poetic craft, rejects the sixteenth-century *Volksbücher*, such as the *Fortunatus* or the Faust chapbook together with Wickram's popular *Rollwagenbüchlein*, and insists, as do all baroque literary theorists, on learning as a prerequisite of poetry:

> Niembt sich auch billich ein Poeten nennet / Wer dGrichisch (*sic*) und Lateinisch Sprach nit kennet.[17]

> [No one who has no knowledge of the Greek and Latin languages is entitled to call himself a poet.]

Behind the technical crudity of these poems, one senses the desire for polish, acceptance of the aristocratic (or perhaps we should say patrician) values of those vernacular literatures, including the Dutch, that had joined the Renaissance club, and a determination that Germany should also gain membership. And this, to their own satisfaction at least, the Germans achieved. The cultivation of German as a literary and intellectually respectable language was vigorously pursued, largely through translation and imitation of foreign models. The new definition of the poet, based, in true humanistic spirit, on the concepts and rules of classical rhetoric, presented the image of a man who performed an elevated and important role in society — an entertainer, yes, but also a teacher and a guardian of public morals — a man of good education and deep learning, a master of correct and polished speech, and above all possessed of a strong intellect and an ingenious wit: a man above the common herd. Opitz himself stated that the poet must be a man "von sinnreichen einfällen und erfindungen" (gifted with ingenious ideas and inventions).[18] Harsdörffer is more frank: poetry, he says, is no trade for the common man.[19] Buchner is brutally frank; he is not writing, he says, "for peasants and idiots."[20]

Some writers, certainly, were more ornate in their style than others, but apart from genres such as the church hymn, where one could arguably talk of special stylistic requirements, the spirit of unsophisticated simplicity, such as might recall the *Volkslied*, was a rarity in the writing of the time, with the exception of the literature of protest, to which we shall come in due course. The unpolished, everyday, essentially middle-class tone of such as Hans Sachs was generally despised. Elaboration became the order of the day, whether in the devising of ingenious titles, the cultivation of intellectually intricate forms such as emblem and allegory, the lavish use of the tropes of which the baroque was so fond, or the concoction of labyrinthine plots. David Schirmer published a volume entitled *Singende Rosen* (Singing Roses, 1654), Philipp von Zesen one with the title *Dichterisches Rosen- und Liljen-Thal* (Poetic Valley of Roses and Lilies, 1670). "Tropisierung," as Manfred Windfuhr has shown, is a prominent feature of seventeenth-century style.[21] In his devotional book *Güldenes Tugendbuch*, Friedrich von Spee writes of sacred songs as "güldne pfeile der liebe, auß einem andächtigen hertzen, als auß einem pfeilköcher gezogen" (golden arrows of love, drawn from a reverent heart as from a quiver).[21] Harsdörffer, in his fancifully entitled theoretical work *Poetischer Trichter* (Poetic Funnel, 1648–53) recommends a dramatic action composed of more than one strand, "weil das Gemüt durch seltene Verwirrung und unerwarte Begebenheit bestürzt / deß Ausgangs mit Verlangen erwartet" (because the mind, taken out of its stride by strange confusion and unexpected events, is eager to know the outcome).[22] As we can see from the foregoing examples, the baroque style, in the hands of the bolder spirits, is capable of far-fetched, even clumsy usage. There is indeed something rather naive about the baroque sophistication; a theoretical awareness of the need — stressed in the rhetorical textbooks of the day — to avoid extremes, but a natural predilection for the massive, the ornate, and, above all, the ingenious, which, in the second half of the century in particular, gave rise to excesses that in turn produced an over-correction in the following period of the Enlightenment, a period equally concerned to achieve a classical sophistication, but imbued with a more moderate and middle-class taste.

There was also a reaction against the new style in the seventeenth century itself, one which has been labelled "anti-courtly" and one that was strongly tinged with conservatism and resentment of foreign influence (neither factor plays a part in the Enlightenment's critique of baroque style). Those whose taste did not run to the more intense levels of baroque style and who, like Andreas Tscherning, preferred what Windfuhr calls the "gebändigter Zierstil" (controlled decorative style)[23] characteristic of Opitz, shared the intellectualistic aristocratism of the baroque, and cannot be seen as reactionaries or rebels. The language of the people, for Andreas Tscherning, should be restricted to works that did not aim at poetic *gravitas*:

> Derer wörter / so nur bey den bauren und gemeinen Pöfel im brauche / zumal in einem wichtigen werke / da nicht etwan bauren oder sonst ihres gleichen eingeführt werden / sol ein Poet nicht gebrauchen.

> [A poet should not use words that are current usage among peasants or common people, in particular in a work of importance, in which no peasants or other such folk are presented.][24]

There were those, however, for whom poetry and polished sophistication did not go naturally together, who saw the latter as a foreign import, a mask for "un-German" insincerity, a morally corrupting influence. Johann Balthasar Schupp was probably one such;[25] the most prominent was Johann Michael Moscherosch (1601–69), whose *Wunderliche und Wahrhafftige Gesichte Philanders von Sittewalt* (1640–50) was known to and undeniably influenced Grimmelshausen. When the latter claims to be writing "satyricè" (in the satirical, or the satyr's mode), he is surely thinking in part at least of the tone adopted by Moscherosch, which, as we shall see, does not always accord with the principles enunciated by Tscherning.

If there is one point at which this trend crystallizes particularly clearly, it is in the criticism of the cult of the "à la mode," the most detailed example of which is the "Ala Mode Kehrauß" in part 2 of Moscherosch's *Gesichte* (1643). It is not simply a matter of being German: the cultivation of the German language was, as we have seen, common ground at that time. The followers of fashion are for Moscherosch "Teutschlinge": un-German Germans.[26] They are guilty of folly, certainly, but the real problem is a moral one, the loss of "alte teutsche Redlichkeit und Aufrichtigkeit" (ancient German honesty and uprightnesss). It is no longer enough, in the age of the *Alamodewesen,* to be an honest, solid citizen:

> Ein fromm Biedermann
> kompt bey Niemand an
> A la mode helff ihm dann /
> sonst er nicht fortkommen kan.

[A good, honest citizen will not prosper anywhere unless he can help himself by becoming "à la mode"; otherwise, he will never get on.][27]

To be "teutsch-gesinnt," as Moscherosch conceives himself and his ideal reader to be, is to deal and speak plainly. It is this plain speaking, for Moscherosch, that is the nub of the satirical posture: "da man kein blatt fürs maul nimbt" (when you call a spade a spade: 75) as he puts it in the preface to the second part of the *Gesichte,* in which he defines "Satyra." In this mode, he says, the truth is told "auff gut bäurisch"(in good, solid peasant style) and while his style is by no means devoid of formality, there is also a strong tinge of the popular. Women who pad out their figures with what they call "Speck" (fat) are "feiste Säuwe" (fat sows); no honest man should touch such a "Schmutzige[n] Garstige[n] Lauß-sack" (dirty, nasty bag of lice: 125). The man who gives his honest German name a fancy foreign form in order to present himself as a "Jünckerlein" is short of a marble or two ("der hat mangel an eim sparren": 114).

Moscherosch's work is a satire also in its moral seriousness, which dominates the work, and, it must be confessed, makes the humour — which is given greater weight in the "style satyrique et comique" of Grimmelshausen's other prime model, Charles Sorel — into a secondary factor. The *Auffschneider,* the man who boasts of his achievements to such an outrageous extent that he becomes inherently ridiculous can be a predominantly comic figure whose incompetence, rather than the fashion he attempts to follow, is exposed by the comic writer. For Moscherosch, though, this figure of the man who pretends to be what he is not is directly linked to the "allgemeine seuche" (general plague: 21) of hypocrisy. We shall see in due course how Grimmelshausen deals with this, or at any rate a very similar problem.

Moscherosch rarely deals directly with literary issues in the strict sense, but one sees the family resemblance when Georg Greflinger remarks, in the preface to his *Weltliche Lieder* (1651): "Belangend die Art zu schreiben / So kehre ich mich an das neue nicht groß... Wir... sind so von den Alten / und nicht a la modo Teutschen." (As far as style is concerned, I don't take much account of the new ways... we... are of the old school, not "à la mode" Germans).[28] Johann Lauremberg makes a similar point, in a more amusing and forceful way, in the fourth of his Low German *Schertz Gedichte* (1652), which bears the title "Van alamodischer Poesie und Rimen."

Nor were these writers, for all their awareness of the popular layers of society and of speech, men of the people, *Volksschriftsteller*. Lauremberg used Low German dialect, but he was also professor of poetry at the University of Rostock. Rist, another who is sometimes counted among the anti-courtly group, did use dialect in the comic interludes of his plays, in which he castigates Germany for having forsaken the "Old German" virtues, but his basic stance, as we have seen, is that of the baroque intellectual who classes himself among the *nobilitas literaria*. Schupp was certainly a robust writer, with an eye for the popular, but he was also an intellectual, who saw himself in the tradition of Lucian and Erasmus. He was certainly no outsider. Greflinger, a peasant's son, who was tossed about by the war and may not have had the opportunity for formal study, was a plain enough poet at times, but he too could conform to the baroque standards, as is evidenced by his witty "Sein gutes Gefängnüß."[29] Gottfried Finckelthaus is known as a poet in the "rough and ready" style, and in particular for his "Der Schäfer Blax an die Allo-Mode Brüder"(Blax, the Shepherd, to the A la mode Brigade), but Antony Harper points out that this tone is by no means dominant in his work as a whole.[30] Moscherosch, a man of obviously "difficult" character, shows resentments and ambiguities in his relation to the dominant baroque culture, but his life and career were played out more or less within the courtly ambit: he was a highly educated man and his *Gesichte,* for all its rough edges, is a work that demands a highly educated reader, who is prepared to concentrate for long periods without any immediate prospect of entertainment. Grimmelshausen is often linked with this tendency in seventeenth-century German literature and in particular with Moscherosch — Haberkamm, for example, describes him as Moscherosch's "disciple"[31] — which may explain why Gaede does not categorize him as baroque, and why Peter Skrine can find no significant role for him in his study. Even if one discounts works of an explicitly polite orientation, such as *Proximus und Lympida* and *Dietwald und Amelinde,* such a separation seems problematic. We shall be addressing this question in our next section.

Grimmelshausen's Intellectual and Social Stance

In a congratulatory postscript to Grimmelshausen's *Dietwalt und Amelinde* (1670), written in verse that is clumsy enough to strengthen the suspicion that it is the work of our author himself, we read that this work by the "Edler Herr von Grimmelshausen" will win him praise "bey dem gelehrten Volck."[32] The assumption of the attribute "edel" (noble), together with the fact that this book is dedicated to an aristocrat — as are the other two that Grimmelshausen published under his own name[33] — may or may not be a direct attempt to establish a social link with the local gentry, but it does seem to indicate a certain sensitivity about his position in society. We know, after all, that on his return to civil life after the war, he reclaimed the family right to the aristocratic "von." He was, of course, far from an "edler Herr" — or at any rate a "großer Herr" — himself. He was, as Quirin Moscherosch (the brother of the satirist) put it in an often-quoted letter of 1674, "nur ein geringer Dorf-Schultes" (no more than a little village magistrate) on whom a clergyman like Moscherosch could look down.[34] Whether he had ever been directly confronted with such a stinging phrase, we do not know, but it is highly likely that in his dealings with social "superiors" he had been made to feel the gap. After considerable direct experience of the lifestyle of the "peripatetics," as G. N. Clark calls them, who were the "exceptional people, moving about in the interstices of a settled world,"[35] he had achieved some stability, but we never have the sense that he feels secure in "belonging."

Nor had he been able to achieve social status and recognition through his writing. The reference to the "gelehrtes Volk" (the learned tribe) quoted above, is either bitter irony or wishful thinking. It is certainly true, as Hans Dieter Gebauer has shown, that his *Simplicissimus* was known and read by people of education and refinement, and indeed appreciated by them.[36] But only, in Leibniz's words, as "un livre . . . fait pour rire" (a book made to provoke laughter).[37] Popular as it immediately became, it was not the key to Parnassus, and Grimmelshausen's energetic rejection of the title of clown and mere entertainer in the opening chapter of the *Continuatio* or sixth book may well indicate that he had become aware that he was being seen as such and wished to correct this false impression. He tried again in the *Springinsfeld* and in the preface to part 2 of *Das wunderbarliche Vogelnest*, where he thunders against members of the establishment such as Christian Weise, who, in his *Die drey aergsten Ertz-Narren von der gantzen Welt* (1672) had dismissed him as a "Salbader" (a purveyor of twaddle).[38] It is true that an impressive body of research has been able to show that Grimmelshausen was not, any more than Shakespeare, "fancy's child," and that his Simplician novels are anything but unsophisticated native wood-notes. He had been untimely ripped from the civil, and plunged into the military world, but he had managed to scramble out of the mire and make himself, in his own autodidactic way, a man of learning. He was a man of high intelligence. He could even manage — as works like *Dietwalt* were perhaps meant to prove — to deal with "polite" subjects in a reasonably polished style, and these and his Simplician writings give evidence of his acquaintance with and ability to handle baroque forms of rhetoric and wit.[39] But none of this was enough to rescue him from what Volker Meid calls the role of literary outsider ("Außenseiterrolle des Literaten": 85).

A desire for recognition and a resentment at its lack do seem to emerge from time to time in Grimmelshausen's work. Attacks on Weise, and on Philipp von Zesen in the *Teutscher Michel* and part 1 of the *Vogelnest*, show that he could be touchy. His background meant that he could not fit easily into the conventional baroque categories. But he manifestly did not wish to be cut off, and he did succeed, above all through the persona of Simplicissimus and the style associated with it, in finding a stance that enabled him to address the deepest concerns of his age in a form that grew naturally out of his unique experience. In view of this he has as much right to be seen as a leading representative of the age as Molière is of his.

The short allegorical fable *Der erste Beernhäuter* (1670) lacks the "instructive secrets" (*KS* 1, 10) it is said to contain, but its function as a counterblast to those who speak scornfully of the social and literary unwashed is not hard to deduce. In it, Grimmelshausen ironically refers to himself on the title page as "Illiteratus Ignorantius, known as 'Idiot'." In part 1 of *Das wunderbarliche Vogelnest*, the bearer of the magic nest mocks the attempts of the "intellectuals," whom he has saved by his intervention, to explain what has happened. All their learning cannot solve the riddle, whereas he, the "ungelehrter Idiot," knows the answer (*VN* 57). In the *Teutscher Michel* (1673), Grimmelshausen seems at one point to be describing himself as an "ignoramus" ("ein Ignorant": *TM* 18). Naturally, he does not think he is anything of the kind. He knows he cannot compete with the highly educated and widely travelled in their style, but he has acquired learning in his own way and is indeed only too willing, at times, to display it. Under the vicious attack of the imaginary pedantic critic, Momus, he feels a certain kinship with Eulenspiegel, but he is careful not to identify himself with him (*SP* 10–11). He certainly knew and must surely have enjoyed the *Eulenspiegel* "Volksbuch," but makes it clear in his *Springinsfeld* that he sees it merely as entertainment for an idle hour and will not have his *Simplicissimus* placed in the same category (*Springinsfeld*, 21–2).

He may not have polish, but he has learning, and more important, he has wisdom. In his persona as ex-musketeer in the *Satyrischer Pilgram* (1667), he can make learned reference to Horace, Aesop, Pythagoras, Democritus,

Homer, and Lucian,[40] but states at the same time that he is writing for "meines gleichen einfältige Leut" (simple people like myself: *SP* 9), people who want not to carp but "to learn something." The moral significance of the word "simple" (that is, free from pride) is more important here than the intellectual sense of the word. It helps Grimmelshausen to build a bridge between himself and the formally educated, from whom he knows he has been separated by circumstances. His whole philosophy is against any kind of pretence, but he feels that he has a right, in his own Simplician way, to a mansion in the house of letters. Perhaps we should speak not so much of a bridge that he can cross as of a tightrope that he must walk. The *Teutscher Michel* — a discourse in explicitly Simplician vein on various linguistic topics and above all on the German language as it should and should not be spoken — is an excellent example of the skill with which he can carry off the trick of remaining himself, yet avoiding isolation. The mature simplicity of Simplicissimus the literary man plays an important part in this.

Precious gifts, he says in the introduction to the second "Caput" (Grimmelshausen's word play for "chapter") of this work, often bring with them great temptations. Intellectual eminence is no exception. The fairest of women, the saintliest of saints, the most valiant of heroes, the most venerable of sages: none are immune against human fallibility. Having thus demonstrated his ability to mount a formal baroque *Häufung* (accumulation), Grimmelshausen then shifts, in characteristically Simplician fashion, into the proverbial mode and adds: "Man sagt, je gelehrter, je verkehrter" (the cleverer you are, they say, the sillier you are). The source of this folly is not learning, but pride, and the source of wisdom is humility, which is allied to a simplicity of heart analogous to that of the hermit in the Spessart, in *Simplicissimus*:

> Gleichwie wir aber das Gute selten erkennen / und das / was uns zur Demut / dem Fundament aller Tugenden / weiset / noch langsamer annehmen; Also bilden sich theils Sprachkundige ein / wollen auch andere Leuth so bereden / sie allein hören das Graß wachsen. . . .[41]

> [But just as we seldom recognise what is good and are slower still to accept that which points us towards humility, which is the foundation of all the virtues, so some linguistically learned men fondly imagine, and try to persuade others as well, that they are the only people who can hear the grass grow. . . .]

The simplicity and indeed ignorance implied in the concept "teutscher Michel" contain positive and negative nuances. The latter are reflected in Grimmelshausen's use of the phrase "albere unwissende teutsche Michel" (silly, ignorant German Michaels: *TM* 35) to describe those who, themselves innocent of all linguistic expertise, insist on larding their communications with foreign words. The recipient does not understand them, but then, neither does the sender. He simply wants it to be thought that he does (36). It is not the lack of knowledge as such, but the moral ignorance behind the action which conditions the use of the word *albern* (silly). Insofar as the "Michel" of the title is Grimmelshausen's (or Simplicissimus's), he is the plain, unvarnished, honest German invoked by Moscherosch, whose attack on the fashion for foreign vocabulary in the "Ala mode Kehrauß" surely provided the jumping-off point for Grimmelshausen's slighter and less learned, but less polemical and more readable work. The *Teutscher Michel* is arguably the most relaxed, the least narrowly satirical, the most truly Simplician of Grimmelshausen's non-narrative "tracts." Signeur Meßmahl (the most transparent of Grimmelshausen's anagrams) is knowledgeable and intelligent, but respectful of and in no way provoked into defensive hostility by the higher learning of the intellectual in whom that learning is not morally flawed.

In real life, Grimmelshausen stood between the nobility, his employers, and the peasantry, whose masters were those same nobles he represented. His relations as an author with these social strata have something of the ambivalence that we have seen in matters intellectual. He understands the peasant, is fascinated by his language and dialect, and can see him at times as a sympathetic figure, possessed of good, solid German simplicity and virtue: "fein im Glaiß seiner Einfalt" like the peasant in the *Teutscher Michel* (31), by no means lacking in intelligence but often unfairly treated. But this figure can also often be coarse and foul-mouthed, ignorant and stupid. And while the peasant is often allowed to air his grievances, the spirit of narrative or discussion is never allowed to become remotely revolutionary.[42] As Eric the Swede says to Simplicissimus's "Knan" (Dad) in the *Rathstübel Plutonis* after the latter has had his long and quite eloquent grumble, "Ihr müsset eine Oberkeit haben" (You have to have an authority over you: *RP* 59).

Similarly, "große Herren" can be arrogant and insensitive, and we cannot but sympathise with the feelings of the would-be clerk, Philarchus, as he is so brusquely turned away in the opening chapter of *Springinsfeld*. The image of the educated man forced to "stand at the great man's gate to tickle his vanity," (*Springinsfeld* 11) and indeed to endure insult from the great man's servants, has considerable poignancy (though Grimmelshausen, in his even-handedness, does not omit to ironise Philarchus's rather inflated estimate of his own importance). Proper respect ("gebührende Ehre": *SP* 10), as Grimmelshausen puts it in the *Satyrischer Pilgram*, should be paid, but vanity and the desire to cut a greater figure on the social stage than is appropriate are always condemned. In his persona as Simplicissimus, if not in real life, Grimmelshausen is able to find a satisfactory relationship with the "grosser Herr" Secundatus in the *Rathstübel Plutonis*.[43] They are not equals, but they meet and discourse on terms of polished politeness. And although the social differences among what eventually becomes a heterogeneous group are always maintained and Secundatus's primacy is consistently recognised, the tone of all the exchanges is one of mutual respect, or at worst amused tolerance (as for example in the case of Courage).

It is a tone that is compatible with the "offenhertzig" (frank) and "Teutsch" ideals that have been enunciated in the opening pages, but hardly yet Simplician. This element, which was previously represented in the socially inferior characters, comes to the fore in the host (Simplicissimus) himself, when, at Secundatus's invitation, he indulges his "satyrical" vein in a long tirade against extravagance and the "Alamodewesen" (*RP* 74–89). The tone changes, not as markedly as would be the case in a less formal, narrative piece, but nevertheless with a certain shift towards the liveliness of the narrative style. The most striking change is the fact that Simplicissimus no longer employs the polite forms of address, but adopts the familiar "du," and he justifies this with an interesting formulation that establishes a modus vivendi of sorts between the Simplician stance and polite society, both in the civil and the literary sense. It represents not a rejection of polite forms, but a licensed exception to them. Simplicissimus sets out to show how "French fashion" can ruin even a rich man, and determines to structure his presentation formally according to the various parts of the body:

> ... wir wollen aber auch particulariter davon reden / und erstlich an deiner (mein Herr verzeyhe mir / daß ich ihn wieder aller jetzigen Menschen Gewohnheit dutze / dann wer die Wahrheit von mir hören wil / der muß auch den Stylum leyden / durch welchen ich die liebe Wahrheit auff gut Simplicianisch anzuzeigen gewohnt bin) Person . . . anfangen. (*RP* 75)
>
> [... what we'll do, then, is discuss it piece by piece , starting, my friend (forgive me, good Sir, for speaking to you, against all proper practice these days, in a familiar manner, but if you want to hear the truth from me, you'll have to put up with the style in which I am accustomed to tell it, in good, plain Simplician language), with the parts of your person.]

Secundatus is in no way offended. The Simplician style fits perfectly well into his scheme of things; indeed, he has invited it, knowing that "der auffrichtige Simplex kein Blat vors Maul nimt" (honest Simplex will call a spade a spade: *RP*, 74). In his closing speech he thanks his "honest German Simplex" ("mein redlicher teutscher Simplice": 89) for his instructive remarks. In the title engraving of the *Rathstübel*, Grimmelshausen unites high, middle, and low social strata in a circle under the linden tree, indulging in intellectual discourse in a format not unreminiscent of Harsdörffer's *Gesprächspiele*, though with a much more Simplician composition. Eric the Swede, the authorial voice of the whole, comments, indeed, on its comic heterogeneity.[43] Like the famous title engraving of *Simplicissimus Teutsch,* it could be seen as symbolic of the "Simplicianische Manier."

Grimmelshausen, then, had raised the concept "Teutsch," together with the figure of the satyr, on his banner in the title of his first Simplician novel. The reader will recall that Moscherosch also had linked the two concepts and used the same phrase ("kein Blatt vors Maul nehmen") to enjoin plain speaking as is employed by Grimmelshausen in the *Rathstübel Plutonis* and in the *Teutscher Michel.*[44] We have seen also how, like Moscherosch, Grimmelshausen does his German duty by satirising, in the conventional sense, the "Alamodewesen." But there is more to his "satyric" tone than that; it is a matter of style as well as of ideological direction. His debt to Moscherosch is clear enough. Manfred Koschlig is also justified in linking the use of the word "teutsch" on the *Simplicissimus* title page with the word "warhafftig" used in the 1662 translation of Charles Sorel's *Francion,* which had an important influence on Grimmelshausen's development. Sorel's *franchise* is clearly relevant here. But whether Koschlig is right to go on to say: "Teutsch bedeutet den Stil"[45] is another matter. It will be instructive to compare Grimmelshausen's practice with that of the earlier writers to see how his differs from theirs.

The metaphor of moral *Sucht,* Grimmelshausen's term for the moral sickness he saw as afflicting society — and for which the German word *Seuche* is a more commonly used synonym —is one that Grimmelshausen shares with and may have adopted from Moscherosch. It forms the foundation of the opening passage of *Simplicissimus.* But there are significant differences in the way in which it is developed. Moscherosch claims that women are particularly to blame for the spread throughout Germany of the passion for novelty:

> Und diese seuche ist allgemein und gehet durch die gantze Welt. Wann solche Thorheit in unserm Vatterland allein geschehe / so wäre es / weil wir mitten in und under den Newbärtigen Frantzosen sitzen unnd wohnen / noch zu verziehen. . . . Aber es ist der Jammer der Newsüchtigkeit biß mitten in Teutschland / biß an das andere Ende unsers Vatterlands / und in der vornehmsten Fürsten und Herren Höfe gerathen.
>
> Und zu forchten / wo durch ernsthafte Rösche Helden-gemüther solchem Wesen nicht gestewret werde / Teutschland dörffte dermahlen durch solche Weiber wiederum zu einem Babel werden. (*Gesichte* 76–77)

> [And this sickness is a general sickness and covers the whole world. If it were in our home territory alone that this folly were going on, then it could be forgiven, since where we live, we are surrounded by these Frenchmen with their fancy new beards. . . . But this miserable state of affairs, this novelty-sickness, has spread into the heart of Germany, right to the other end of our fatherland.

⁹ Cf. Greflinger, op. cit., 16: "Wann Gott nicht selber wil mit deinen Feinden kriegen. . . ."

¹⁰ Opitz, *Gesammelte Werke*, ed. G. Schulz-Behrend, vol. 1 (Stuttgart: Hiersemann, 1968), 217.

¹¹ Cf. G. Spellerberg, *Verhängnis und Geschichte. Untersuchungen zu den Trauerspielen und dem "Arminius"-Roman Daniel Caspers von Lohenstein*, (Bad Homburg: Gehlen, 1970), 36–40: "Der Souverän und die Geschichte."

¹² Cf. *Keuscher Joseph* 125. All man can do, says Grimmelshausen, is repent, and hope, as a "demütig-büssender Bekenner begangner Sünden" (a meekly penitent confessor of one's sins) for Grace.

¹³ Cf. Peter Skrine, *The Baroque* (London: Methuen, 1978), 111–14.

¹⁴ *De Werken van Vondel*, vol. 5, ed. J. M. Sterck et al., (Amsterdam, 1931), 605. Grimmelshausen sees Wallenstein as an exemplar of vaulting ambition (*Rathstübel Plutonis,* 64–5).

¹⁵ Johann Rist, *Sämtliche Werke*, ed. E. Mannack, vol. 2 (Berlin: de Gruyter, 1972), 21. This is part of a tirade in the preface to *Das friedewünschende Teutschland* (1647) against a lampoonist and "slanderer" who persistently attacks the "Great" . . . and other men of "fame and learning" (including Rist himself).

¹⁶ Quoted from V.-L. Tapié, *The Age of Grandeur*, (1957) trans. A. Ross Williamson (London: Weidenfeld, 1960), 77.

¹⁷ Cf. K. Hanson, ed., *Theobald Höck. "Schönes Blumenfeld." Kritische Ausgabe*, (Bonn: Bouvier, 1975), 264.

¹⁸ Martin Opitz, *Buch von der deutschen Poeterey*, ed. R. Alewyn, (Tübingen: Niemeyer, 1963), 11.

¹⁹ Harsdörffer, *Frauenzimmer Gesprächspiele*, vol. 6 (1969), 163.

²⁰ August Buchner, *Anleitung zur deutschen Poeterey*, ed. M. Szyrocki, (Tübingen: Niemeyer, 1966), 29.

²¹ Cf. M. Windfuhr, *Die barocke Bildlichkeit und ihre Kritiker* (Stuttgart: Metzler, 1966).

²² Friedrich von Spee, *Güldenes Tugendbuch*, ed. T. G. M. van Oorschot (Munich, 1968), 199.

²³ G. P. Harsdörffer, *Poetischer Trichter* (1648–53; reprint, Darmstadt: Wissenschaftliche Buchgesellschaft, 1969), part 2: 75. The title is derived from wine-bottling.

²⁴ See Windfuhr, *Die barocke Bildlichkeit*, 349, 351.

²⁵ See the extract from *Unvorgreiffliche Bedenken über etliche Mißbräuche in der deutschen Schreib- und Sprach-Kunst* (1659) in *Poetik des Barock*, ed. M. Szyrocki, (Reinbek: Rowohlt, 1968), 168.

²⁶ For Schupp, see Windfuhr, *Die barocke Bildlichkeit*, 357–63.

[27] J. M. Moscherosch, *Wunderliche und wahrhafftige Gesichte Philanders von Sittewalt*, ed. W. Harms, (Stuttgart: Reclam, 1986), 129 ("Ihr Teutschlinge..."). Subsequent references to this work will be indicated by the page number in parentheses, and with the short title *Gesichte* where this may be unclear.

[28] Cf. E. Blühm, "Neues über Greflinger," *Euphorion* 58 (1964), 76.

[29] See A. Schöne, ed., *Das Zeitalter des Barock*, (Munich: Beck, 1963), 811.

[30] Cf. A. Harper, *David Schirmer. A Poet of the German Baroque* (Stuttgart: Heinz, 1977), 150.

[31] K. Haberkamm, "Johann Michael Moscherosch," in *Deutsche Dichter des 17. Jahrhunderts*, ed. H. Steinhagen and B. von Wiese (Berlin: E. Schmidt, 1984), 192.

[32] *Dietwalt und Amelinde*, 102, 103.

[33] The others being *Proximus und Lympida* and *Ratio Status*.

[34] Quoted from: Volker Meid, *Grimmelshausen. Epoche-Werk-Wirkung*, (Munich: Beck, 1984), 84.

[35] Cf. G. N. Clark, *Early Modern Europe*, vol. 4 (London: Oxford U P, 1966), 1.

[36] Hans Dieter Gebauer, *Grimmelshausens Bauerndarstellung* (Marburg: Elwert, 1977), 424 ff.

[37] Letter from Leibniz to Duchess Sophie of Hanover (24 April (?) 1688), quoted from Gebauer, *Grimmelshausens Bauerndarstellung*, 424–5.

[38] See *Springinsfeld*, chapters 3 and 7; *Vogelnest*, 149.

[39] See for example P. Heßelmann, "Dessen Schwall mache Jesuiten verstummen. Grimmelshausen und die Rhetorik," *Simpliciana* 15 (1993), 105–22, and D. Breuer, "Der sinnreiche Poet und sein ungewöhnlicher neuer Stil. Grimmelshausen und die europäische Argutia-Bewegung," ibid., 89–103.

[40] *Satyrischer Pilgram*, 11. For Homer, cf. G. Weydt, "Grimmelshausen und Homer," *Simpliciana* 8 (1986), 2–17.

[41] *Teutscher Michel*, 12. Rolf Tarot has pointed to the original theological meaning of the concept of simplicity, a tradition of submission of oneself to God that culminates in the New Testament admonition to "become as one of these" ("Grimmelshausens *Simplicissimus* und die Form autobiographischen Erzählens," *Études Germaniques* 46 [1991], 62.) While the present context is not theological, there is clearly an analogy. At the same time, it is worth pointing out that in Simplician writing, such *sancta simplicitas* can be at the same time praiseworthy and comic, as in the instance in which the trusting Herzbruder expresses the belief that Simplicius (who has boiled the peas on which he is walking on the pilgrimage to Einsiedeln) must be exceptionally blessed with God's grace (*Simplicissimus*, 377: cf. below, chapter 3).

[42] On Grimmelshausen as social critic and "reformer," cf. Gebauer, *Grimmelshausens Bauerndarstellung*, 102–24 and 199–216. That Grimmelshausen sympathised with many of the problems of the common people seems beyond doubt, but

to assert that he sides with them in "Ausfälle gegen die Standeshierarchie" (425) seems to be overstating the case.

[43] Cf. *Rathstübel Plutonis,* 10: "Es sahe in Wahrheit recht lächerlich auß / weil sich so unterschidliche Leuth da beysammen befunden." The Simplician principle of variegation is also expressed in the curious mixture of the *Simplicissimus* engraving, and in the preface of the *Ewigwährender Kalender:* " . . . hoher gelehrter Leut Meinung und Sentenz . . . zwischen der unansehnlichen Bauren-Practic."

[44] *Teutscher Michel,* 37.

[45] Cf. M. Koschlig, *Das Ingenium Grimmelshausens und das "Kollektiv,"* (Munich: Beck, 1977), 82–3. See also: J.-M. Valentin, "Grimmelshausen zwischen Albertinus und Sorel," *Simpliciana* 12 (1990), 135–57 and "Du rire au plus haut savoir. Sur les écrits poétologiques de Sorel et Grimmelshausen," *Études Germaniques* 46 (1991), 95–119.

[46] For a discussion of Grimmelshausen's relation to Garzoni, see J. H. Scholte, *Zonagri Discurs von Waarsagern* (1921; reprint, Wiesbaden: M. Sändig, 1968).

2: Grimmelshausen and Baroque Dualism

The Two Realities

EVEN THOUGH, AS we saw in chapter 1, Grimmelshausen's relation to the intellectual and literary establishment of his day was somewhat ambivalent, he was in many respects still a man of the baroque, not least for the fact that he partook — albeit in his own way — in the dualistic view of reality that is characteristic of that period. In the heyday of *Geistesgeschichte*, the dominant critical method of the 1920s and 30s, the concept arose of a "Baroque Man" riven by the tensions of a dual perception of reality. He was inwardly torn, split, confused,[1] pulled this way and that between Christian belief and "the joy of the modern in the things of this world";[2] he had been "born with a double nature."[3] These fruits of an uninhibitedly inductive method are perhaps a little overripe in their schizophrenic implications, but the dualism to which they refer was real enough. As Conrad Wiedemann points out in his *Barockdichtung in Deutschland,* one of the best short introductions to the baroque, the "neo-Aristotelian metaphysics" of the time presented the seeker after knowledge with a world which was meaningful only in its "conceptual," not in its actual material existence. Justus Lipsius, whose *De Constantia* was a key text for baroque thought, saw a dichotomy between philosophical judgements on universals ("recta ratio") and "opinion" on the objects of the material world, which could be riven with contradiction.[4] For the writer, the direct representation of the world of reality without the mediation of an intellect that could abstract from the actual to the universal would be of doubtful cognitive value; what was required was the "second reality" available through symbolic modes of perception,[5] such as the *Sinnen-Bild,*[6] or emblem which was so popular in those days. The *Schein,* or apparent reality, of an often highly attractive world was therefore very often seen as being in itself unstable and untrustworthy, relatively transitory and vain when placed alongside the *Sein,* or universal reality.

The aspect of relativity needs to be emphasized here. It is easy, in the face of the powerful and deeply felt rhetoric of an Andreas Gryphius, to think in terms of a negation of the world. Yet even when he portrays the spiritual reality breaking through the physical, as in the sonnet "Über die Geburt Jesu," and calls the night of the Nativity a "night, brighter than the day," the physical darkness of night and brightness of day are essential factors in the metaphorical equation. Gryphius speaks with an organ voice of the mortality of man, of the transitoriness of the world and the fleeting nature of earthly time, yet the message is surely the need to emancipate oneself from *mental* subservience to material reality, as the only way to live properly *within* it. Friedrich Gaede is right to emphasize the dichotomy of the temporal and eternal,[7] but we must remember also that human existence inevitably links the two spheres, even if there is no philosophical possibility, for the baroque age, of harmonising them. Gryphius's famous sonnet "Es ist alles eitell" (All is Vanity, 1643) does not deny the reality, or even the attractiveness of the things of this world; rather, it is an attempt to persuade man of the danger for his immortal soul of an overestimation of their importance and validity. Man, as the initial stage directions for Gryphius's play *Catharina von Georgien* graphically remind us, stands between heaven and hell and should be mindful of the fact, but the ground on which he stands is that of this earth.

The relation between the two poles of the baroque duality is most commonly one of tension, which is at its most acute when our minds are in temporal mode. It is in the moment of present time that the two realities meet and the consciousness of disparity between them becomes most pressing. In the self-examination that leads to his initial conversion, Simplicissimus realises that his life has been a spiritual death: "Ich sahe nur auf das Gegenwärtige und meinen zeitlichen Nutz" (I considered only the present and my temporal welfare: *ST* 456). Seen in relation to eternity, the present is trivial, impermanent. Yet the present is the location of our human life and its joys. Here is a potent source of tension and it makes itself felt strongly in the verse of one of the most sensuous of baroque poets, Hoffmann von Hoffmanswaldau (1617–1679). Aware, as he puts it in his *Verliebte Arie* "Wo sind die Stunden," that "what pleases our spirit arises out of presentness," but simultaneously that "all pleasure is transitory,"[8] he can celebrate the fascination of beauty and at the same time feel it slipping away from him, as in the sonnet "Vergänglichkeit der Schönheit" (The Transitoriness of Beauty). There is an even more acute tension between a rather cool, rational spirituality and the almost overwhelming power of sensuality in the work of Daniel Casper von Lohenstein (1635–1683), Gryphius's most important successor in the theatrical field, and an important novelist and poet. The extremes of passion represented in Lohenstein's characters and the saturation of his style with sensory impressions earned him the epithet *geil* (lascivious) from Enlightenment critics, yet the vantage point from which he views his material is one of abstract detachment and his ideal is clearly that of a rationally-based Virtue.

Grimmelshausen himself, of course, ends the fifth book of his *Simplicissimus* with a rejection of things earthly. It is a prelude to the hero's withdrawal from the world to return to the point from which he came into it, the life of the hermit. The dualism — which can also manifest itself in other contrasts, for example that of the comic and the serious — here takes the form of the opposition of worldly and spiritual, temporal and eternal. This is a constantly recurring theme throughout the cycle and is introduced early through the figure of the Einsiedel, the hermit in the wood, who is Simplicius's spiritual and, as it later turns out, also his natural father.

The Einsiedel is clearly meant as an ideal, a yardstick by which human spirituality can be judged. The man himself dies in chapter 12 of book 1, but there are frequent subsequent references that make him a presence throughout *Der abentheurliche Simplicissimus*. Ilse-Lore Konopatzki has documented Grimmelshausen's interest in and knowledge of the lives of the Early Fathers and makes a convincing case for the assumption that they were the inspiration behind this figure. The Einsiedel represents the ideal of saintliness, the "longing for the highest values": a thread that runs though the whole work. Konopatzki recognises the humour that plays a considerable part, alongside deep religious seriousness, in the narration of the episode in which the young Simplicius meets the Einsiedel, and which she contrasts with the monotone solemnity of the passage from the *Vitae patrum* that could well have been the initial model. Similarly, like almost all critics, whatever the angle from which they approach Grimmelshausen, she notes the strength of his response to the "Buntheit des Lebens" (colour and variety of life), which also affects the narration of the whole episode. But there is no sense here of a fruitful polarity that would allow two perspectives to coexist, each with its own validity. The reality of the material world "conceals" the didactic meaning; it is merely a "foreground,"[9] so that defining the relation between the two sides involves a devaluation of being in the interests of meaning, and a consequent disruption of the balance of the Simplician manner.

Clearly, the eternal has to have philosophical priority. In theory, there is an opposition between the two poles of the duality. In his normal practice, though, Grimmelshausen handles the relationship in a way that creates an independent space or — as we shall argue in chapter 3 — a path for each. He makes it unnecessary to devalue the first in order to give due weight to the second. Only in the occasional set piece, such as the final chapter of book V already referred to, in which he adapts a meditation by the Spanish court chaplain Guevara, does the theme of *vanitas mundi*, so central to Gryphius's philosophy, dominate. And even then, there is a characteristic final adjustment that dilutes the sense of finality: it is by no means certain that Simplicius will remain permanently in the state of a world-denying hermit. The possibility of a step sideways is left open ("stehet dahin"). Grimmelshausen's outlook allows of a genuine coexistence of the two realities. Chapter 7 of book I of *Simplicissimus*, which follows the initial meeting, provides a good example of this coexistence.

The boy's fear of the strange and in some ways comically outlandish person with whom he has come into contact has caused him to faint. He comes to with his head in the other's lap and seeing him in such close proximity, begins to "scream blue murder, as if he were about to tear my heart out of my body" :

> Er aber sagte / Mein Sohn / schweig / ich thue dir nichts / sey zu frieden, etc. je mehr er mich aber tröstete / und mir lieb-koste: je mehr ich schrye / O du frisst mich! o du frisst mich! du bist der Wolf / und wilst mich fressen: Ey ja wol nein / mein Sohn sagte er / sey zu frieden, ich friß dich nicht. Diß Gefecht währete lang / biß ich mich endlich so weit liesse weisen / mit ihm in seine Hütten zu gehen. (*ST* 23)
>
> [But he said: "Be still my son, I am not going to hurt you, calm down" and so on. But the more he comforted and caressed me, the more I cried out: "O, you're going to eat me! You're going to eat me! You're the wolf and you want to eat me up!" "No, no, not at all, my son," he said, "calm down, I am not going to eat you." This wrestling match went on for a long time, until I finally allowed myself to be persuaded to go with him into his hut.]

Soon after, the boy's exhaustion causes him to fall asleep. Eventually he awakes, "at about midnight," and hears the hermit singing the hymn "Komm Trost der Nacht / o Nachtigal," whose naive charm has given it a deserved place in many an anthology of German verse. But we are not discussing it here as a piece of lyric poetry, and indeed it would be misconceived to think of it as a spontaneous lyrical outburst of the type that graces so many Romantic novels and stories, particularly those of Eichendorff. Its function is not to distil a mood, but to act as a crystallising agent for religious thought. Grimmelshausen, who was in fact *not* a poet of great talent or expertise, chooses the lyric form here, not because it is particularly congenial to him on aesthetic grounds, but because a hymn is what the occasion requires. Though it is based on the popular and often imitated hymn of Philipp Nicolai known as the "Morning Star"("Wie schön leuchtet der Morgenstern"), it is a nocturn hymn, a hymn of vigil, of ascetic spiritual self-discipline and devotion to the spiritual dimension. As such it is fitting for a figure based on the early anchorites, one of whom, St. Antony, was one of Grimmelshausen's favourite saints, and a prime model for the picture of Simplicissimus the hermit that is painted in book VI. The saint's reputed remark that Nature was a "book" in which one could read about God is quoted there (chapter 23) and is part of the background to our hymn as well. Heribert Rosweyde's commentary on this moment in the *Life of St Antony* contains, as Konopatzki shows (64), a reference to the psalmist's "The heavens declare the glory of God" (Ps. 19).

Grimmelshausen takes his hermit seriously, and he takes the virtuous life, in which the anchorite's devotion to God is carried out into the world, equally seriously. The linkage between the two is clear in his non-Simplician "heroic" novels, *Proximus und Lympida* and *Dietwalt und Amelinde*. When writing in the Simplician manner, however, he cannot maintain the tone of unrelieved seriousness that characterises the two books just mentioned. Indeed, one is tempted to ask whether he can take seriousness itself — even his own seriousness — entirely seriously, although he is severe in condemning frivolity, or *Leichtfertigkeit*, which he links to lack of spiritual awareness. There is, as we shall see when we discuss the relevant episode in chapter 6, more than a hint of criticism of the tone of the preacher himself, as he focusses the light of criticism on Springinsfeld's sins.

Scarcely have the last notes of the nightingale hymn died away in the forest before we are in a different atmosphere. The coda, so to speak, of chapter 7 moves us back towards the theme of the child's naive ignorance and the long conversation in chapter 8 oscillates between two poles. Grimmelshausen sympathizes with the hermit's deep spirituality and his horror at the "bestial" condition — that is, ignorance of God — of the boy whom he is catechising and whom he christens "Simplicius." On the other hand, he responds as a narrator to the reality of the young lad who has grown up in ignorance, talks in a thick dialect and is prone to comic misunderstandings of unfamiliar words. The whole episode in the isolation of the forest (chapters 7 to 12) is indisputably directed towards the Truth that transcends earthly reality. It is a piece set apart from the general action so that it obtains a symbolic status. Later on, the mere mention of the word Einsiedel will evoke a nexus of spiritual associations. But at the same time, here are two real people, living in a real forest, feeding themselves on a detailed menu of vegetables and wild plants, trapping and fishing and even fattening up a wild pig (chapter 11), almost like the castaways on Ballantyne's Coral Island.

The description of Simplicissimus's life as a musketeer at Philippsburg (book IV, chapter 11) is one in which the lasting symbolic significance of the Einsiedel episode, and the way in which it runs in tandem with the reality of earthly life, become clear. Simplicius has become "ein recht wilder Mensch": "No one would have believed that I had been brought up by such a pious hermit." He is called to account by the Regimental Chaplain, "ein recht frommer Seeleneiferer" (a really zealous soul-saver), but admonitions do no good, nor does the chaplain's bloodcurdling threat that if he should die in this condition, he will not grant him a Christian burial. We feel a duality of perspective here: the religious seriousness associated with the Einsiedel running alongside the soldier's reaction to the bible-puncher who does not have to risk his life in the field. Still in serious mood, the retrospective narrator exclaims over his great folly:

O ich großer Narr! Ich erzehlte offt meine Bubenstück bey gantzen Gesellschaften / und log noch darzu / aber jetzt / da ich mich bekehren / und einem einigen Menschen / an Gottes statt / meine Sünden demütig bekennen solte / Vergebung zu empfangen / war ich ein verstockter Stumm!"

[O what a terrible fool I was! I would often go on before the company at large about the mean and low tricks I had got up to, and invent a few for good measure; but now that it was a question of turning to God, and humbly confessing my sins to just one person, standing in God's place, so that I might obtain forgiveness, I hardened my heart and kept my stubborn mouth shut tight.]

The adumbration of the Confession theme (which is to recur with full weight at the end of the *Vogelnest*), leaves us in no doubt as to the seriousness of the danger Simplicius's soul is in. But then there is a characteristically Simplician change of mood. Firstly, the hardened sinner comes away from the confrontation with the chaplain, if not exactly on equal terms, then without humiliation. Grimmelshausen moves from the almost catechising tone of the retrospective narrator to that of the soldier, whose life is bounded by the present moment. Objectively, of course, this is still a reflection of Simplicius's spiritual limitations, but we are not now seeing him in pure contemplative retrospect. The narrative perspective has shifted and even if we do not share his realistic fatalism, we experience the reality (and vitality) of his life. For his grave, he replies, the soldier may have "to make shift with an open field, a ditch, or the belly of a wolf or a raven." There is an acceptance, here, of bleak reality that even has a hint of Shakespearean grandeur about it. Grimmelshausen goes on to accord the sinner a humorous victory over the zealous "saint":

Also schiede ich vom Geistlichen / der mit seinem heiligen Seelen-Eyfer anders nichts umb mich verdient / als daß ich ihm einsmal einen Hasen abschlug / den er inständig von mir begehrte / mit Vorwand / weil er sich selbst an einem Strick erhenckt und umbs Leben gebracht / daß sich dannenhero nicht gebühre / daß er als ein Verzweiffelter / in ein geweyhtes Erdreich begraben werden solte. (*ST* 326)

[Thus I parted from the preacher, and all that holy man's zeal for souls got him from me was that I once refused to give him a hare that he begged of me most earnestly, on the grounds that since it had strung itself up and taken its own life, it was not fitting that a creature that had died in a state of desperation should be granted a burial in consecrated ground.]

The serious tone, which recalls the "theological" coda that Ägidius Albertinus added to his translation of Alemán's *Guzmán de Alfarache* and recurs in the final section of the *Vogelnest*, gives way here to one in which real life in the here and now, in both its harsh and its comic aspects, speaks for itself. This reaffirmation of the perspective on life from within is not a denial of the importance of the truth perceived from the transcendental point of vantage. It simply re-establishes the coexistence of the two perspectives as separate and valid entities, and the ability of the Simplician narrator to move directly from one to the other without self-contradiction. In the later stages of the cycle, when Simplicissimus is more mature at the time the action occurs, there is necessarily less difference between his perspective on an event when it occurs and his view of it retrospectively. Without these contrasting perspectives — which form the "equilibrium" of which J.–M. Valentin has spoken — Simplicius becomes a less suitable channel for the Simplician manner.[10] His is too austere a piety. He sees the world too exclusively from one point of view to be able to encompass the parallel existence of two valid realities, and the "Simplician author" (or authorial principle) then has, as we shall see in due course, to take on other shapes.

This is perhaps the appropriate place for a brief discussion of the vexed question of Grimmelshausen's supposed "realism." Certainly since Richard Alewyn's comparison of Grimmelshausen with the Austrian baroque novelist Johann Beer in 1932, it has been seen as problematic, yet not even the advent of what Volker Meid calls the spiritualistic (*spirituell*)[11] method of interpretation has killed the debate. Alewyn is right to observe that Grimmelshausen is not concerned with creating a sense of "objective actuality";[12] Rohrbach also in asserting that his characters are often more correctly designated as "figures," whose true meaning often lies outside the material world that they inhabit.[13] For all that, even in the midst of blatant allegory, we sense life.[14]

It could well be this sense of an earthly vitality that explains the attempts that are still made to rescue the term "realism" for Grimmelshausen. But what we have in mind is covered neither by Tarot's ingenious blend of reality and allegory in the phrase "deutender Entwurf von Wirklichkeit" (interpretative sketch of reality),[15] nor by Haberkamm's concept of interdependent layers of meaning, in which the "literal" sense "has the function of a vehicle."[16] Friedrich Gaede is on less risky ground in associating the term "realism" with the satirical presentation of a "verkehrte Welt" (topsy-turvy world).[17] For satire does indisputably give a kind of description of the everyday world. But it does so in a generalised way that robs it of much of its individual vitality. And in both allegory and in satire, meaning and validity lie not within, but outside the "reality" presented.

Grimmelshausen does, of course, indulge in both allegory and satire. But both are comprehended within and shaped by the Simplician manner, and Grimmelshausen's attitude toward reality has much to do with this. We can agree with Alewyn that Grimmelshausen is not as true to everyday life as

Beer is, but the Simplician novels convey a vivid sense of the reality of the life described, of its essentially dynamic vitality. Grimmelshausen is no relativist or "libertin" like at least the younger Sorel, but a sincere Catholic Christian who places the spiritual firmly above the material in his view of life. Still, this does not stifle his *experience* of life or his awareness of the validity of that experience in its own right. A settled existence, such as Simplicius eventually achieves, is important for a true perspective on the world. He could not have endorsed Francion's dictum; "Mon naturel n'a de l'inclination qu'au mouvement" (My nature has no other inclination than that toward movement).[18] But insight must not be achieved at the expense of the stasis that derives from a radical detachment from life, in which some degree of mobility is endemic. *Francion*, as we know from its title, is an "histoire comique" (though "satyrique" is added later in the text), and it did give an important impetus to Grimmelshausen's development into a Simplician author, that is, at least in part, a comic one, for whom responsiveness to the dynamic vitality of this life on this earth — of what is, even if the moralist thinks it perhaps ought not to be — is extremely important. There is a true polarity between the moral and the comic in Grimmelshausen that we miss in Sorel. When Springinsfeld rejects the idea of a godly and contemplative life in favour of the freedom of the open road, Simplicius, no doubt with his creator's approval, describes the latter as simply an imagined freedom ("vermeinte Freiheit": *Springinsfeld* 47). Yet, as we shall see in chapter 6, Springinsfeld's view is not simply swept aside as nugatory.

Constancy and Comedy:
Didactic and Humorous Responses to the World

The reality in which a baroque literary figure had to live was subject to sudden and violent change. Grimmelshausen is one of many who refer to the idea, which can be traced back to Ovid (*Tristia* V, 8, 18), that "nothing is more constant in the world than inconstancy itself" ("das nichts beständigers in der Welt ist / als die Unbeständigkeit selbsten": *ST* III, 8). It is through the constancy of change that we become most acutely aware of Fortune, who, with her "erbärmlich Unbestand" (lamentable inconstancy) as Syphax calls it in Lohenstein's *Sophonisbe* (II, 2–3) "plays with us as if we were bubbles." But it is possible to see beyond this apparent moral chaos to the realm of Divine Providence and this insight is the foundation of the greatest of all the baroque virtues, that of *Beständigkeit* (constancy).

Grimmelshausen's Proximus and Lympida and Dietwalt and Amelinde, though tossed about by Fortune, remain models of heroic constancy and are duly rewarded, though Lympida seems to conflate Fate with Fortune when she laments: "O du unbarmhertzig- und ohngerechtes Verhängnus / wie spilestu mit denen so grausamb / die doch in Unschult zuleben sich befleissen und sonst nichts als Tugend lieben?" (O pitiless and unjust Fate, how cruelly you play with those who strive to live an innocent life and have no other love but virtue!: *PL* 94) A clearer insight into the situation of virtue under the assaults of fickle Fortune emerges in an episode from Anselm von Ziegler's *Asiatische Banise*. Like all heroic novels of its type, this book boasts a whole chorus line of pure, noble, beautiful, and, above all, constant heroes and heroines, who are led through labyrinthine but carefully planned cycles of fortune and misfortune to eventual happiness. One of these, Higvanama, endures a rapid-fire sequence of changes, from power and glory to captivity and humiliation and rescue, through Divine Providence ("Die Schickung der Götter")[19] all in the space of a single page.

Conditions in the so-called *niederer Roman* (low, that is, picaresque or comic novel), to which category the Simplician books belong, are different. The hero is by definition *not* constant, and as soon as he does achieve constancy through conversion, his function is reduced to that of retrospective narrator. Grimmelshausen, as we know, was a man of sincere faith and deep moral seriousness, and he introduces constancy as an ideal in characters such as Herzbruder and, above all, the Einsiedel, whose *Beständigkeit* impresses Ramsay (*ST* 65) and who, in fact, enjoins that same virtue on the young Simplicissimus just before he dies. The inconstancy of the world is given as a prime motive of the older Simplicissimus at the end of book V, when he withdraws from it to become a hermit himself. And frequent use is made in the Simplician novels of devices that allow the perspective to be shifted from the hectic present, dominated by Fortune, to a point of relatively timeless stillness from which events can be seen *sub specie constantiae*.

But can this be achieved without casting a blight on the humour and vitality of life in its dynamic state? Surely we either lose a high proportion of these qualities, or we have the feeling, as with the didactic reflections in the later versions of Sorel's *Francion*, that such passages have been simply tacked on in the interests of an external or internal censorship, and are not sincerely meant? Emile Roy points to the fact that in the second edition of 1626, when "le libertinage devenait dangereux" (libertinage was becoming dangerous), Sorel's book was "allégé de saletés et additionné de sermons édifiants"(cleansed of improprieties and supplemented with edifying sermons).[20] Sincere or not, such passages produce the impression, not of a polarity, but of a breakdown of continuity between two attitudes in the same character.

It is the distinctive virtue of the Simplician manner to achieve a dynamic balance between zeal and zest. We are equally convinced of the integrity of the moralising and of that of the *Histori* within the wider context of life in its wholeness.[21] We may take a narrative example from the fifth chapter of book IV of the *Simplicissimus*.

Our hero's physical beauty has attracted the attention of sundry amorous ladies in Paris and he has been sent for under mysterious circumstances to present himself under cover of night at a strange house. He finds that he has been brought thither for the purpose of fornication, a deadly sin in itself and aggravated in his case by the fact that it will be adulterous. The situation is, then, one with strong moralistic overtones. Grimmelshausen has underlined this by including, in the heading of chapter 4, in which the episode begins, a reference to the medieval legend of the *mons veneris*. He makes the atmosphere sultry and threatening. The thoroughly sinful nature of the old German woman who acts as interpreter and general mistress of ceremonies is made very clear, and we can disapprove of her, interesting as she is. Yet the author's sense of humour, and of graphic actuality, is not inhibited by the symbolic potential of the scene. The woman is also described as "ein altes Geribb" (an old bone-bag) and when what she sees as a naïvety on Simplicissimus's part makes her laugh, she does so, not in the manner of a sinister Hoffmannesque crone, but as a comic figure: "hierüber fieng sie an zu lachen / daß man ihr alle vier Zähn sahe." (This made her laugh so heartily that you could see all four of her teeth: *ST* 306). Simplicissimus succumbs to temptation, of course, and later receives what is explicitly designated as a punishment for his sin. We shall be discussing this sequel a little later.

First, though, it seems appropriate to consider the phenomenon of the Simplician coexistence of the serious and the comic in the context of a longer sequence, and we have chosen an example from part 2 of *Das wunderbarliche Vogelnest*, where the formal narrative framework is of a somewhat different kind. The anonymous second owner of the magic bird's nest is writing his life history in a deeply penitent state of mind. He sees his former self as a driven man: the melancholy and despair induced by the theft of his money, together with his subsequent "inconstancy" in backsliding from the wholesome attitude of his meditation on the flower-bulb in chapter 2, have separated him from God, the only source of constancy. Even in this context, the Simplician manner creates the conditions for the presence of the two sides of the Simplician polarity as separate entities. The obvious comic and purely narrative potential of the bird's nest (which makes its holder invisible) can still be exploited with little or no inhibition, even though the style changes in the surrounding text and a sternly disapproving narrator makes his presence felt.

The narrative perspective shifts easily and directly between the now and then, between the sternly repentant sinner and the blithely confident trickster. J. H. Petersen, who speaks rightly of the dual character (*Duplizität*) of this perspective, invites us to see this in terms of a division of the authorial perspective between a narrating and a narrated (or experiencing) persona.[22] But the necessary polarity is present in neither picaro nor penitent; it has to be provided by the somewhat shadowy figure (if indeed it *is* a figure!) of the "Simplician author" referred to in the preface to this work. Through his mediation, the trickster can, in a sense, take over the narration, inviting us to enjoy the fun with him. In the episode in question (chapters 5–9) he uses the nest to frustrate his wife's attempt to cuckold him, to punish her and at the same time to seduce the housekeeper, his wife's cousin.

In chapter 6, the housekeeper is manoeuvred, by an entertainingly narrated trick, into a situation in which she can be seduced. There is no sense of regret: this is a comic deception; a foolish virgin and her "treasure" are soon parted. In the two paragraphs that follow, we are shifted abruptly sideways to the perspective of the Judgement Day, and the narrator brands himself as an "Ehebrecher und Jungfrauen-Schänder" (adulterer and violator of virgins), only to dart, just as abruptly, back into the "Posse" (prank) that he is playing on his wife. "Then" becomes "now": "Vor dißmahl aber betrachtet ichs nicht so weit / sondern war nur drauff bedacht / wie ich den Possen / welchen ich meinem Weib auch reissen wolte / Werckstellig machen möchte" (For now, though, I didn't give the matter that much thought, but concentrated solely on how I could put the other trick, the one I wanted to play on my wife, into practice: *VN* 184). The tone is almost dismissive; the sobersided older narrator is thrust into the background and the younger prankster is left in charge. We accept the shift because we have become acclimatised to the Simplician mode of narration.

The excitement and continuous flux of present living reality, which also raises in the mind the allied idea of *vanitas mundi*, and hence, by implication, that of the Eternal, is itself a prominent theme. A striking example of this is the sequel to the Parisian episode in *Simplicissimus*, on which we touched earlier. It is of particular value because it shows how the Simplician manner, through the style and technique of narration, keeps the two sides of the polarity in a state of creative balance. Chapter 7 of book IV of *Simplicissimus* begins: "Womit einer sündiget / darmit pfleget einer auch gestraft zu werden" (That wherewith a man sins is usually also the instrument with which he is punished). Simplicissimus is suddenly struck down by a loathsome disease that renders him weak, penniless and so ugly that he becomes thoroughly unattractive to women. He begins to reflect on his life in a serious tone, replete with images suggestive of constancy and inconstancy: fortune and misfortune, the pious Einsiedel and the theme of the Prodigal Son. Finally he bursts out with a reflection on the theme of mutability:

> O schnelle und unglückselige Veränderung! Vor vier Wochen war ich ein Kerl / der die Fürsten zur Verwunderung bewegte / das Frauenzimmer entzückte / und dem Volck als ein Meisterstück der Natur / ja wie ein Engel vor kam / jetzt aber so ohnwerth / daß mich die Hund anpißten. (*ST* 311–12)

[Oh what a swift and melancholy alteration! Four weeks ago, I was a fellow who moved princes to admiration and women to ecstasy, and the common people to think me a masterpiece of Nature, an angel indeed. And now I was sunk so low that the dogs would come and piss on me.]

Logically, perhaps, this final phrase is a kind of rhetorical climax, the nadir of a descent into degradation. Stylistically, though, it is a shift of register and comes closer to being a piece of comic bathos, a return to the vigorously earthy: for all its grotesqueness, a comic exaggeration of the self-description that preceded this reflective passage.

Constancy, then, is as much a cardinal virtue for Grimmelshausen as it is for the heroic author in his aristocratic context. But while we would concur that the Simplician novels deserve to be taken seriously, they cannot be described as a straightforward and serious attempt to preach the gospel of constancy. There is a clear moral and religious message, and it clearly has what we might call theological primacy. But as Grimmelshausen himself states in the opening chapter of book VI, he is not writing here in a theological style. And this, as we shall see, is more than a mere matter of sugaring a moral-satirical pill. In Grimmelshausen's case, the style and general manner is crucial to any judgement we may wish to make as to authorial intention. He places himself, most notably in his descriptive subtitles, firmly within the traditional concept of the poet's role, which is accepted by the baroque as a whole, namely that he should edify as well as entertain. But a significant Simplician nuance can be discerned in the application of that principle: the Horatian maxim "miscere utile dulci" (to mix the useful with the pleasant) does not apply for him, if we take the idea of mixing literally. In this context, the ending of part 1 of the *Vogelnest* is as important as the more often cited preface to part 2.

The first owner of the bird's nest, having finally decided to renounce the life of the picaro, tears the nest "into seventeen hundred pieces" and then contemplates the ants and learns the lesson of constancy from their industry. But he is soon taught that "the world has not devoted itself to you [to Constancy], but to your arch-enemy, Inconstancy."(And indeed, we never learn whether he himself remains steadfast in the path of virtue.) He sees the nest acquire a new owner, and takes his leave of the reader with the pious hope that the latter has duly absorbed his moral message. This, surely, should be the end of the book. But instead, the Simplician principle seems to invade Grimmelshausen's concept of the reader. Just as the flux of life goes on in spite of the moral ending, so there is another legitimate way to read the novel. Indeed, the Simplician duality — or in this case, perhaps, plurality — penetrates into the concept of authorship as well. The Simplician author sheds the persona of the reformed picaro and looks forward to the publication of part 2. Individual picaresque figures can leave the world, or rise above it, but the world itself goes on and it is as fascinating as it is sinful. There is a second kind of reader who may not find, or if he finds them, may not heed "concealed teachings":

> ... so wird ihm jedoch diß Wercklein anderwerts contentirt / und ihme verhoffentlich die Zeit eben so wol und vielleicht nützlicher und besser vertrieben / als wann er in dem Amadis gelesen hätte.(*VN* 140)

> [... this little work will nevertheless have brought him satisfaction in other ways and, I hope, provided him with as pleasant, and perhaps a more useful and beneficial way of passing his time than if he had been reading the *Amadis*.]

It would be too much to expect, particularly at this point in the story, that Grimmelshausen should overtly accord the "lustig" equal status with the "nützlich." The official position that dominated seventeenth-century literary theory, that art should be edifying, must have priority in a programmatic passage such as this. But our author's genuine moral and didactic vision coexists with a perhaps instinctive comic vision of the world, and the fact that he can conceive of a reader who may or may not see the message, but who responds more spontaneously to the comic vision as being "usefully" employed hints at a degree of acceptance of the world as it is. This is not necessarily approval, for he is no more ready than is Cervantes to tolerate man's unstable and fallen nature with moral indifferentism. He does, though, have an ingrained respect for and responsiveness to the force of life itself; the activity of human beings who are being merely human, and the world, with all its inadequacies, is the only place in which that life is to be found. In the final analysis, the solution of the hermit, for all its moral grandeur, is for Grimmelshausen false, or at any rate, non-Simplician, for it is one-sided.

Reality and Meaning: Allegory

Our task in this and the following section is to pursue the theme of the baroque dual reality into the field of established practice and technique; to test the formulations that can and have been adduced to describe Grimmelshausen's narrative procedures. The basic question may be stated thus: if the true meaning of life can only be discerned from a viewpoint that transcends the individual man and moment, what approaches to the task of portraying life are open to the writer with ambitions to poetic status? That Grimmelshausen harboured such ambitions there can be no doubt. His position, though, is complicated by the fact that, although he shared the baroque conception of truth as transcending earthly reality, he responded with great intensity to the vitality of that reality. His predilection for a form of the novel in which the dynamic principle — the event, action — at the very least holds the balance against the more static one of contemplation must surely reflect that fact.

A marriage, therefore, had to be arranged between reality and meaning, and in this situation, two methods were of special relevance in the seventeenth century. They can certainly be said to overlap, but are sufficiently discrete to permit of separate treatment. The first, allegory, which Benjamin characterizes as the baroque form of a "history of significant nature,"[23] is evidence of the strong links between the baroque and the medieval mentality; the second, satire, is of at least equally ancient lineage, but has survived into modern times less radically transmogrified. It should come as no surprise, then, that satire has always been recognised as a prime factor in Grimmelshausen's art, whereas the case for allegory languished for a long time in relative neglect and has, in a natural reaction, been the dominant preoccupation in Grimmelshausen scholarship and criticism in more recent years. Our aim here is not to challenge the validity of these two approaches as such, but to suggest the need for some modification in Grimmelshausen's particular case and to use this discussion to gain greater insight into the workings of the Simplician manner as it affects narrative technique.

The word allegory is used here in a broad sense, to include all those procedures, including figurative forms of exegesis, which were popular in the seventeenth century. That Grimmelshausen should have remained immune to the influence of this trend is inherently unlikely. Nor did he: his frontispieces, for example, are at least partially allegorical in this sense.[24] Our argument will be that he does at times write allegorically, but that there is in his handling of allegory a Simplician dimension that needs to be taken into account. Theoretical analysis, fascinating as it is, has to feed on scraps in Grimmelshausen's case, and must remain speculative. It is at least worth considering whether the analysis of concrete *practice*, and in particular style, can take us further. We have chosen here to examine three examples, of somewhat different types, in which there is an allegorical presence that seems to have been conditioned by a Simplician spirit.

The "Schermesser" Episode

Every so often, Grimmelshausen sets an episode apart from the general run of his narrative, perhaps as a dream-vision, perhaps by presupposing the suspension of the laws of nature, or by some other kind of signal (for example, a chapter heading) that tells us that the episode stands to a certain extent on its own. It is in episodes of this kind that we have the greatest expectation of finding what many call the allegorical layer in Grimmelshausen's work, that which, in the words of Hubert Gersch, has the function of making a statement that has "eine über den unmittelbaren Erzählzusammenhang hinausreichende Aussagefunktion" (a function of expression that goes beyond the immediate narrative context).²⁵ An obvious candidate for such status is the sequence in *Simplicissimus* in which the hero has an encounter with a piece of toilet-paper (book VI, chapters 11–12). The paper tells the story of its life and hard times and pleads, unsuccessfully, for mercy. Rolf Tarot has interpreted this as a figure of the sinful and frivolous state of the hero's soul, of his *superbia* and *curiositas*, which override the sympathy he should feel for the poor, abused, indeed martyred object over which he has the power of life and death.²⁶

What is disturbing about this interpretation is not so much the specific thrust of the argument — indeed an ingenious case is made out — but its one-sidedness. That the episode has representative status is undeniable, but the single-minded drive to document the presence of allegory tends to obscure the productive polarity between two realities. When the concept of martyrdom appears, we can sense the seductive power of the idea threatening to stifle the critic's sense of humour. Tarot certainly concedes that Grimmelshausen's is a "realistic portrayal," but claims that an allegorical element "breaks through" the realism here. Therefore he treats the text almost as if it were a homily by St. Augustine, and required to be interpreted strictly according to medieval exegetic methods. He speaks of the "kernel within the shell of the external action" and indicates that the author is telling the reader that he must not allow the entertaining aspects of the book to distract him from the "higher" meaning. We could as well say that if the author had wanted this meaning to emerge clearly, he ought not to have allowed his attention to be distracted by so much interesting and amusing detail, which leaves us with a polarity of moral allegory and comic fantasy. Tarot's apparent disregard of style and tone is the main problem here. He can certainly point to the fact that Grimmelshausen himself used the shell/kernel image in referring to his work in the opening chapter of the *Continuatio*, but there, as will be discussed in greater detail in our next section, Grimmelshausen was protesting against those critics who would consign him to the category of a mere sub-literary entertainer, and using the image to claim the status of a satirist, rather as Johann Beer does in the preface to his *Teutsche Winter-Nächte*.²⁷

The problem with the shell/kernel image, in our context, once it is taken beyond the stage of the standard terminology of satire, is that it drastically reduces the validity of one factor in the equation. It requires, as Sigmund von Birken wrote, that we "crack the [shell of the] nut in order to enjoy the kernel,"²⁸ a formula that subordinates narrative to didactic interest. It also raises, in an acute form, the question of Grimmelshausen's "hidden" meanings. He certainly does speak, as we saw in the preceding section, of "hidden teachings" and castigates, in chapters 7 and 8 of *Springinsfeld*, the "grobe[r] Verstand" (coarse understanding) of those who cannot understand him, and think him a mere "Gaukler" (juggler); but a spiritualistic interpretation that takes these and similar phrases further than the justified self-defence of the satirist and moralist is entering dangerously speculative methodological territory and risks upsetting the Simplician balance and destroying the very quality that makes the work unique. If Grimmelshausen is being consistently misread, it must surely be because he has *not* written in the way in which — for the moment at least — he may wish he had. Urs Herzog, for example, propounds the theory that the Christian idea of Pity or Mercy is the "hidden theology" of *Simplicissimus*, and is forced to argue that Grimmelshausen uses a "code" to enable the reader to discover lights hidden — too well, apparently — under bushels. He maintains that the simile of the bagpipes (in book I, chapter 3) "crying out so pitifully" when Simplicissimus falls on top of them, "as if they were trying to move the whole world to pity" is a "Chiffre,"[29] and we have to agree that this is possible. Many, if not all things are possible with this method. But no really convincing argument is advanced for the view that this was Grimmelshausen's intention, and a reading of the whole passage makes it seem more likely that enjoyment, rather than edification, was his chief aim here. One is reminded of the "lamentation" of the bed in part 1 of *Das wunderbarliche Vogelnest*, when Gretl lets Clausen Hansens Georg into her room, and a "wildes Wesen" (disorderly conduct) ensues (*VN* 35). Grimmelshausen may not morally endorse these goings on, but amusement predominates in this description.

What one misses in Tarot's account is an appreciation of Grimmelshausen's direct response to the liveliness of life and to its humour. No amount of special pleading or learned reference can remove the comic content from a situation in which a man in a privy sits in judgement on a piece of toilet paper and hears it plead for its life, or at least for a more honourable death. It is perfectly true, as Tarot says, that Simplicissimus lacks humility and deserves to be reminded of his mortality, but how humble is the "Schermesser"? It flaunts its ancient lineage — as hemp-seed, it is mentioned in Pliny — and thinks itself worthy to wipe a king's backside: "oder warum werde ich nicht in eines Königs von Frankreich Secret gebraucht / dem der von Navara den Arsch wischt?" (or why should I not see service in the privy of the King of France, who has his arse wiped by the King of Navarre?) The two kings were, of course, one and the same person.

The pathos of a piece of paper that, with its coarse reference to the royal hindquarters, does, as Simplicissimus says, seem to be something of a "grober Gesell" (coarse fellow), has both its serious and its ridiculous side. The paper's account of its life-cycle is both symbolic and imbued with a solid and palpable reality. What we have is a Simplician, not a pure allegory. If the latter is to work successfully, its "reality" must be transparent and it must eschew true humour, which ties us to this world (and which suffocates, conversely, in an abstract vacuum). Don Quixote's illusions are comic only in so far as they bring him into collision with present and all-too-solid reality. They can certainly have *representative* significance, but if we did not believe in the material reality of the windmills, we could not laugh at Quixote's assault on them.

In tracing the stations of the paper's pilgrimage from dust to dust, Grimmelshausen is constantly, it seems, succumbing to the temptation to digress into the physical reality and develop the humorous or narrative potential of his material. (For an allegorist of the Classical school, that is, this would be a temptation to be resisted; the Simplician manner encourages such indulgence.) Here is his description of events at the paper-mill:

> ... daselb wurden wir etlichen alten Weibern übergeben / die uns gleichsamb zu lauter Streichpletzen zerrissen / allwo wir dann mit einem rechten Jammer-Geschrey unser Ellend einander klagten; damit hatts aber drum noch kein End / sondern wir wurden in der Papiermühl gleich einem Kinderbrey zerstoßen / daß man uns wohl vor kein Hanff- oder Flachsgewächs mehr hette erkennen mögen / ja endlich eingebeitzt in Kalch und Alaun und gar in Wasser zerflöst. (*ST* 520)

[... and there we were handed over to a party of old women, who ripped us apart until we were nothing but dishrags as it were, while we exchanged loud cries of anguish, bemoaning our miserable fate. But that was not the end of it: rather, we were taken to the paper-mill and pounded into a porridge you could have fed to a baby, so that no-one could have told us for hemp or flax any more and finally, we were steeped in lime and alum and indeed, dissolved in water.]

It is perfectly proper to see this as an episode with a representative function. It is clearly set apart, and has obvious applicability to the situation of Simplicissimus in particular, and to life in general. Its ground-plan, then, could be said to be allegorical, but the manner of its realisation makes us want to qualify the statement somewhat. Is not the development of full-blown allegory inhibited by the independent and self-validating vigour of the narrative and the style? Could we not speak of reality and individuality "breaking through" apparent allegory in this case? Not, to be sure, in such a way as to destroy or even obscure its representative significance, but rather in free coexistence with it within the framework of a Simplician view of the world? Having been "anatomisiert" (dissected) in one incarnation by one group of old women wielding their flax-combs, our hero is now torn limb from limb by another. These are real people, doing real work. The humour with which Grimmelshausen turns the sound of rending linen into cries of pain militates *against* an interpretation of the event as a martyrdom and helps, indeed, to underpin the actuality of the scene. The introduction of the idea of baby-food not only enlivens the style, but contributes to our impression of a narrative set in the present, everyday world. The details of the paper-making process add an obvious realism; however, although one has some sympathy with Knopf's reaction against "spirituelle Deutung," to imply that Grimmelshausen is setting out here to describe the "frühkapitalistische Realität" is perhaps imposing yet another perspective from outside.[30] That generalised and abstracted reality may well be reflected in what he writes, but if we derive a sense of realist intention from the text, it is that of a response to being rather than meaning. It is true that the paper has the last word and that its message, *qua* message, is a bleak and stern one. As Simplicissimus is dealing with the paper, so Death will deal with him (*ST* 521–2).

A serious *memento mori*, and meant as such: it is written in a uniformly serious style. But we are aware at the same time that these words are spoken by a piece of paper held by a man who is sitting on a judgement-seat ("daselbst hinsetzte ich mich eilends zu Gericht") that is also a toilet-seat. The allegory of life stands alongside a piece of comic baroque parody and the curious nature of the episode is highlighted by the use of the word "seltzam" in the chapter heading. Oddity is not an eternal and universal, but a temporal and individual quality. One is reminded of a remark at the beginning of chapter 4 of book V: "es gehet wohl seltzam in der veränderlichen Welt her" (It's an odd life in this mutable world of ours: *ST* 383). This formulation, in which the two poles, the temporal and eternal, stand side by side, could be a formula for the Simplician manner.

Courage and the Campfire: Matter and Substance

Though he must surely have been aware that he had written a genuine and consistent allegory, Bunyan felt the need to append an "Explanation" to part 1 of *The Pilgrim's Progress*. An awareness of the inherent power of narrative to grip the imagination seems to resound in his warning to the reader against confusing the apparent actuality, which is meant as a "figure or similitude," with "the substance of my matter."

Grimmelshausen's often-quoted introductory remarks to book VI of *Simplicissimus* show a similarity of approach to that of Bunyan. He distances himself firmly from the "clowns and pranksters" whose aim is "to make people laugh." "Viel lachen ist mir selbst ein Eckel" (To me personally, frequent laughter is repellent), he asserts, in a phrase borrowed from Moscherosch's satirical credo,[31] and he goes on to justify the "possierliche" aspects of his work with the standard satirical formula of the sugared pill, and to make the remark about the shell and the kernel to which we have already referred. He is using, he says, the technique of the charlatan in the marketplace rather than that of the preacher because the former is so much more successful in drawing a crowd. He is indeed discussing his "manner," and above all its "lustig" element, but says nothing about its effect on the quality of the message. It is true that we would not expect high critical sophistication of him, or of the baroque age in general, but that a man with such a mastery of style should not have had at least a subliminal awareness of its importance seems improbable. There is likely to be another tactical consideration at work here: Grimmelshausen certainly has a serious didactic purpose, but he is also serious about his status as a writer, and on this and similar occasions he is asserting his right to be taken seriously. The category that represents his best route to recognition is satire, which is after all part of his armoury. The "Marckschreyer" in this passage is not just a poetological metaphor, however. In the presentation, and through the style itself, he becomes a living, interesting, indeed amusing reality. The preacher, called here "eyferig[s]te Seelen-Hirt" (most zealous shepherd of souls), a figure which occurs on several occasions in the cycle and by no means in an entirely flattering light, pales into ineffectual insignificance by comparison.

In the *Courasche*, a work published in the year following the appearance of the reflections we have just discussed, we have a striking case of this dynamic and productive polarity. The autobiographical narrator Courage is an unrepentant sinner, a defiant example and practitioner of all seven deadly sins and in particular that of *luxuria*, a sin particularly laden with devilish associations and yet so very much alive and graced — through the medium of the Simplician style — with so much humour that one could almost be misled into reading the portrait as sympathetic. An episode from the sequence in which Courage lives with Springinsfeld shows this style at work in a more thoroughly mundane and narrative-oriented context than is the case with the "Schermesser." Courage has established complete dominance over Springinsfeld, made a fool and a flunkey of him and completed the process of his corruption. He is beginning to rebel — though he is still sexually in thrall to her — and one night, while the army is encamped by the Danube, he resorts (for the second time, in fact) to violence. He snatches her from her bed and runs off towards the camp fire. A scene of great animation ensues: Courage, finding herself being carried "quite naked" towards the fire, begins to scream as if she had fallen into the hands of a gang of murderers. The officers come running, expecting to find a mutiny, and find instead:

> ... nichts anders als ein schönes lächerliches Einsehen und närrisches Spektacul / ich glaube auch / daß es recht artlich und kurtzweilig anzusehen gewesen sein muß; Die Wacht empfinge dem Spring-ins-felt mit seiner unwilligen und schreyenten Last / ehe er dieselbige ins Feuer werffen konte / und als sie solche nackend sahen / und seine Courage erkanten / war der Korporal so ehrliebend / mir einen Mantel um den Leib zu werffen. ...

Als indessen Spring-ins-felt sich wieder witzig stellte / oder (ich weis selbst schier nit / wie es ihm ums Hertz war) als er wieder zu seinen sieben Sinnen kommen; fragte ihn der Obriste / was er mit dieser Gugelfuhr gemeint hatte? da antwortet er / ihm hätte geträumt / seine Courage wäre überall mit giftigen Schlangen umgeben gewesen / derowegen er sie seinem Einfall nach / zu erretten und davon sich befreyen / entweder in ein Feuer oder Wasser zu tragen vors beste gehalten. (*Courasche*, 118–19)

[. . . only to find a ludicrous spectacle, a comic diversion. And I think myself that it must have made a highly amusing and entertaining show. The guard intercepted Springinsfeld with his reluctant and vociferous burden and when they found that this latter had no clothes on and was in fact Springinsfeld's Courage, the Corporal's sense of modesty moved him to wrap a cloak around my body. . . . And when, in a while, Springinsfeld went back to behaving like a rational being or (and I really have no idea what his state of mind was at the time) when he was once more in full possession of all his faculties, the Colonel asked him what sort of stupid game he thought he had been playing. He answered that he had dreamed that his Courage was covered all over with poisonous snakes so that (as he thought, to save and free her from them) he had thought the best thing was to put her into fire or water.]

No one who is at all familiar with the theme will have failed to recognise in Springinsfeld's dream an explicit reference to the medieval allegory of My Lady World (Frau Welt), the seductive female figure which turns out on closer inspection to be full of corruption and repellent. Mathias Feldges, who devotes a whole section to this theme, is justified in claiming that "Courage is identified here with Frau Welt."[32] But that identification does not allegorize the whole episode retrospectively. The narrative is insulated against such an effect by its lively style and essentially comic vision. When Feldges quotes the narrative itself in support of his thesis (the fact that Courage is naked is said to confirm that she is Frau Welt, for she is "unverhüllt," that is, exposed), he illustrates very well the problematic nature of all-embracing allegorical interpretation. The comment represents an unwelcome and inappropriate attempt to integrate morality with farce. Courage's unclothed condition needs no abstract explanation — and indeed it will not, as presented, support one — and her own admission, looking back, that she must have made a laughable spectacle, is most likely an authorial signal, an indication of the way in Grimmelshausen, for all his warnings against an exclusively comic interpretation in other places, must have expected and intended this episode to be read.

This would seem to be an example of the Simplician process of shifting between poles, from real to representative, from comic to serious. Feldges argues that Grimmelshausen has carried out a measure of integration of the two sides by making Frau Welt into a human being rather than an ageless allegory. "Die Kluft zwischen Zeichen und Leben," he says, "ist ausgefüllt" (the gulf between the [symbolic] sign and [real] life has been filled: 92). But integration surely means that the real person and the allegorical meaning are linked, not just at one particular moment (a conclusion with which we would gladly agree), but consistently and permanently. It is in the nature of Frau Welt to be young and fair, and Courage, as a wrinkled gypsy of a more advanced age, cannot sustain the parallel. And integration, if we are to take it seriously, means also adulteration (for example, of reality by moral satire). That there is a "geistiger Sinn" (spiritual meaning) in Grimmelshausen's novels is perfectly true, but it lies neither "behind" the reality, as Feldges says, nor in it: it stands alongside it. Solid reality cannot be allowed to exclude, nor can it be allowed to become subordinate to, what Weydt calls an "allegorising exegesis." The *Courasche*, for example, cannot be described (as it is by Weydt) as picaresque at most in the sense that it has a picaresque foreground ("höchstens vordergründig noch").[33] We cannot accept Feldges's assertion that Grimmelshausen's humorous vivacity is no more than a device used as a means ("ein bewußt eingesetztes Mittel") to a "higher" end, a sop to the average reader (152). It is an essential part of a view of the world that combines religious conviction and deep moral awareness with an ingrained respect for the vitality of life itself. Courage is very much a case in point. In spite of her acknowledged wickedness, she retains a certain respect, if not exactly sympathy, in the reader's mind and heart, by virtue of an apparently indomitable, if incurably sinful spirit.

An Image of War

As was observed, the precise detail and overriding issues of the Thirty Years' War cannot (with the possible exception of the *Springinsfeld*) be said to constitute the primary reality of the novels in which it plays a part. The war is, however, a constant presence, and there are moments when it is brought to the forefront as a theme in its own right. Chapter 4 of book I of *Simplicissimus* is one such, as its introductory paragraph makes clear. It is true that the narrator also stresses the importance of this episode (the plundering of his foster-father's farm) as a means employed by Providence to bring him out of a state of bestial ignorance and to eventually launch him out into the world where he will acquire understanding. But the detailed narrative would not have been necessary for this purpose. Grimmelshausen excuses himself to the "peace-loving reader" for leading him into a scene of violence, on the grounds that he must inform "the gentle reader of posterity" of the "cruel deeds that were done, here and there, in that German war of ours" (*ST* 17). The boy — who has not yet even acquired a name — has been forced to guide a group of marauding soldiers to the farm. On arrival, they set to with a comprehensive and almost demonic energy which makes it hard for us to think of them as no more than an ordinary group of soldiers. Everything they do spells devastation and ruin:

dann obzwar etliche anfiengen zu metzgen / zu sieden und zu braten / daß es sahe / als solte ein lustig Panquet gehalten werden / so waren hingegen andere / die durch-stürmten das Hauß unden und oben / ja das heimlich Gemach war nicht sicher / gleichsam ob wäre das gülden Fell von Colchis darinnen verborgen; Andere machten von Tuch / Kleidern und allerlei Haußrat / grosse Päck zusammen / als ob sie irgends ein Krempelmarckt anrichten wolten / was sie aber nicht mitzunehmen gedachten / wurde zerschlagen / etliche durchstachen Heu und Stroh mit ihren Degen / als ob sie nicht Schaf und Schwein genug zu stechen gehabt hatten / etliche schütteten die Federn auß den Betten / und fülleten hingegen Speck / andere dürr Fleisch und sonst Gerät hinein / als ob alsdann besser darauff zu schlaffen gewest wäre; Andere schlugen Ofen und Fenster ein / gleichsam als hätten sie einen ewigen Sommer zu verkündigen / Kupffer und Zinnengeschirr schlugen sie zusammen und packten die gebogene und verderbte Stück ein / Bettladen / Tisch / Stül und Bänk verbrannten sie / da doch viel Clafter dürr Holz im Hof lag / Hafen und Schüsseln muste endlich alles entzwey / entweder weil sie lieber gebraten assen / oder weil sie bedacht waren / nur ein einzige Mahlzeit allda zu halten. (*ST* 17–18)

[For while some of them fell to butchering, boiling and roasting, so that it looked as if a jolly banquet was to be held, there were others, in contrast, who rampaged through the house upstairs and down, and even the privy was not safe from their attentions, just as if the Golden Fleece of Kolchis lay hidden there. Others made up great bundles of material, clothes and other household objects, as if they intended to hold a flea-market somewhere or other; anything they didn't intend to take with them, on the other hand, was smashed to pieces. Others thrust their swords into the hay and straw, as if they hadn't already had sheep and pigs enough to stick them into, some shook the feathers out of the beds and re-filled them with bacon, dried meat of other kinds, and other stuff, as if this would make them more comfortable to sleep on. Others smashed in the stove and the windows, as if they had come to proclaim an eternal summer. They crushed the copper and pewter vessels and packed up these bent and ruined objects, they burned bedsteads, tables, chairs and benches, even though there were many cords of dry wood lying about in the yard and finally, all the pots and dishes had to go down the road to ruin, either because they preferred their meat roasted, or because they meant to eat only one meal here.]

After this, Grimmelshausen, who is clearly working, here, according to a formal plan, turns from the maltreatment of the inanimate, to that of the human occupants of the farmstead. What we have seen is a Bruegelesque picture, or rather part of one, and its formal structure helps to underpin its representative function as a kind of compendium. At the same time, while the general burden is the cruel and senseless nature of war, the narrative style is more than a mere vehicle for a catalogue of atrocities. It describes a representative scene, but it reflects also the vivid actuality of a specific incident.

There is repetition, but there is also variation of rhythm. The main thrust is all in one direction, but there is also a great sense of variety. Grimmelshausen's moral outrage at this manic destruction in which, as he repeatedly underlines, the world of healthy normality is stood on its head, cannot be doubted. Neither, however, can his fascination with the narrative and even humorous potential of the scene. We disapprove of the soldiers' activity, but we catch a sense of its bustle and excitement. And in the detail, the objects are often endowed with a living and specific reality. The looters do not simply "empty" the beds, they are graphically depicted shaking the feathers out of them and then stuffing them full of booty. Likewise, we seem to see the bent and twisted drinking-vessels as they are packed away. The drive towards reflection is balanced by that towards storytelling, and if this is an allegory, it is a very Simplician one.

The baroque tendency to expand from the individual into the universal is found in Grimmelshausen as well. But the principle of individuality is also present in his mind in great strength, and there are occasions, too, on which we can speak of a significant measure of individualisation of the exemplary figure, as for example in the case of Colonel Lumpus in the chapter 11 of the *Springinsfeld*. Lumpus exemplifies well enough the general truth that the soldier finds it hard to see further than the end of his nose and escape from the deadly treadmill, even when Fortune favours him. But as Grimmelshausen warms to telling Lumpus's story, he acquires individuality. We remember him, for example, tossing coins to the sentries who salute as he passes, in his days of wealth and extravagance. Allegory, then, is a factor in Grimmelshausen's mental constitution, and he sometimes makes use of allegorical forms in his work. But the tendency to full-blown abstraction is foreign to him.

Reality and Meaning: Satire

Satire, as F. J. Stopp has said, is a literary mode which tends not to evolve its own genres, but to be parasitic on those of others,[34] and it very early recognized the epic genres as suitable hosts. In the context of the classicistically-oriented literary theory of the seventeenth century, however, it could repay some of its debt by conferring literary respectability. Novels could claim to improve and instruct, as it was the duty of all literature to do, by exposing and criticising faults as well as by celebrating the heroic virtues. The *niederer Roman*, as Vosskamp tells us, leaped gratefully on to this bandwagon.[35] Its need was particularly great, since the reality that it described was not only "low" and un-heroic, but also often comic, or entertaining in a way which did not appeal immediately to the intellect. Nothing in it pointed beyond the merely mundane. So we find that Grimmelshausen and others make great play with the standard satirical formulae. To take as example the prefatory apologia given by Johann Beer in his *Teutsche Winter-Nächte* (1682), the author recommends his book as a product that contains a sweetened ("versüßet") medicine and, in a phrase borrowed from Horace, claims to instruct through laughter ("lachend unterrichten").[36] The truth referred to is that of the "higher" reality and is reached in this case not by an allegorical alienation, but by a process of abstraction from the individual to the general, and judgement of human behaviour from the point of view of recognized moral universals. The story told may be *possierlich* (trivial; comic or curious), but it can attain official literary recognition if it can find refuge under the umbrella of a definition of satire such as Opitz's: "die harte verweisung der laster und anmahnung zue der tugend" (sharp condemnation of vice and admonition to virtue).[37] On its own, the word *Posse* — which could mean a prank, a funny story, a curious incident, or a nonsensical trifle — always contained associations of mere frivolity, associations that the "low" novelist was always having to fend off. Harsdörffer, for example, damns the three best-known Spanish picaresque novels in a single phrase when he exclaims scornfully against "ärgerliche Possen ... nicht höher zu achten / als Guzmana, Lazarillo, oder die Picara Justina" (tiresome trifles, no more deserving of respect than Guzman [de Alfarache], Lazarillo [de Tormes] or the Picara Justina).[38]

The theory, then, is that the storyteller's principal aim is to instruct and improve his readers, and that he may legitimately amuse them if, and only if, he does so in order to achieve his didactic purpose more effectively. We are close, once more, to the doctrine of the shell and the kernel, which we met in the preceding section, and there will be some similarities in our line of argument. We shall be looking to see whether the relation of two contrasting impulses, the entertaining and the didactic — or, to use the terms employed by Grimmelshausen himself in his descriptive subtitles, the "lustig" and the "nützlich" — coexist and interact as interdependent entities in a Simplician polarity, or whether the relationship is one of predominance and subservience. In a properly satirical context, we would expect the dominant didactic intention to inhibit the development of the narrative and comic potential of the material; conversely, such development should be detrimental to the effectiveness of the relevant episodes or passages as satire. Beer has his serious side, it is true, and there are satirical parts even in the *Winter-Nächte*, but if we place it alongside other works by the same author in which the satirical impulse is a clear and strong motivating factor, works like the *Jungfer-Hobel* or even *Bruder Blaumantel*, we can see that in describing such an entertaining book as "mehr einer Satyra als Histori ähnlich" (more like a satire than a story),[39] he is belying the strengths of his own work. That he should have done so is not too surprising, in the literary climate of the baroque age. He will not have wished, any more than did Grimmelshausen, to be seen as a "Schalksnarr und Possenreisser" (fairground charlatan and entertainer).

Stories certainly *can* be told for primarily didactic purposes. Preachers themselves can make use of them to soften somewhat the abstract rigours of the strict theological style. But whereas narrative as *story* gives real weight to the concrete and individual, the moralist's use of it tends, as Wolfgang Harms observes of Moscherosch, to direct the reader's gaze "towards the general."[40] Moralistic storytellers retain strict control of the narrative element: it is clear from the style and technique that the message remains paramount. Since the evidence we shall have to seek in deciding Grimmelshausen's position is made up of stylistic and technical relativities, the best procedure seems to be to work through comparison, and we have chosen for this purpose someone who had a penchant for telling stories in his sermons and indeed attracted criticism for doing so, the cleric and satirist Johann Balthasar Schupp. Schupp was, like Grimmelshausen, a man who combined deep moral seriousness with a strong sense of humour, and who, although he had enjoyed an academic training denied to our author, had a natural responsiveness to the living reality of the world. It was this latter, in fact, that in the 1650s involved him in a bitter polemical battle with colleagues in Hamburg, out of which arose the satirical novel *Corinna* and a series of tracts to which we shall make reference.

Schupp defends his use of material deemed unsuitable for the theological style on the ground that he is writing and speaking for "Herr Omnis,"[41] a figure whom Grimmelshausen also conjures up in chapter 1 of the *Continuatio*, to represent his reader. But Schupp's departure from the theological format is not as radical as might at first appear. He uses narrative, either as a framework for or as an exemplary episode inset into an argument, but in each case, it is argument rather than storytelling that is the dominant motive. A case that offers a basis for direct comparison with Grimmelshausen is the story of the innkeeper's daughter in Schupp's *Deutscher Lucianus*. Schupp here mounts a systematic attack on the hidebound academic system within which he is being called upon to work, and as a part of that attack he sets out to make the various philosophical systems look ridiculous, among them the supposed philosophy of "Heraclitus the Weeper." He integrates more or less seamlessly into his argument the tale of the innkeeper whose daughter's hand has been asked for in marriage. He tells her of this and then sends her to the cellar for some wine. When half an hour has passed with no sign of her, the mother goes to the cellar and finds her weeping bitterly. She is weeping, she says, because she has been thinking of the many and various disasters that might occur if she were to get married and have children. Her mother, overcome by the sad prospect, joins in: "Darauff habe die Mutter einen *Alt*, die Tochter einen *Discant* geheulet, und das habe eine ganze viertel Stunde lang gewehret." The father comes down and finds them in this tearful state: "Als er aber die Ursache gefraget, habe er angefangen, einen *Bass* zu heulen und da sey es angegangen auff drey Stimmen, und habe eine geraume Zeit gewehret" (Then the mother began to lament in the alto, and the daughter in the soprano line and this went on for a full quarter of an hour.... When he had found out the reason, he began to lament in his bass voice and off they went in three-part harmony and continued for a considerable time).[42]

The musical conceit is neatly presented and it has an undeniable enlivening effect. But it has no existence independent of the satirical intention of arguing a point. It is given in bare outline for the sake of its point, rather than *told* with a truly narrative evocation of the quality of real, individual life. None of the three figures who participate in it have any other function. The facts are not presented as a continuous action, but rather structured as a formal triad of examples of one and the same folly. The style is nondescript, repetitive ("heulen," for example, is used three times) and rhythmically flaccid.

In *Der stoltze Melcher*, a little pamphlet written to express opposition to the Dutch Wars of Louis XIV, and above all, to deter young Germans from joining the French army, Grimmelshausen makes use of the same conceit. The framework is the parable of a Prodigal Son. Melcher has run away to enlist, against his father's express command, but has now returned, broken down and in rags. His mother brings out some fresh clothes and begins by berating him:

> Solches nun war der Anfang der ersten Sermon die sie thät / das Mittel war etwas gelinder / und als ihr Sohn seine Lumpen auß und hingegen die Kleider / die sie mitgebracht / wieder anzog / so / das sie beobachten konde / wie mager / ellend und jämmerlich er am Leib aussahe (maßen er gantz verdorben / von Fleisch kommen und erbärmlich abgefallen war) beschlosse sie auß Mütterlichem Mitleyden das End daran mit weinen; Tochter und Sohn stimbten mit an / welches zusammen die artlichste *Harmonia* einer *miserablen Music* abgab; der Vatter, welcher seines Sohnes Ankunfft erfahren / kam mit einem starcken *baculo* herzu geloffen / ohnzweiffel des Vorhabens / den tact auff seines Sohnes *Buckelorium* zuführen.
>
> (*KS* 35)

[Thus she began by preaching him a sermon; as she reached the middle, her tone became somewhat gentler and when her son had pulled off his rags and pulled on, in exchange, the clothes she had brought him, giving her the opportunity to observe how thin, miserable and pitiful his body looked (for he had gone really to the dogs, shed pounds of flesh and descended to a pitiably wasted state), her motherly heart was touched and she brought her speech to a conclusion by bursting into tears. Her daughter and son joined in and all three voices were most prettily blended in harmonious musical misery. The father, who had heard of his son's arrival, came running up with a big thick baton, intending, no doubt, to beat out the rhythm by laying it on the back of his son.]

The reader will have noted that Grimmelshausen introduces the musical conceit *after* he has made his point: Melcher's rags and his emaciation serve as an awful warning. The second half of the passage is pure comic narrative; making its little joke (the intention to amuse is underlined by the use of the word "artlich") and bringing in the most colourful of the book's characters: the prodigal's father, a stubborn, choleric peasant who represents a highly individual and idiosyncratic variation on the Biblical model. Even before that point is reached, however, the narrative as opposed to satirical impulse has begun to assert itself. The mother in Grimmelshausen's piece is characterized as a mother, whereas Schupp's is merely labelled as one, and the language of the former is more colourful and specific and less repetitive. Grimmelshausen, like Schupp, uses a triadic structure; however, its function is not to drive home a point by threefold repetition, but to produce a rhythmical climax.

Novels too can, of course, contain satire without themselves becoming satires, and many a passage and episode in the Simplician cycle is satirical in nature and conception. Some of these are more or less formal set-pieces; in others, the narrative can temporarily become an overt vehicle for social criticism, after which the author often carries out an explicit shift back into full narrative gear with an "I must get back to my story." We will look here at one example of each type.

In chapter 9 of *Springinsfeld*, Simplicissimus asks his former comrade why he has no wife. The latter, in reply, refers to the bad experiences he has had with a woman (not Courage, in this case, but the "Leirerin" [hurdy-gurdy girl] whom we are to meet later in the book). The fact that Springinsfeld has had bad luck, says Simplicissimus, does not mean that he could not find himself an honest woman who would make him a faithful wife. A wife, says Springinsfeld, means trouble and expense:

> ... hab ich ein Weib / so ist nichts gewissers / als daß mir ein jede von meinen Ducaten hinfort nit mehr als einen Taler gilt; spinnet sie mir und ihr ein Stück Tuech an Leib so mus ich Flachs / Woll und Weberlohn bezahlen; soll sie mir was kochen / so muß ich Speiß / Holtz / Saltz und Schmaltz sambt dem Küchen-Geschirr herbey schaffen; wolte sie mir bachen / wer mus anders das Meel hergeben als eben ich? also auch / wer zahlt Holtz / Saiff und Wäscherlohn / wann sie mir und ihr das leinen Geräd saubern läst? Und wie gehts allererst / wann man mit einem Haufen Kindern beladen wird? Welches ich zwar nit erfahren habe / aber auch nicht zuerfahren begehre; wann nemblich eins kranck: Das ander gesund: Das dritte faul: das vierte muthwillig: Das fünffte eselhafftig und das sechste sonst widerspenstig / ungehorsamb und nichts nutz ist. (*Springinsfeld* 55)

[Once I've got a wife, there's nothing surer than that from that day forth, each of my ducats will be worth no more than a thaler. If she spins cloth for her back and mine, then I've got to pay for the flax and wool and find the weaver's fee; if she's going to cook something for me, then it's me that has to provide the food, the wood, the salt and fat as well as the kitchen utensils. Suppose she takes it into her head to do some baking: where does the flour come from except from yours truly? And then again, who's going to pay for the wood, the soap and the washerwoman when she decides to have all our linen done? And what if, to cap it all, she hangs a bunch of kids round my neck? It's not an experience I've had, but it isn't one I want to have, either. There'll be one that's sick, another well, the third one lazy, the fourth with butterflies in the head, the fifth thick as a plank and the sixth stroppy, disobedient and good for nothing.]

This passage fits easily into the tradition of *Weibersatire* (satirical misogyny). It takes the form of the standard review or tirade that is featured so often in Moscherosch, or indeed in the tradition stretching back to Sebastian Brant. But when we place it alongside the work of Moscherosch, we find significant differences in the style and technique, which seem to point to the fact that the more generalized technique and style of the satirical tradition is under pressure from a more individualistic, more pronouncedly narrative force. Moscherosch writes with vigour, but he lacks the natural variety and ease of flow that Grimmelshausen achieved. His speakers have names and identities, it is true, but they are all of them — Philander and Expertus Robertus included — cogs in a satirical machine, and have no real existence apart from it. In Grimmelshausen's passage, we sense the presence of a narrative element, the character of Springinsfeld himself, the "alter Kracher" who, says Simplicissimus, is "not worthy of a decent woman," and we sense the reality of the things he is describing. Grimmelshausen's mind has been engaged by the image of a busy housewife in the real world, and a curmudgeonly old creaker and groaner of a husband who is forever grumbling at the expense she is putting him to.

We conclude this section with the examination of an episode in *Simplicissimus* in which the main character is presented in the context of overt moral and social satire. The principal aim, in other words, is explicitly to inform and improve the reader. There are certainly times when Grimmelshausen writes within this tradition, drawing vices, in the image commonly used, through the hackle (*durchhecheln, durchziehen*), while maintaining the discourse at the level of generalisation; "ohne Verletzung eines Menschen Ehren," (without injuring any man's honour) as Joachim Rachel wrote in the preface to his *Satyrische Gedichte* (1664). Grimmelshausen, using Simplicissimus as a mouthpiece at this point, puts forward the same programme in chapter 4 of *Springinsfeld*: "Ich habe andern die ihrige [Laster] (doch da es ihnen an ihren Ehren nicht nachtheilig seyn kann) unter fremden Namen auch rechtschaffen durchgehechelt" (I have put the vices of others through the mill, though under false names, in such a way as not to expose them to public dishonour: *Springinsfeld* 23).

The period that the young Simplicissimus spends in Hanau, full of the pious ideas instilled by the Einsiedel, with whom he has been living in the forest, but largely bereft of worldly wisdom, affords obvious opportunities to expose social vices to the criticism of one whose moral standards have not yet been tarnished by social experience. The story of the dance and the goose pen, which straddles the divide between books I and II of *Simplicissimus*, is one example of such satire. The naive young Simplicissimus, having been misled by a malicious fellow-page into thinking that the leaping and stamping of the dancers — who must, he thinks, be mad — is an attempt to make the ground open and swallow him up, and that the only way to save himself is to hold on tight to the nearest female, follows this advice, becomes more fearful still at the reaction he provokes, fills his trousers and is finally shut away in the goose pen as a punishment. As he lies there, miserable and afraid, he hears someone fumbling with the bolt on the door and positions himself by the doorway, as inconspicuously as possible. A man and a woman enter and he cowers there, "awaiting the end in fear and trembling." After some conversation between the gallant lover and his lass, the boy hears some strange noises:

> Hierauff hörte ich küssen / und vermerckte seltzame *Posturen* / ich wuste aber nicht was es war oder bedeuten solte / schwieg derowegen noch fürters so still als eine Mauß. Wie sich aber auch sonst ein possirlich Geräusch erhube / und der Gänsstall / so nur von Brettern unter die Stege getafelt war / zu krachen anfienge / zumaln das Weibsbild sich anstellte / als ob ihr gar wehe bey der Sache geschehe / da gedachte ich / das seynd zwey von denen wüthenden Leuten / die den Boden helffen eintreten / und sich jetzt hieher begeben haben / da gleicher weis zu hausen / und dich umbs Leben zu bringen. So bald diese Gedancken mich einnamen / so bald nam ich hingegen die Thür ein / dem Tod zu entfliehen / dadurch ich mit einem solchen Mordio-Geschrey hinauß wischte / das natürlich lautet / wie das jenige / das mich an denselben Ort gebracht hatte . . . Günstiger Leser / ich erzehle diese Geschicht nicht darumb / damit Er viel daruber lachen solle / sondern damit meine Histori gantz seye / und der Leser zu Gemüt führe / was vor ehrbare Früchten von dem Tantzen zu gewarten seyen. (*ST* 96–7)

[Whereupon I heard kissing going on and became aware of odd positions being taken up. I had no idea what all this was or what it all meant, so I continued as quiet as a mouse. But then, when some kind of comical commotion arose and the goose pen, which was just a few boards fixed under the steps, began to make cracking noises and at the same time the woman behaved as if she was being hurt, I thought: "These are two of those mad people who are trying to stamp a hole in the ground and make an end of you." No sooner had this thought entered my mind than I was entering the doorway, rushing out in headlong flight from death with the same cries of fire and slaughter as had got me here in the first place.... Dear reader, I am not telling you this story just to give you a good laugh, but so that my History shall be complete and so that my reader shall consider how moral are the consequences to be expected from dancing.]

It is not too difficult to relate this description of a dance and its aftermath to the kind of satire of seventeenth-century fashions and morals that we met in Moscherosch's *Ala Mode Kehrauß*. There is no doubt of the satirical nature of the general framework within which this story appears, and the parody of baroque Petrarchism in a sordid setting emphasises that aspect of the story. But the general manner of its telling raises questions as to the purity of its satirical motivation. Unlike Schupp, Grimmelshausen feels the need to add a corrective against his reader's laughter. He is sincere in his serious criticism, but less monolithically consistent in his seriousness. He knows, not only that he *has* told this story in a laughter-inducing manner, but also that it was his intention to give the reader a good laugh. This is also signalled in his chapter heading: "Wie sich ein Ganser und eine Gänsin gepart" (A gander and a goose get together); and like the noise that this copulating couple makes at a crucial moment, the whole thing is *possierlich*: amusing — and worth telling — for its own sake. The duality of the young Simplicissimus's naiveté is exploited in a truly Simplician manner: he is both a vehicle for satire of the folly of those only apparently "wiser" than he, and at the same time himself a fool, at whom they and we can and must laugh.

Strong as the impetus given by *Francion* undoubtedly was, the Simplician style is more than simply "realistic" in Sorel's sense, as Koschlig maintains (110).[43] It is true that Grimmelshausen borrowed some of Sorel's theoretical phrasing, but whereas in practice, the latter's "style comique et satyrique"[44] can be reduced to the formulation "[voir les choses] dans leur naifveté" (to see things in their natural state: i.e. the unvarnished truth), there is a more genuine and dynamic polarity between serious and comic in Grimmelshausen. The polarity of the Simplician manner enables the narrator to step sideways to add his moral reflection, without producing a sense of inconsistency, as happens with the moralising passages in Sorel's work, or inhibiting the comedy by its full integration into satire, as seems to be suggested by Petersen's comment on this passage.[45] Grimmelshausen is sincere in his serious *addendum*, but he is not cancelling out what has gone before, any more than the opening of the *Continuatio* can cancel out the effect of the narrative method and style of *Der abentheurliche Simplicissimus* and send us back to read it again in a different frame of mind. It is not a "retrospective preface;"[46] at most, it is a reminder of the Simplician polarity.

Grimmelshausen's natural method is not to entertain so that he may moralise the better, but to encompass both the entertainer *and* the moralist. Nor is he averse to saying so quite openly at times. In the concluding section of the *Courasche*, for example, at a point when we would not expect a consequential moralist to indulge in inconsequentiality, he has his "heroine" tell a story for no better reason than that her scribe still has a blank sheet of paper left. In his *Bart-Krieg* (The War of the Beards), Grimmelshausen tells the story of the Elector of Cologne and his fool, Veitel (*KS* 64-5). The point that governs — or is ostensibly meant to govern — the telling of this tale is that black-beards are envious of red-beards, and when he has gone far enough to make the point clear, the author draws a specific line: "Hieraus sihet man nun / wie neidig ... die Swartzbärt seyn" (That shows how envious black-beards are). But that is not the end. "Ob nun gleich das End dieser Histori zu meinem Vorhaben nichts taug," the narrator continues, "so ist es doch lustig zu hören / wils derowegen auch erzehlen" (Although the ending of this story has nothing to do with the point I was making, it's a good story, so I am going to tell it). He marks off the serious (in the context of this work) from the merely comic and places the two side by side, flaunting the fact that the latter can be its own justification. This is no self-contradiction, but a more than usually explicit assertion of the principle of coexistence that lies at the heart of the Simplician manner. Koschlig is justified in stressing the importance of the stimulus given by Sorel's comic style to the development of this manner. And it is true that Sorel also lays claim at times to the satirist's mantle as justification for his comic narrative.[47] But in his case, this sounds like an afterthought. Grimmelshausen is also a satirist with serious moral intent and a storyteller for whom the inherent quality of "life" that gives a story its vitality has a validity of its own. His Simplician manner is more than simply a style in the narrower sense: it is also a formula for the meaningful — that is, essentially equal — coexistence of those apparently disparate elements.

There are implications here also for the formal and above all structural aspects of the works we have to consider. The storyteller, to be accommodated, and in his turn to accommodate the vitality and variety of life, requires a more open and flexible form than that of pure satire, which may be seen as episodic in terms of plot (A. B. Kernan says it has "the form of a newsreel"),[48] but whose episodes are always organised on the principle of the subordination of the individual "Bild" to the general "Norm," as Schönert puts it.[49] We shall pursue this topic further in our discussion of the key work in which the Simplician manner was triumphantly demonstrated, *Der abentheurliche Simplicissimus*.

Notes

[1] "... in sich zerrissen, zwiespältig und verwirrt." Arthur Hübscher, "Barock als Gestaltung antithetischen Lebensgefühls" *Euphorion* 24 (1922), 531

[2] "... neuzeitliche Diesseitslust." Emil Ermatinger, *Barock und Rokoko in der Lyrik* (Leipzig 1926), 23–4

[3] "... als Doppelwesen geboren." Herbert Cysarz, *Deutsches Barock in der Lyrik* (Leipzig 1936), 43

[4] Cf. Friedrich Gaede, *Poetik und Logik. Zu den Grundlagen der literarischen Entwicklung im 17. und 18. Jahrhundert* (Berne/Munich: Francke, 1978), 33. Chapter 4 of this work deals with the philosophical roots of baroque dualism at some length.

[5] Conrad Wiedemann, "Barockdichtung in Deutschland," in B. Könnecke and C. Wiedemann, eds., *Deutsche Literatur in Humanismus und Barock* (Frankfurt am Main: Athenaion, 1973), 51–2.

[6] On the emblem, see Mario Praz, *Studies in Seventeenth-century Imagery*, 2d ed. (Rome, 1964); Albrecht Schöne, *Emblematik und Drama im Zeitalter des Barock* (Munich: Beck, 1964), especially 17–59; Dietrich-Walter Jöns, *Das Sinnen-Bild. Studien zur allegorischen Bildlichkeit bei Andreas Gryphius* (Stuttgart: Metzler, 1966), Wolfgang Harms, "Emblem. Emblematik," in *Theologische Realenzyklopädie* (Berlin, New York, 1982).

[7] Friedrich Gaede, *Humanismus, Barock, Aufklärung* (Berne/Munich: Francke, 1971), 118–21.

[8] *Herrn von Hoffmannswaldau und anderer Deutschen... Gedichte*, pt. 1, ed. A. G. de Capua and E. Philippson (Tübingen: Niemeyer, 1961), 46.

[9] "vordergründige Buntheit des Lebens." Ilse-Lore Konopatzki, *Grimmelshausens Legendenvorlagen* (Berlin: Schmidt, 1965), 8.

[10] Cf. Valentin, "Du rire au plus haut savoir," 106. Valentin speaks of an "équilibre de deux excès," that is, of "theological" solemnity and "comic" laughter. Further to this topic, see my article: "The 'Simplicianische Manier' in a Satirical Context: Grimmelshausen's *Teutscher Michel,*" *Modern Language Review* 81 (1986), 646–54. Though Valentin (and the majority of critics) discuss this and similar themes in the theoretical or "poetological" context, this is more an aspect of narrative *practice* and will accordingly be discussed in detail later, under the heading of "Grimmelshausen's Artistry" (below, chapter 3).

[11] Meid, *Grimmelshausen. Epoche-Werk-Wirkung* (Munich: Beck, 1984), 142.

[12] See R. Alewyn, "Realismus und Naturalismus," in *Deutsche Barockforschung*, ed. R. Alewyn (Cologne/Berlin: Kiepenheuer & Witsch, 1965), 362. See also more recently M. Kremer, "Wirklichkeitsnähe in der barocken Literatur. Zur Gestaltung der Realität bei Grimmelshausen und Beer," *Simpliciana* 13 (1991). In Grimmelshausen, Kremer argues, "[fungiert] die reale Welt nur als Kulisse."

[13] See Günther Rohrbach, *Figur und Charakter. Strukturuntersuchungen an Grimmelshausens Simplicissimus* (Bonn: Bouvier, 1959).

[14] For example in the "Baldanders" episode: see chapter 4.

[15] Rolf Tarot, "Grimmelshausens Realismus," in *Festschrift Weydt*, ed. W Rasch et al., 259.

[16] See K. Haberkamm, "'Fußpfad' oder 'Fahrweg'? Zur Allegorese der Wegwahl bei Grimmelshausen," in *Festschrift Weydt*, ed. W. Rasch et al., 306: "Der Realismus hat als Buchstabensinn der Erzählung Vehikelfunktion für den 'sensus allegoricus.'"

[17] Gaede, *Humanismus*, 79–81.

[18] Charles Sorel, *Histoire comique de Francion*, ed. E. Roy (Paris 1924), 3: 24.

[19] Heinrich Anselm von Ziegler, *Asiatische Banise* (1689; reprint, Munich: Winckler, 1965), 377.

[20] Sorel, *Francion*, 1: xii-xiii.

[21] On the question of loose or "open" structure in Grimmelshausen, see my article: "Grimmelshausen, the Picaresque and the Large Loose Baggy Monster," *The Seventeenth Century* 1 (1986), 1–26. The theme of structure will be considered in detail in chapter 8.

[22] Cf. J. H. Petersen, "Formen der Icherzählung in Grimmelshausens Simplicianischen Schriften," *Zeitschrift für deutsche Philologie* 93 (1974), 489. More recently, R. Tarot has pursued this theme in "Grimmelshausens *Simplicissimus* und die Form autobiographischen Erzählens," *Études Germaniques* 46 (1991), 55–77.

[23] Walter Benjamin, *Ursprung des deutschen Trauerspiels* (Frankfurt, 1963), 290.

[24] Cf. my articles: "Simplician Emblematics? The Title-sequence of Grimmelshausen's *Springinsfeld*," *The Seventeenth Century* 9 (1994), 77–91 and "Cutting Linguistic Capers: The title-sequence of Grimmelshausen's *Teutscher Michel*," *German Life and Letters* 48 (1995), 277–91.

[25] Hubert Gersch, *Geheimpoetik. Die "Continuatio des abentheurlichen Simplicissimi" als Grimmelshausens verschlüsselter Kommentar zu seinem Roman* (Tübingen 1973), 104.

[26] R. Tarot, "Simplicissimus und Baldanders. Zur Deutung zweier Episoden in Grimmelshausens *Simplicissimus Teutsch*," *Argenis* 1 (1977), 107–29.

[27] Cf. the discussion of the image in the context of the *Continuatio* (Chapter 4 below).

[28] "Frangenda nux, ut nucleo fruamur." Quoted by E. Kleinschmidt in: "Die Wirklichkeit des literarischen Fiktionsbewußtseins und das Problem der ästhetischen Realität von Dichtung in der frühen Neuzeit," *Deutsche Vierteljahrsschrift* 56 (1982), 176.

[29] Urs Herzog, "Barmherzigkeit — die im Roman "verborgene Theologie." Zu Grimmelshausens *Simplicissimus*," *Argenis* 1 (1977), 277.

[30] Cf. J. Knopf, *Frühzeit des Burgers. Erfahren und verleugnete Realität in den Romanen Wickrams, Grimmelshausens, Schnabels* (Stuttgart 1978), 76. That there is reference to seventeenth-century actuality as well as moral-didactic "Allegorizität" in Grimmelshausen's depiction of war — and specifically, in scenes of brutality — is the burden of G. Hillen's article: "Allegorie und Wirklichkeit. Untersuchungen zu Prosatexten von Moscherosch und Grimmelshausen," *Daphnis* 19 (1990), 67–80. Van Ingen, in his "Krieg und Frieden bei Grimmelshausen," (*Études Germaniques* 46 [1991]), points to the importance of money and sees the "Wirklichkeitsbezug" of reference to plundering, extortion, the "Kipper und Wipper" and so on as an underpinning of the "deeper meaning." He is quite right, of course, but our point concerns not the undisputed fact that the "Teutscher Krieg" is being depicted, but the individual vitality and immediacy of its *depiction*.

[31] "Von Natur zwar ist mir viel lachen ein Eckel": cf. the "Teutsche Zugabe" of part 1 of Moscherosch's *Gesichte* (60).

[32] Mathias Feldges, *Grimmelshausens "Landstörtzerin Courasche." Eine Interpretation nach der Methode des vierfachen Schriftsinnes* (Berne, 1969), 87.

[33] G. Weydt, Nachwort (afterword) to Grimmelshausen, *Courasche* (Stuttgart: Reclam, 1971), 177.

[34] Frederick J. Stopp, "Reformation Satire in Germany," *Oxford German Studies* 3 (1968), 57.

[35] W. Vosskamp, *Romantheorie in Deutschland. Von Martin Opitz bis Friedrich von Blanckenburg* (Stuttgart 1973). Pages 29–44 deal with the "niederer Roman."

[36] Johann Beer, *Teutsche Winter-Nächte/Die kurtzweiligen Sommer-Täge* (1682–3; reprint, Frankfurt: Insel, 1963), 9–10.

[37] Opitz, *Buch von der deutschen Poeterey*, 20. Weise describes his own *Ertznarren* as outwardly "possierlich."

[38] G. P. Harsdörffer, "Vorrede" to *Der große Schau-Platz jämmerlicher Mord-Geschichte[n]* (1656; reprint, Hildesheim/New York: Olms1975), paragraph 7.

[39] Beer, *Teutsche Winter-Nächte*, 7.

[40] W. Harms, "'Hic et nunc.' Satirische Funktionen lokalisierter Handlung in Moscheroschs 'Philander' und Grimmelshausens 'Simplicissimus,'" *Études Germaniques* 46 (1991), 82. Whether Grimmelshausen is "satirical" to quite the same extent is another matter.

[41] J. B. Schupp, *Der Bücherdieb*, in *Streitschriften I*, ed. C. Vogt (Halle 1910), 9.

[42] Schupp, *Streitschriften II*, ed. Vogt (Halle 1911), 11–12.

[43] M. Koschlig, *Das Ingenium Grimmelshausens*, 110. Cf. the whole section, 108–14.

[44] Sorel, *Francion*, 3: 125–6: "N'est-il pas vray que c'est une tres agreable et tres utile chose que le style comique et satyrique. L'on y voit toutes les choses dans leur naifveté."

[45] J. H. Petersen, *Formen der Icherzählung,* 493: "Daß es Grimmelshausen . . . um die Enthüllung menschlicher Torheit geht . . . zeigt der Schlußsatz." Petersen sees the relation between the two sides not as a coexistence, but as a "Verknüpfung" (490).

[46] "Nachgeholte Vorrede": cf. E. Mannack, "Grimmelshausen und das Monströse," *Simpliciana* 15 (1993), 152, 153.

[47] E.g. Sorel, *Francion*, "Avertissement," iv: "Il faut que j'imite les Apothicaires . . . ."

[48] See A. B. Kernan, *The Plot of Satire* (New Haven and London, 1965), 97.

[49] J. Schönert, *Roman und Satire im achtzehnten Jahrhundert* (Stuttgart, 1969), 29.

Part Two:
The Simplician Cycle

Figure 1: Title engraving from Der abentheurliche Simplicissimus

3: *Der abentheurliche Simplicissimus Teutsch*

The Dualistic World

IN THIS PART of the book, we shall be considering Grimmelshausen's novels as individual and discrete wholes. We shall inevitably be returning at times, albeit in a changed context, to topics discussed in part 1. Thus, when we set out to take an overall view of the wide-ranging and multifarious narrative that is *Simplicissimus Teutsch* (cited in the text as *ST*), we are confronted once more by the dualism that we treated under the heading "Reality and Meaning" in chapter 2. The choice seems at first glance to lie between a panoramic chronicle of life whose main content is life itself: the interpretation of Romantic readers such as Eichendorff,[1] which is echoed in the conclusions of Hayens[2] and even Negus,[3] and a unifying approach, based on an elaborately calculated structure, dictated by an underlying theme: a tendency begun by Johannes Alt in 1936, and still in the ascendant.[4] In the first approach, the element of entertainment dominates, in the latter, that of edification. Each recognizes the existence of the other, but in neither case is a satisfactory relationship between the two sides achieved.

In looking for a conceptual basis, we could do worse than begin by returning to Grimmelshausen himself; not to the so-called retrospective preface at the beginning of the *Continuatio*, but to the title sequence of *Simplicissimus Teutsch* itself, that is, the title page and frontispiece, which, although unsigned, is generally agreed to stem in all probability from Grimmelshausen, at least in its design (See fig. 1, opposite). The title page gives us one of the most succinct general descriptions of the book available, and one of the most helpful. Firstly, we are told that it is not constructed in terms of plot; rather, it has a central *thread*: it is, in the Spanish picaresque tradition, a *vida*,[5] "the description of a life." It is certainly arguable that Grimmelshausen's book has a much higher degree of structural integrity than the standard picaresque novel, but it undeniably follows the picaresque tradition in its constant forward movement, in a linear progression that is primarily event-driven, along the path defined by the career of a single central figure, up to the point from which the retrospective narrative takes place. Certainly, Grimmelshausen is more aware of transcendent thematic contexts,[6] and makes more thorough and effective use of the potential dual perspective of autobiographical narrator and narrated life than is usual in the picaresque genre. The presence of a mature narrator is established through the sovereign irony of the first chapter of book I, and anticipated indeed by the reference to a state of rest (*Rhue*) in the verses appended to the frontispiece. But that mood is hardly dominant, either in the book or in the title sequence. Rather, there is a polarity between contemplative rest and a movement that is certainly the engine of change, but should not be confused with the *idea* of change (*Wechsel, Veränderung*), which after all can be thematically subsumed as an essentially negative aspect of "the world," as the church would see it. We are thinking here of the dynamic and unsuppressable energy of life itself, a phenomenon to which Grimmelshausen responded more positively.

No one would wish to classify our novel among the loosely assembled collections of stories of the *Volksbuch* tradition such as *Till Eulenspiegel, Fortunatus* or the *History of Doctor Faust*, but Grimmelshausen certainly knew this tradition and was not wholly hostile to it. Even if he knew himself to be more than a mere *Possenreisser* (purveyor of comic anecdotes and pranks), he was by no means averse to the *Posse* as such, and he emphasises in his title another aspect of this tradition when he designates his hero as "abenteuerlich," a word that can have both the connotation of oddness (which we shall pursue later, as we shall the significance of the adverb "Teutsch") and that of "having a propensity to be involved in adventures." The Simplicissimus of the novel's action, like Eulenspiegel, is constantly on the move (he is identified on the title page as a "Vagant") and he is the kind of person to whom things happen. Eberhard Lämmert says of works of the *Eulenspiegel* type that the chief formal principle is an orientation towards "Buntheit, Mannigfaltigkeit ... rasch wechselnde Abenteuer, Heldentaten und Possen."[7] Whatever the more serious aspects of the work, variegation and rapid change ("rasch wechselnde Abenteuer") are certainly features of *Simplicissimus*.

To continue with our reflections on the title page, we note a deviation from the normal practice of the popular and picaresque traditions in Grimmelshausen's careful and formal triadic structuring of his hero's career and its careful concentration on a single point, the word "Welt"; to be precise, "diese Welt" (this world), the world into which the hero "comes" and which he eventually "voluntarily leaves." To be sure, the concept "world" has the duality (of vitality and *vanitas*) that we would expect of Grimmelshausen the baroque writer, but in the tug of war between the two sides, the former more than holds its own. All four elements are invoked in the frontispiece and its accompanying verses, but it is the earth that predominates, and nowhere more so than in the language. The twofold identification of the hero as odd or curious (*abentheuerlich, seltzam*), also helps to place his feet firmly on the earth: it is to the material rather than the transcendental dimension that curiosities belong.

The "Bub" (boy) who is later to acquire the name of Simplicius Simplicissimus is discovered at first living on a farm with his "Knan" and "Meuder" (Dad and Ma, as he calls them: in fact, they are his foster parents) in a kind of limbo of ignorance and illiteracy, a creature totally without knowledge of the spiritual dimensions of life. An immediate response to the present and a reflective intellectual and spiritual contemplation, comedy and religious seriousness, lie side by side in this introductory sequence, thanks to the Simplician vision of Grimmelshausen, which can allow the wisdom of a polished and enlightened retrospective narrator to work in tandem with a spirit of direct involvement in the reality described. That this description is not an outrageous falsification (as might be undertaken for allegorical purposes) of the actualities of peasant life we can confirm by reference to Harsdörffer. Although he, being a pastoral poet, could idealise the country life, he was also well aware of life's harsh realities. In his novella *Der Vatermörder* (The Parricide) he reports a case from actual life that had occurred "jüngst verwichener Zeit / alhier" (that is, a short time ago in the Nuremberg area). He gives a chilling account of how far removed from civilised conditions rural existence could be. The criminal, Bossecker, has been brought up by a father who sent his children neither to school nor to church,

> ... sondern sie der Säue hüten lassen / daß sie von den Zehen Geboten / dem Vater Unser etc. und anderen Hauptstücken Christlicher Lehre nichts gewust / und ein Leben geführet / wie das thumme Vieh.[8]

[... but rather made them tend the swine, so that they knew nothing of the Ten Commandments, the Lord's Prayer and other principal tenets of Christian doctrine, and lived the life of the dumb beasts.]

It is in this sense that Grimmelshausen's "Bub" (who is also employed as a swineherd) is a "Bestia."

When the farm Simplicius lives on is pillaged by soldiers (the book is set in the period of the Thirty Years' War[9]) he runs away into a forest, where he is taken in and educated in a form of naive Christianity by a hermit, who is in fact, as later transpires, his natural father and who gives him his Christian name of Simplicius. He lives there for two years, until the hermit's death, but after the Battle of Nördlingen, marauding soldiers drive him out of the forest and he eventually arrives at Hanau (chapter 19). It is at this point that, for the purposes of the novel, he "comes into the world," as we can see from his reflections at the time when, under suspicion of being a spy, he is threatened with torture. He is receiving his just reward, he feels, for having run away from God's service into the world ("auß dem Dienst GOttes in die Welt geloffen": 57).

From this point on, the hero, who is given the surname Simplicissimus by the Governor of Hanau, is truly "in the world" — the world of the human condition, that is — though insulated for a time both from its corruption and from its wisdom by the innocence and ignorance he has brought with him from the forest. He is not, though, protected against its changing, inconstant nature,[10] and is soon plucked from Hanau by a Croat patrol and driven on by a long series of changes of fortune and condition (*Veränderungen*), that are often as rapid and radical as they are unexpected. As viewed from the vantage point of constancy that religious insight can give — and the narrator is supposed to have achieved — this quality of rapid change in earthly life exposes its essential folly and vanity. When the narrator reflects on events, this aspect certainly emerges. When he narrates, on the other hand, that change and the movement it brings is part of the substance of life, of its excitement and fascination. Simplicissimus goes through a sequence of identifiable phases: involuntarily satirical comic fool, consciously satirical jester-fool (after the Governor has attempted to drive him mad by making him think he has been to hell and instead succeeded only in causing him to be born fully and finally *into* the world, "like the phoenix, through fire") then a piece of flotsam on the waves of the war until he rises, as the "Huntsman of Soest," to the status of successful military adventurer, then sexual adventurer in Lippstadt and Paris (the *mons veneris*). He then takes a slide down the slope of civil and military misfortune from which, thanks to the duality of powers that rule his destiny, the goddess Fortuna and the Providence of God, he is rescued into the settled life of a farmer. He is still, however, exposed to the vicissitudes and temptations of the world, the flesh, and the devil, so he decides to become a hermit once more, though, as he says, whether he will remain constant in this way of life until death is an open question ("Stehet dahin": 463).

The world is viewed almost simultaneously from the transcendental and ideal, and from the earthly and realistic perspectives. On the one hand, satire and religiously tinged moral reflection and a thoroughly baroque sense of *vanitas*.[11] On the other, true comic vision, a vivid sense of dynamic movement, and a strong savour of vitality, both in the events of the *Histori* and in the language in which they are conveyed. The two perspectives neither vitiate nor inhibit one another, and yet the duality seems dynamic and productive rather than disruptive. How, then, do the two sides relate to each other? At this point, it is helpful to turn to the frontispiece, where, since the medium is no longer purely linguistic, simultaneity of representation is more nearly achievable (See figure 1). And here, thanks to the fact that the research of recent years has established beyond doubt that the work shares the deeper transcendental concerns and intellectual insights of its age, we no longer have to concentrate exclusively on that aspect of the work as a corrective to the view of Grimmelshausen as a mere *Volksschriftsteller*, and to the detriment of its terrestrial dimension.

Characteristically for Grimmelshausen, the frontispiece is emblematic. The tripartite structure of the emblem is reproduced in the strip containing the title (*inscriptio*), the figure of the monster with the book and masks (*pictura*) and the verse commentary (*subscriptio*). The function of the *inscriptio* is to introduce in cryptic form a puzzle contained in a picture, and perhaps give a veiled hint at its solution. To this end, the adjective "abentheurlich" and the adverb "Teutsch" are significant. The first, as we have seen, suggests both a series of unusual and exciting events, and a quality of oddness.[12] "Teutsch" is used here, surely, to indicate not that the work is a translation, but the honest, plain-speaking approach and style of the satirist and moralist.[13] The basis of the figure portrayed in the *pictura* is the satyr, which was in the seventeenth century routinely linked with the genre of satire. The head has the satyr's horns and long ears, one of the legs has the statutory goat-like quality, and as Walter-Ernst Schäfer has shown, the thrust-out middle fingers of the hand reproduce a traditional gesture indicative of derision — among other things — and associated with the satyr in a number of contemporary illustrations, not least one included in the first edition of Moscherosch's *Gesichte*.[14] The development of this theme, the satire of folly, in the *subscriptio* ("so that the reader should depart from folly and live in peace") suggests a related, but more contemplative state, an at least moral withdrawal from the world, such as could be symbolized by Simplicissimus's eventual decision to become a hermit. Such a withdrawal, as we see in the penultimate chapter of the work, is based on the achievement of self-knowledge, which in turn is closely related to an awareness of the essential vanity of earthly and bodily things. The comedians' masks with which the ground is strewn could well be a reference to this idea of vanity (that life on earth is nothing more than a series of roles in a play). Satire, in our normal understanding of the word, certainly brings a degree of self-knowledge, but its application is basically to this life on earth. The *Simplicissimus* contains social satire, but not only that: it is full of reminders of the needs of the soul, and of its primacy.[15] Time also has its duality: "die edle Zeit" (for instance, *ST* 456) is noble precisely because in it, the soul can be saved for eternity ("[die Zeit] zu meiner Seligkeit wol anzulegen": 456.) Sybille Penkert, indeed, believes that the fact that the creature's fingers in the *pictura* are pointing to the child and the tree has eschatological significance,[16] and there is support for this in the facts that the work opens with a reference to the Last Days, that the hermit's summary of the essentials of religion (28) ends with the Day of Judgement, and that the King of the Sylphs in the Mummelsee episode is worried about rumours that the Last Judgement is imminent (book V: 425).

But the chiliastic thinking that was not uncommon in the seventeenth century, and which is referred to in the opening sentence of *Simplicissimus*, does not truly permeate the work. Grimmelshausen certainly knows that this is a world of sin[17] and that it can be too much with us, but neither sombre piety and apocalyptic imaginings nor the Messianic enthusiasm of a Quirinus Kuhlmann are his line. He can see that the "Phantast" who imagines himself to be the god Jupiter has much right on his side in condemning the wickedness of the world, but he still regards him as an essentially ridiculous dreamer. There is no negation of the world and its reality in *Simplicissimus Teutsch*. It is entirely in character that Grimmelshausen should give us, in the principal "Jupiter" episode (*ST* III, chapters 3–8), a picture that conveys a sense of variegation and of shifting perspectives. There is nothing inconsistent, in the Simplician scheme of things, in both sympathising with the man's idealistic vision of a harmonious and peaceful world and simultaneously laughing at him when he posits a "Teutscher Held," a hero with powers to rival those of Superman or Wonder Woman, who is to bring about his — "Jupiter's" — millennium. Grimmelshausen deliberately switches between perspectives, often signalling the switch with an introductory remark. The most notable example occurs in chapter 6, which begins with a speculation that the man may not, after all, be mad, and ends with a scene derived from Fischart's *Flöhhatz* (1573), in which Jupiter drops his trousers to gain some relief from the fleas which are plaguing him; his reward, he says, for his kindness in offering them asylum from the bloody persecution they have been suffering at the hands of womankind. Mathias Feldges makes a manful attempt to show that "the fleas stand for [fallen] mankind in an allegory of the world,"[18] but a Deity without dignity cannot function allegorically, and a "Jupiter" with his trousers round his ankles, picking out the fleas whose attentions have liberally speckled his skin, has no dignity. The comic intention is underlined by the opening sentence of the next chapter (220).

That this is a comic rather than a strictly satirical intention is worth re-emphasising. The man (whose name we never learn) has driven himself into this state by an excess of devotion to learning and poetry ("der sich überstudiert / und in der Poeterey gewaltig verstiegen": 209), and while he does have lucid periods, he is also in the habit of mingling the fruits of his reading with reality, somewhat in the manner of Don Quixote. Grimmelshausen's dynamic polarity, in which the serious and the ridiculous can exist side by side (as they do also in Cervantes's masterpiece), is not really compatible with the strict logic of satirical vision, which presents a reasoned criticism of life as measured against the generalised norm of what should be. But such a dynamic polarity does fit into the comic approach, which accepts life as it is, with all its individual heterogeneity. The variegated nature of the creature on Grimmelshausen's frontispiece — which could be said to be replicated in the variety of objects represented on the pages of the book it displays — has been interpreted as an attempt to underpin its satirical status.[19] But while it is true that from ancient times the principle of the medley (the *satura* [mixed dish], or the *farrago* [mixed fodder] of Juvenal) had been seen as a distinctive feature of satire, this was surely a matter of the variation of subject *matter* within a collection of pieces rather than that of the *manner* of representation (*Darstellungsweise*). As Gifford puts it in his version of Juvenal's first satire:

> Whatever passions have the soul possessed . . .
> Shall form the motley subject of my page.[20]

The subject changes; the method, manner and mood are, however, consistent. So even if we assume that Grimmelshausen knew and intended to apply the correct meaning of *satura* (he seems generally to have accepted the common equation with the word "Satyr" and the Satyr-play), the deliberate impression he gives here of a curious jumble, of oddness, seems out of harmony with the spirit of traditional satire. It is easier to link it with the "abentheurlich" of his title and to his characterisation of his hero as a "seltzamer Vagant" (odd vagrant) on the title page.

That would fit better, also, with the fact that while he certainly is satirically critical of reality at times, especially in the Hanau phase of books I and II, he is also unashamed in his appreciation of the vigorous animation, humour, excitement, and sheer vitality of a world that is not only "veränderlich" (which contains the idea of inconstancy), but simultaneously "seltzam";[21] disturbing at times, perhaps, but stimulating, and of interest in its own right. The emphasis on unceasing movement in the references to the four elements in the *pictura*, and in the words "wandert," "raist," and "umschwermen" (wander, travel, roam about) in the *subscriptio* is not cancelled out by the motif of rest on which the latter ends. Both rest and movement are necessary to the overall structural stability of the Simplician style, and both contain a polarity. "In Ruhe leben" can, as is implied in the *subscriptio*, stand for the state of contemplative wisdom that serves as a guard against folly. But it can also carry the idea of slothfully "living at one's ease," as in the case of Musai in the "Simplicianized" version of *Der keusche Joseph*:

> "wie ein kleiner Herr so in Ruhe leben: oder wie man bey uns Teutschen sagt / mit einem schmutzigen Maul zum Fenster hinaus sehen." (*KJ* 131)

> [to live like a little Lord and be able to look out of one's window, as we Germans say, with a dirty mouth.]

It is from a "life of ease" that Simplicius is jolted by the appearance of Baldanders in the *Continuatio* (509) into *accepting* the "inconstancy of this world" (Unbeständigkeit dieser Welt) and going out into it once more.

The dualism of Grimmelshausen's Simplician perception of the world is dynamic — and, with all due respect to Kenneth Negus, is based not so much on thought as on instinctive feeling. It is characterised by a polarity that enables him to shift from perspective to perspective without producing the sense of "irreconcilable contradiction"[22] that would occur if the methodology were determined by strict philosophical logic. At the beginning of book III, the narrator draws the reader's attention once more to the "Ehrgeitz" and "Thorheit" of his former self in Soest, but the fascination of the curious soon reasserts itself when he thinks of his "wunderliche Einfäll" (curious inventions): "dahero erfand ich eine Gattung Schuh," he goes on, "die man das hinderst zu vorderst anziehen konte . . . " (So I invented a kind of shoe that you could put on back to front: 200). The idea that this was a reprehensible "folly" stands, but it does not inhibit the interest of the invention itself.

An excellent example of this *modus operandi* on the larger scale is provided by the effortless — if abrupt — transition from serious to comic, or "nützlich" to "lustig," in the terminology of Grimmelshausen's title page, in the sequence in book IV (chapters 15–24) in which Simplicissimus lives the life of a highway robber, as the passive partner of the evil Olivier. We first meet this black character, and his "white" counterpart, Herzbruder, in the Magdeburg sequence in book III (chapters 19–27) in which, through the use of black magic, he cheats his virtuous rival out of the post of regimental "Musterschreiber" (a kind of secretary). Simplicissimus's relationship with these two characters hardly bulks large in the novel taken as a whole, but it is significant as a variant of the constant theme of the battle between the forces of darkness and light for his soul. When Olivier reappears, he is a "Merodebruder," a renegade soldier who has dropped out of the social and disciplinary framework of the army and now kills, robs and steals on a private basis. Out of fear of his companion's bloodthirsty ruthlessness, Simplicissimus goes along with him, while trying to avoid complicity in his evil ways and principles. He fears that he is on the path to hell (342), and protests against the use of a church as a robber's cache, occasioning a sardonically ironic outburst on Olivier's part (which, in spite of a later corrective reflection by the hermit-narrator, one cannot but feel that Grimmelshausen the storyteller thoroughly enjoys). Whereupon Olivier tells Simplicissimus the tale of his "ruchlose[s] Leben" (wicked life, 345). And a thoroughly black tale it is, until Simplicissimus asks him where he got the marks on his face.

The Simplician flexibility shows itself here in a shift within the character of the narrator-persona: a trait that, as we shall see, becomes more pronounced from the later stages of the *Continuatio* onwards. It is Grimmelshausen the comic writer rather than Olivier, the ostensible narrator, who tells this story. It all happened, we learn, when Olivier was in winter-quarters in Pomerania, where he kept a pretty mistress, with whom he was wont to lie in his landlord's bed. They are disturbed, however, by the latter's cat, which has also been wont to lie there.

Olivier's lady love swears that he shall enjoy no further favours until he has got rid of the cat, so, thinking to have some fun and get his revenge on the intrusive animal, he puts it in a sack, and taking his landlord's two big dogs with him, goes out into an open meadow, on which there are no trees where the cat can seek refuge:

> Aber potz Stern! es gieng mir nit allein Hunds-übel / wie man zu sagen pflegt / sondern auch Katzen-übel (welches Übel wenig erfahren haben werden / dann man hätte sonst ohne Zweiffel vorlängsten auch ein Spruchwort darauß gemacht) massen die Katz / so bald ich den Sack auff thate / nur ein weites Feld / und auff demselbigen ihre zwey starcke Feind / und nichts hohes vor ihr sahe / dahin sie ihre Zuflucht hätte nehmen konnen: Derowegen wolte sie sich nicht so schlechtlich in die Nidere begeben / und ihr das Fell zerreissen lassen / sondern sie begab sich auff meinen eigenen Kopff / weil sie keinen höhern Ort wuste / und als ich ihr wehrte / fiel mir der Hut herunder; je mehr ich sie nun herunder zu zerren trachtete / je fester schlug sie ihre Nägel ein / sich zu halten : Solch unserm Gefecht konten beyde Hunde nicht lang zusehen / sondern mengten sich ins Spiel / sie sprangen mit offenem Rachen hinden / vornen und zur Seiten nach der Katz / die sich aber gleichwol von meinem Kopff nicht hinweg begeben wolte / sondern sich beydes so wol in meinem Angesicht als sonsten auff dem Kopff / mit Einschlagung ihrer Klauen hielt so gut sie konte . . .(356—7)

[But damn it all! It wasn't just a case of being dogged, as they say, by misfortune: I was catted as well and there can't be many as have had that experience, or they'd have made a saying out of that too, a long time since. For no sooner had I opened the sack than the cat, seeing nothing before it but an open field and its two powerful enemies and no high place where it could take refuge, and not wanting simply to take the low road and get the fur torn off its back, made its way right up on to my head, there being no higher perch on offer. And when I tried to stop it, my hat fell off and the more I tried to wrench it down, the harder it dug in its nails, to keep its footing. The two dogs were not content for long just to watch this wrestling match, but rather joined in and jumped up, jaws gaping, from in front, from behind, and from both sides, trying to get at the cat. The cat, however, showed no inclination to quit my cranium, but clung on as best it could by sinking in its claws into my face as well as the other parts of the head.]

Eventually, brutality reasserts itself: the dogs kill the cat, Olivier kills the dogs and then proceeds to beat his mistress mercilessly. She then runs away and leaves him, "no doubt because she couldn't love such an ugly mug any more." In chapter 23, Grimmelshausen signals the comic intention of the story he has just told by showing Simplicissimus having to bite back his laughter, and then switches immediately to the serious mode. The two rob a coach, and Olivier, having already murdered a guard and the coachman, is about to butcher the women and children inside it when Simplicissimus intervenes. The theme of the immortal soul emerges clearly in the irony of Olivier's description of his companion as "ein heilloser Kerl." Simplicissimus is "a hopeless case," one assumes because he is incapable of rising to the heights of Olivier's Machiavellian philosophy.[23] It is Olivier, however, who is in danger of placing himself beyond the reach of salvation (*Heil*) in the religious sense because — unlike Simplicissimus — he is totally unaware of any need for it. In a way, Simplicissimus plays in this relationship the same role of idealistic *ingénu* as he did in book I, coming straight from the forest full of simple Christianity and devoid of knowledge of the world. And it is noteworthy that here too, much as he disapproves of the more worldly-wise Olivier, Grimmelshausen cannot resist savouring the down-to-earth liveliness of the worldly mentality. Olivier wants to murder the children in cold blood, but his practical reasoning comes out in the proverbial form of which Grimmelshausen is so consistently fond: "Eyer in die Pfannen / so werden keine Junge drauß" (358: Break the eggs into the pan and you won't get any chicks).

So the women and children are shut up in a cellar and the robbers ride into a wood, where Simplicissimus is scared by the figure of a man standing against a tree. Olivier's callousness is again in evidence: it is a Jew whom he has left tied in that position and who has frozen to death. In fond remembrance of the money he has stolen from the dead man, he chucks the latter playfully under the chin. And then, when we are ready for a moral tirade, the narrator switches moods again and the comic and curious principle comes to the fore. It turns out that the poor man had tried to save a few of his coins and valuables by secreting them in his mouth. Having fished this booty out of its odd hiding-place, Olivier gives Simplicissimus a ruby as a reward and leaves him to mind the horses with the jibe: "Watch out that the Jew doesn't bite you" (359). Words spoken by a villain, but with a panache that is savoured by the author, who does not recall his narrator to redress the balance.

And so it goes on: Simplicissimus prays to "God, in His goodness" (360) to rescue him, and in due course, he is saved and vice is punished, but not before we have had an exciting and graphic fight scene in which Olivier receives a blow that sends his brain spurting out, while Simplicissimus, in fulfilment of the prophecy that caused Olivier to trust him in the first place, avenges him by despatching the man who dealt the blow to join his comrade in the dance of death (362). The moral is not lost, but the language conveys a vivid perception of the actuality. The variegated effect that results from what we have called Grimmelshausen's dynamic polarity of vision does not have a contradictory or confusing impact, because he resists the temptation to attempt a *blend* of the two sides. What makes this possible, however, is the fact that, if the narrative is not always of this world, it is always in it. Everything, even the dream vision of the trees, which represent society in time of war (I: chapters 15–18), the gruesome and odd ("greulich seltzam") witches' dance (144), and the underwater adventure of the Mummelsee (V: chapters 12–17), is charged with a vitality of narrative vision and linguistic expression.

The coexistent awareness of absolute truth on the one hand and of individual life on the other is nowhere more apparent than in the reflective and satirical passages. In an episode, for example, which is graphically illustrative of the abrupt reversals of fortune and the vanity of this world, Simplicissimus is reunited with Herzbruder, who formerly rescued him from misery, but now himself has need of rescue. The degradation to which this good man has fallen is screwed to a high pitch: he limps, his head is bandaged, his arm in a sling, his clothes not worth a penny, he stinks: a litany of wretchedness in the formal baroque style of accumulation of which Grimmelshausen is fond and which he often uses in set-piece passages. Not only that, the poor man is full of lice, so full "daß man die gantze Schwabenhaid[24] damit besetzen könte" (that you could have covered the whole of the Schwabenheide with them: 366). When, in the camp at Magdeburg, Simplicissimus is taken by the elder Herzbruder to see the soldiers indulging in gambling, the hateful devil's own invention ("deß leydigen Teuffels eigene Invention": 154), we are given a detailed description of the "Spielplatz," which is both formal and replete with lively language and detail. The false dice known as "Niderländer," for example, which have to be rolled with a slow, "dragging" action, have the fives and sixes "on sides as sharp-edged as the backs of the donkeys the soldiers have to ride on" (Die hatten so spitzige Rücken / darauff sie die fünffer und sechser trugen / als wie die magere Esel darauff man die Soldaten setzt: 152).

All the deadly sins are represented, and the presentation of each is dualistic in the sense that each is an object of serious contemplation, but also rendered with all the smell and taste of its living, earthly reality, which can of course include even humour. Pride, for example, is exposed in the episode during Simplicissimus's superficially glorious career as "Huntsman of Soest" in which he robs a priest of his ham and bacon (II: chapter 31). The primary motivation of this exploit is the love of fame ("wann ich nur muthmassete / daß ich Ruhm bey den Leuten dardurch erwecken möchte": 188–9). The tale culminates in the moment when the hero, who has climbed down the chimney and cannot get up again, blackens his face with soot and assumes the role of the devil in the face of the priest who has come in all solemnness to exorcise him. The manner of the narration, which we shall discuss in the next section, ensures that the pleasure we take in this story in no way diminishes our awareness of the truly devilish associations of Simplicissimus's behaviour.

The sin of luxury (that is, lust) is not neglected and is crystallized, as is common practice with Grimmelshausen, in specific representative episodes: one, in Lippstadt (III: chapter 21) in which Simplicissimus sets out in search of sexual gratification and acquires a wife instead, and the quasi-allegorical "Venusberg" episode in Paris (IV: 4–5) in which he commits adultery and is used as a male prostitute. We will look a little more closely at the Lippstadt episode. Simplicissimus's career as the freebooting "Huntsman of Soest" is brought to an end when he is taken prisoner by the Protestant side. He is allowed freedom of movement in Lippstadt and since he has managed to rescue some of his wealth, is in a position to enjoy the pleasures of the flesh. In spite of the warning he receives from a preacher ("Er hüte sich vor dem Thier das Zöpff hat": beware of the beast which wears its hair in plaits: 266), he indulges in frequent intercourse (in the full sense of the word) with "die liebe Jungfrauen," in which activity he is materially assisted by his physical beauty, his skill on the lute, and by the novels that become his favourite reading-matter and help to fuel the flames of passion and to hone his gallant skills. Looking back, he describes himself as "ein gottloser böser Bub" (a godless, wicked scoundrel: 269). He becomes infatuated with the daughter of a Lieutenant Colonel. Eventually, he overcomes the various obstacles placed in his way: "Es ist ohnnöthig / alle Thorheiten meiner Leffeley umbständlich zu erzehlen / weil dergleichen Possen ohne das alle Liebes-Schriften voll seyn" (It is not necessary to give a detailed account of all the silly things I said and did in the course of my amorous pursuit, since the romantic novels are full of such nonsense: 272).

The reference to "Possen" here is no doubt a moralistic gesture of rejection. At the same time, it is in all probability a signal that we are about to be amused. One night, our amorous hero succeeds in gaining admittance to his beloved's room and bed. Though he promises marriage with the most bloodcurdling of oaths, she will not allow him to enjoy her. She permits Simplicissimus to continue to lie beside her, however, and worn out by his frustration, he sinks into a gentle slumber:

> Ich wurde aber gar ungestümm auffgeweckt / dann morgens umb vier Uhr stand der Obrist Leutnant vorm Bett / mit einer Pistol in der einen / und einer Fackel in der andern Hand: Crabat / schrye er überlaut seinem Diener zu / der auch mit einem blossen Sebel neben ihm stunde / geschwind Crabat / hole den Pfaffen! Worvon ich dann erwachte / und sahe / in was vor einer Gefahr ich mich befande; o Wehe / gedacht ich / du sollest gewiß zuvor beichten / ehe er dir den Rest gibt! Es wurde mir gantz grün und gelb vor den Augen / und wuste nicht / ob ich sie recht auffthun solte / oder nit? Du leichtfertiger Gesell / sagte er zu mir / soll ich dich finden / daß du mein Hauß schändest? Thät ich dir unrecht / wenn ich dir und dieser Vettel / die deine Hur worden ist / den Hals breche?

Ach du Bestia, wie kan ich mich doch nur enthalten / daß ich dir nit das Hertz auß dem Leib herauß reisse / und zu kleinen Stücken zerhackt den Hunden dawerffe? damit bisse er die Zähn ubereinander / und verkehrte die Augen / als ein unsinnig Thier. . . .(272–3)

[I got a very rough awakening, though, for at four o' clock in the morning, there was the Lieutenant Colonel standing by the bed with a pistol in one hand and a torch in the other. "Crabat," he bellowed to his servant, who was standing beside him and was armed as well, in this case with a naked sabre, "quick, Crabat, go and get the priest!" On which I woke up and saw the danger I was in. "O calamity!" I thought "you'd surely better get your confession made before he finishes you off!" I saw flashing lights before my eyes and wasn't sure whether I ought to open them fully or not. "You unprincipled villain," he said to me, "am I to find you here bringing shame on my house? Would it be any more than you deserve if I were to break your neck, and that of this trollop here, who has become your whore? Oh, you filthy creature, I don't know how I can stop myself from tearing your heart out of your body, cutting it into little pieces and throwing it to the dogs!" And with that, he began to grind his teeth and roll his eyes like a senseless beast. . . .]

Eventually, practical considerations prevail — though not before the outraged father has been reduced to complete incoherence, "foaming at the mouth like a wild boar" (274) and talking wildly of broken necks and hands washed in blood — and the marriage rites are performed over the two technically innocent delinquents as they sit there in bed. In due course, the family is reconciled to the *fait accompli*. The dualism is clear enough: the whole chapter is not only an accomplished piece of moral satire, but a masterpiece of comic narrative.

Grimmelshausen's Narrative Artistry

Dynamic Coexistence

The theme of Grimmelshausen's narrative artistry is hardly a new departure at this point. The general thrust of our argument has been (and will be) that the moralist and satirist in him should not be allowed to obscure his achievement as a storyteller. We have, in a sense, been discussing the theme for some time and will continue to do so in later chapters, if in less detail. But it is not inappropriate that we should devote special attention to it here, for it was in *Simplicissimus* that it reached its fullest development; in the later works, it is under a greater or lesser degree of inhibition. We began by identifying a polarity, one which we have traced in a number of different contexts, and could have traced in many more. We have attempted to characterise this polarity as dynamic, in that the two sides are genuinely discrete and autonomous and yet compatible and complementary. In their interrelation, they constitute a world in which the moral ideal and the merely human reality can — indeed must — coexist. Sex, for example, can be seen as a negative, under the rubric of "luxury." The Paris episode is one in which Simplicissimus, as "Beau Alman," is involved in what is uncompromisingly designated as sin.[25] But Simplicissimus the sinner is at the same time a human creature of flesh and blood. He thinks of his wife, but it does him no good. He was a human being, alas! ("leyder ein Mensch") and would have had to be a block of wood to come away in a chaste condition ("daß ich wol ein Ploch hätte seyn müssen / wenn ich keusch hätte darvon kommen können" (307)). This is not an excuse, but a statement in plain, convincing terms, of the simple reality, juxtaposed with the ideal. Each exists independently, and this is not incompetence or neglect on the author's part, but a principled refusal to dissolve duality into integration.

It is Grimmelshausen's artistry, his awareness of the importance of *manner* in narration, that enables him, in the majority of cases at least, to maintain this dynamic coexistence of apparent contradictions. Philosophically, as we have said, the universal and eternal must have priority over the individual and momentary. When the Prince of the Sylphs, in book V, chapter 14, strikes the note of *vanitas* in referring to the "Augenblick eurer nichtigen und flüchtigen Zeitlichkeit" (the [passing] moment of your valueless and transitory temporality: 423), we acknowledge the rightness of the remark. But what man would want, literally or metaphorically, to be a sylph and live under water? A counterweight is constantly present in the Simplician manner, the "lustigere Manier" that is foreshadowed at the end of the *Satyrischer Pilgram* (cf. *SP* 160), and which observes from a point inside actual temporal life, rather than at a satirical remove from it. Through narrative art, language, and structure, it distils the *vitality* of the moment so much despised by the sylph, the quality of life itself, which, of course, can adhere in art to the fantastic, and even to the allegorical as well as to what is more routinely true to life. There is nothing ethereal about Grimmelshausen's description of life at the bottom of the Mummelsee.

The allegorical school of criticism is led by its logic (the overemphasis on meaning) to undermine this principle. Manfred Kremer asserts that in Grimmelshausen, "die reale Welt [fungiert] nur als Kulisse" (the real world functions merely as stage-scenery).[26] So what of the cat-and-dog story that we considered earlier? Could it be worked into an allegory? No doubt it would not be beyond the wit of man — particularly that ingenious creature, "Baroque Man" — to do so, given just the bare bones of the story. As we have observed, the whole sequence forms part of the battle between the forces of darkness and light. But this would work only if we could divest the figures involved of a large part of their individual actuality. And how is the story told? With conscious humour and irony, a strong emphasis on action and movement, and above all, a clear sense of the sharp reality of the claws which dig into Olivier's head and rend his visage, all of which qualities militate against allegorisation. An ugly and disfigured face, as a relatively static object of contemplation, can have symbolic moral connotations. But that is not what we are given here; the life principle more than holds its own against the moral principle at this point. This is storytelling, not allegory.

The detail in description and narration in passages that can and in some cases clearly do have representative, if not indeed allegorical force, is often such as to imbue a scene with at least a measure of that life principle. The great chapter on gluttony (I: chapter 30), which ends with a moving reference to the beggar Lazarus, is also immensely alive in this sense. Much the same can be said of the Notary of Cologne, who is clearly a representative figure: the epitome of avarice (III: chapter 34). Grimmelshausen accumulates, in a formalised, if lively manner, examples of his meanness in "feeding" his lodgers, to whom he serves up stinking fish that anyone else would have thrown away. Thus far, the moralist has maintained a certain distance, but the storyteller is tempted by the idea of the miser prowling in the fishmarket:

> dann er kieffe alles der Wohlfeile nach / und ließ sich die Mühe nicht dauren / zu solchem Ende auff den Fischmarckt zu gehen / und anzupacken / was jetzt die Fischer außzuschmeissen im Sinn hatten. (284)

> [For he was always out to buy cheap and with this in mind, he would take the trouble of going to the fishmarket and grabbing the stuff that the fishermen were going to throw out.]

By taking us down into the marketplace, the narrator turns those reject fish from a generalisation into something actual and individual. They acquire narrative life within a representative framework.

There are many stories told in the *Simplicissimus* that are patently, to use a phrase we have met before, "lustig zu hören."[27] Some are "Possen" (often tricks played or odd and comic misfortunes suffered). They may well stand in a meaningful relation to the serious and more abstract themes of the work, but they are not subordinated to them. The tricks that the young Olivier plays on his schoolmaster (346), such as releasing crickets in the school in summer, or sneezewort when a boy is undergoing corporal punishment, are certainly the acts of a "böser Bub," but as reported, they savour of the devilment not of a Mephistopheles but of Max and Moritz. They form a kind of comic counterpoint, perhaps, to the evil deeds of the grown-up figure. The deceptions practised on Simplicissimus by his naughty brother-page in Hanau in book I certainly throw his innocence into relief, but they are hardly a peg on which we could hang a denunciation of the wickedness and corruption of the world. They are funny, and meant to be funny, and even if we sympathise with the victim and disapprove of the culprit, we are faced with the situation that often confronts us in the reality of life as opposed to the laboratory conditions of satire; that is, in the common phrase, "we have to laugh," for this *is* life, and boys will be boys.

Some stories fall into the category of what we can call, with Grimmelshausen, "Stücklein" (exploits, escapades). The famous ham and bacon episode (II: 31), to which we have already referred, is explicitly designated as such (188). Clemens Lugowski says of this narrative form, which is closely related to the traditional *Schwank,* the entertaining short tale or anecdote which was so popular in the seventeenth century, that it possesses "Sonderbündigkeit," that is, it is self-contained and self-justifying.[28] Hans Geulen, who shows a very welcome sensitivity to the fact that Grimmelshausen "does not preach, but narrates," nevertheless insists that this narrative is supported on a spine of meaning, which is achieved by "strukturell integrierte Allegorik" (structurally integrated allegoricism).[29] Somehow, without breaking the flow of narrative at the "actual" level, the storyteller refers ("verweist") to a higher level of supra-literary, universal significance ("außerliterarisch Allgemeines").[30] We must, apparently, read as the ideal, educated baroque reader would have read, for Grimmelshausen relied on that reader for a correct interpretation of his work. We have touched on this problem in an earlier chapter.[31] It is surely by no means certain that Grimmelshausen always *wants* us to find the "hidden meanings" which the text can certainly yield to the interpreter with the full arsenal of exegetic instruments at his disposal. Grimmelshausen's own announced motivation for his "Stücklein" — that he intends to amuse us — is not to be dismissed so lightly, or retrospectively brushed aside by reference to the opening chapter of the *Continuatio* or the remarks of the more sober-sided Simplicius in the framework section of *Springinsfeld.*

Grimmelshausen's introductory remarks to the "Stücklein," which he relates to "make complete" his account of his life as a musketeer (IV, 10–11) make it quite clear that he is aware of the relation between them and the moral-religious dimension (he refers specifically to the dualism of danger to "body and soul." But the form that this takes need not be "integrated allegory." True, the author reminds us of his "German" frankness: "Ich wil meine Untugenden so wenig verhelen als meine Tugenden" (I no more want to conceal my vices than I do my virtues), but he does this "damit nicht allein meine Histori zimlich gantz sey / sondern der ohngewanderte Leser auch erfahre / was vor seltzame Kautzen es in der Welt gibt" (not just for completeness' sake, but to give the untravelled reader the benefit of his experience of this strange and fascinating world and of the odd specimens that it contains: 319). The figure is of legitimate interest, not just as an *exemplum,* but also on account of its "abentheurlich" quality.

As we saw in the preceding section, the story of the ham and bacon contains a clear adumbration of the moral and religious dimension. But it is still identified and narrated as a "Stücklein," told because it is "lustig zu hören" (because it will entertain the reader: 188). While it is being told, the story is not only amusing, but also very concretely "real" in the Simplician sense. The world in which it occurs is observed with a genuine storyteller's interest: the detail of the peasant "plastering over his baking-oven, which had big loaves of pumpernickel in it that would need to stay there for twenty-four hours," the priest "opening the night-lock on the stout oaken door that led into the churchyard," Springinsfeld hallooing his animal imitations down the chimney, and the cook with a coat hanging from her shoulders which "brushed against [Simplicissimus], so close did she come": all this holds us in that world and affords no purchase to the abstracting intellect. Our awareness that the hero is guilty of the sin of pride is in no way integrated with the storytelling proper. It is only after he has got away with the theft of the ham and bacon that Simplicissimus takes the action that reveals his "freveln und ehrgeitzigen Kopff" (wicked, fame-hungry mind: 195) by paying for the food he has stolen in a would-be "splendid" gesture.

Much the same point could be made about the equally famous episode related in book IV, chapter 10, when Simplicissimus is fighting for his life in the river, clinging desperately to a large branch. Certainly, his conscience is aroused and he turns to God for help, but the solemnity of this theme runs parallel with the immediacy and excitement of a real man buffeted by the waves of a real river. The same Simplicissimus who describes beginning "to pray as piously as if I had been brought up in a monastery" is thrown about so violently that he also says "I could have spewed up my liver and lungs" (321). This is not a phrasing that lends itself to allegorisation; rather, it suggests that this world is as prominent in the narrator's mind as the next and it certainly ensures that that is so in the reader's case. We are preoccupied simultaneously but separately with the danger to soul and to body, and our attention can shift easily and directly between the two because their coexistence is an essential part of the whole life we lead, which is the perspective that the Simplician manner sets out to establish.

The young Simplicissimus, watching the cleaners at work after the gluttonous banquet (II: chapter 2), sees an image of "the folly and madness of this world" by comparison with his godly-oriented, simple life in the forest (99). This in no way blunts the sense of specific, individual reality conveyed by the author's description of a floor covered with "the debris of broken glasses and window panes, scattered heaps of substances that had been brought up or down, and in other places, large puddles of spilt wine and beer" and of a smell so repellent that it drives the boy away to the kitchen. It is above all the presence of the cleaners that fixes this as the description of the almost tangible sordidness of an actual banqueting hall after an actual orgy. It is a mess with a clear symbolic potential; at the same time, it needs to be cleared up. The life principle, which may not have meaning, but is imbued with an unquenchable force, impels us forward, as moral reflection directs us upwards. Life has gone on (in the orgy), is going on (in the activity of the cleaners), and will go on, when the room has been made fit for human habitation again.

The Structure of Parallel Paths

The search for structure has been a very prominent theme in studies of *Simplicissimus*, as is evident from Weydt's review of works seeking to demonstrate its "mögliche Tektonik."[32] As that last remark indicates, the structure in question is consistently conceived in architectonic terms, and since the formal narrative technique is essentially the additive one of the picaresque novel, any such structure could only be thematic. There is thus a close relation, for this school of thought, between structure and what we have called "meaning," or in Weydt's expression, "Gestalt und übergeordneter Sinnzusammenhang" (17). In that word "übergeordnet," suggestive of the priority of a universal, abstract, and above all, consistent ideological framework over individual and living reality, we catch, once more, an echo of our perennial theme. It is not that there can be any dispute over the fact that Grimmelshausen raises and pursues many of the great themes of the baroque worldview (*vanitas*, Fortune, the presence and pre-eminence of God, and so on), nor indeed that these do not very probably provide elements of tectonic form. The problem is the implied *sub*ordination of life: life, that is, seen as a dynamic principle that informs all our physical, mental and spiritual activities and unites them into a whole whose meaning (insofar as it is proper to talk in these terms) lies in the fact that it *is*. For our purposes, these themes do not constitute a transcendent framework within which everything that occurs on earth must be viewed, but rather fixed points of reference within the ambit of life as we have defined it. We need not an over-arching *unitary* framework, but a more flexible *dual* structure, something analogous, perhaps, to the "equilibrium" that Valentin discerns, in a more theoretical context, between Albertinian seriousness and Sorelian laughter.[33]

The constant, if not always visible presence of the great themes means that the path traced by the hero in the narrative is always open to review from the spiritual perspective. Reminders of the two eternal realities of God and the devil are frequent enough to establish, alongside the path of events, a parallel path onto which the narrator can step with a sideways movement when it suits him to do so. Possibly the most important single structural motif of this kind is that of the hermit, which lays down the religious ground bass in book I (crystallized above all in the "Nachtigallenlied," which we discussed in chapter 2). The memory of this episode remains with Simplicissimus throughout his life, and with it goes the theme of self-knowledge, which is part of the hermit's valedictory message to Simplicissimus (I:12) and recurs in the penultimate chapter.[34] The weight of seriousness that this brings into the book can be illustrated by reference to the concluding paragraph of book V, chapter 1. Simplicissimus has resolved to accompany Herzbruder on a penitential pilgrimage to Einsiedeln in Switzerland and to emphasize the element of penance, to walk, as his friend does, "auff Erbsen" (that is, with peas under the soles of his shoes). But his feet hurt so much that he boils the peas. Despite and without prejudice to the seriousness of the underlying theme, Grimmelshausen does not repress his response to the humorous effect when the trusting Herzbruder, whose feet are killing him, remarks, when he notices the ease with which his friend is walking: "You are greatly blessed with the grace of God." Then, the mood switches directly into the didactic mode. Simplicissimus tells him what he has done and has then to listen to an earnest remonstration, which brings us back to the question of the salvation of the soul and the memory of the hermit in the forest:

> Von dieser Zeit an folgte ich ihm traurig nach / als einer den man zum Galgen führt / mein Gewissen fieng mich an zu drücken / und in dem ich allerley Gedancken machte / stelleten sich alle meine Bubenstücke vor Augen / die ich mein Lebtag je begangen / da beklagte ich erst die verlorne Unschuld / die ich auß dem Wald gebracht / und in der Welt so verschertzt hatte. . . .(377).

> [From this time forth, I followed him in sadness, like a man being led to the gallows; I began to feel the keen pinch of conscience and as all kinds of thoughts ran through my head, all the misdeeds of which I had been guilty throughout my life rose up before my eyes. Then I lamented the lost innocence which I had brought with me out of the wood, and so thoughtlessly thrown away in the world. . . .]

From this perspective, wood and world (*Wald* and *Welt*) provide what looks like a convincing framework for the understanding of events. The tone here is uniformly serious, the deliberate pairing of "Wald" and "Welt" makes clear that it is right to see earthly things *sub specie aeternitatis*. It is good that a man should reflect on his world and himself, either in the narrated time or from the retrospective position of the narrator, who not infrequently condemns his own youthful folly (e.g. 325: "Ich großer Narr!") But as we saw earlier, the *author's* perspective (as opposed to that of the narrator, perhaps) enables moral seriousness to go hand-in-hand with a direct response to the intrinsic interest of the comic and curious in life. We find it hard to judge Simplicissimus's cooking of the peas too harshly, hard, indeed, not to smile: he falls short of the — no doubt admirable — religious zeal of Herzbruder, but we like him better, if anything, for being only human. "Welt," which includes humanity and humour, refuses to be suppressed by the ascetic ideal. It is right and proper that we should recognise the ideological superiority of the hermit mentality and the sincere feeling with which it is communicated, but in the Simplician context, the pith of this world is not sicklied o'er with any pale cast of thought.

The structural consequence of this reasoning is that the apparent framework to which we have just referred — and it is a term that of course has tectonic implications — needs to be seen not as all-inclusive and dominant, but as a part of a wider tapestry whose presiding spirit is more flexible, more open and more free. As foreshadowed in the *Satyrischer Pilgram*, Grimmelshausen is writing here not in a theological tone, but in a "lustigere Manier," a manner that is not predominantly didactic. The Simplicissimus who stands behind this work as narrator, and whom we meet later in the *Springinsfeld* and *Rathstübel Plutonis*, has certainly acquired a relative stability and gravitas by comparison with the figure we see within it, but he remains a free, and in many ways an odd spirit. The Simplician manner is the ubiquitous element that possesses the flexibility needed to accommodate the variegation and constant movement of human life to which, as we saw, the frontispiece refers us. There is an interesting potential analogy between this emphasis on what we call manner and the distinction in modern narratological theory between story, which exercises what Frank Kermode has dubbed an "arbitrary" authority and seeks an effect of "closure" that imposes limits on the variety of life, and discourse, which Bruce Robbins defines as "the mode of recounting or presenting the events." Although it is hardly likely that Grimmelshausen would have been concerned to stress the fictionality of his fiction, and although one suspects that he was not by nature a theorizer, he may instinctively have been seeking, in his way, to find a way of narrating that allowed for a plurality of perspectives beyond what was offered by the standard contemporary forms.[35]

Weydt, after careful examination of the available evidence, concludes that the question of a possible knowledge of Cervantes's *Don Quixote* on Grimmelshausen's part must remain open.[36] But that need not prevent us from referring to it for evidence of the viability of a form of novel that has, as the Canon of Toledo puts it in chapter 47 of part 1, commenting on the possibilities of the chivalric romance, an "escritura desatada" (a "loose plan," in J. M. Cohen's translation) and emerges as "a beautiful and variegated fabric."[37] Quixote himself is, after all, a character whose career is modelled on the principle of the knight-errant, and the unity of the work is provided in the main by the polarity of the different perspectives of Quixote and Sancho, which in turn relies on the polarity of idealistic fantasy and pragmatic realism in the human mind. There is a corresponding polarity within the Simplician manner, which, once the author has made us accustomed to it, is in no way disruptive in its effect, and which is the basis of the shifting perspectives to which we have already referred. If we were never to be able to step back and see the essential vanity of material things when measured against a spiritual ideal, we would hardly be truly human. On the other hand, if we could see nothing but vanity, we could hardly live at all. The phrase "That's life" contains a recognition of the mixture of disparate and sometimes apparently contradictory things which make up our existence: it is the spirit of life and its varied and shifting constitution that lies at the root of the Simplician manner and of the flexible structure of *Simplicissimus*.

The capacity of the novel to accommodate a response to humour, even in a serious passage, contributes materially to the flexibility of its structure, its freedom to range over the whole variety of life. Even in the mouth of the mentally disturbed "Jupiter," the punishment of the godless (III: chapter 4) is a serious idea, and the decapitation of an enemy army by the "Teutscher Held" is no joke, yet there is a comic image here that Grimmelshausen manages to bring to the fore as well: "also daß die arme Teuffel ohne Kopff da ligen müssen / ehe sie einmal wissen wie ihnen geschehen!"(So that before they know what's hit them, there they are, poor devils, lying on the ground with no heads: 211–12). This effect of variegation through humour is a constant feature of the work. Conversely, the narrator has the freedom at any time to vary his tone with a serious note that prevents laughter from becoming a kind of blinkered frivolity.[38] To that extent, perhaps, Leibniz's judgement needs qualification, but the serious note does not clash with the laughter.

The potential of a switch between serious and comic is one source of the sense of freedom and movement that is characteristic of the novel. And indeed, the Simplician dualism, the potential of movement as well as tectonic stability is present in many of the themes we have already identified as recurrent in the book. Fortune as an agent, a presiding deity in the world, is a constant, but it can also be seen in terms of movement, as in the rapid sequence of "unglückliche Zufäll" suffered by Simplicissimus after his marriage to the peasant girl (403). Change obviously involves not only constancy and inconstancy, but also ends and new beginnings. Chapter 7 of book IV contains not only one of the most impressive set piece reflections on the eternal theme ("O schnelle und unglückselige Veränderung . . ."), but also a fine example of the sideways shift between two paths in the narrative to which we referred a little earlier. As soon as his reflection on the swiftness and violence of change is over, the author switches directly and abruptly to the narrative path: "Ich machte wol tausend und aber tausenderley Gedancken / was ich angreiffen wolte . . ." (I must have turned over in my mind a thousand, and then a thousand more ideas about what to do next: 312).

The war is seen (not least in the "Jupiter" episode) as an example of God's intervention in human affairs, but it is also an endlessly and restlessly moving sea on which the hero is borne along. And the theme of fate ("fatum" or "Verhängnis") has a similar duality. In essence, it means: "whatever happens to us." This is sometimes seen under the rubric of Divine Providence (cf. 355: "die göttliche Vorsehung"), as when, in reflecting on the assault on the farm that had sent him out into the forest, the author remarks that such evils are often sent upon us ("verhängt") by God "for our benefit" (17). At other times, the word "fate" denotes simply "the course of events": man in his inability to control his destiny, as when Simplicissimus explains his failure to grasp the opportunity to climb the ladder of advancement with the phrase "weil mein fatum ein anders beschlossen" (because fate had decided on a different course for me: 383) or in the same chapter, the narrative takes an odd twist when, by a "sudden and unexpected turn of fortune," Herzbruder loses his "testiculi" (385). That, indeed, is life — with a vengeance.

It is improbable that the principle of life, which we identified earlier as the presiding spirit of Simplician structure, can be precisely defined, since its indwelling spirit is not one of consistency (except in the sense of consistent variety). There is a strong sense of the presence both of a reader and of an active author, speaking through a narrator who frequently has to remind himself of the necessity to "tell my story."[39] The potential for digression, or sideways movement, is always there. And this does not produce the impression of the "loose straggle of actions" identified by A. A. Mendilow as characteristic of the picaresque genre,[40] but rather of the constant presence of a unifying but flexible force. Nor would the idea of an "open form" of satire, as invoked by Volker Meid, which "does not seek to resolve contradictions by harmonisation,"[41] help us in such a quest; satirical form (often marked by the treatment of a variety of subjects) cannot be divorced from satirical purpose, which imposes a non-narrative framework at least as rigid and consistent as that of a plot or a spiritualistic ideological perspective. The structure of Grimmelshausen's *Satyrischer Pilgram* is indeed genuinely satirical: the work subdivides into a series of discrete thematic modules, but despite the apparent variety of material, leaves the impression of rigidity rather than flexibility of format. The overall effect, (as also in the superficially Simplician *Verkehrte Welt*) is, measured against that of the *Simplicissimus*, one of sameness. The satirical author is working, to use an expression employed by the narrator-Simplicissimus, "unter einer Botmäßigkeit" (under a higher jurisdiction, in a state of subjection: 278).

It may not be possible to come any closer to a definition of our Simplician principle of life than "the spirit of freedom," a freedom *in* the world which goes beyond the standard Christian-Stoic view of freedom "im

Gemüt" and of the world as a "Babylonian captivity."[42] It includes, of course, even the freedom to be an outsider and a sinner: even, like Courage, a lost soul. If, as Simplicissimus is to say to his old comrade in the *Springinsfeld*, you don't want to go to heaven, "nobody's going to pick you up and carry you there" (cf. *Springinsfeld* 131). In the latter novel, indeed, the idea of the "free life" can be said to become an important central theme. We will not anticipate discussion of that topic here, nor have we the space to launch into an examination of the idea of freedom in Grimmelshausen's oeuvre as a whole.[43] But it is worth noting that hints of it appear in *Simplicissimus* as well, and nowhere more strikingly than in the episode cited at the end of the previous paragraph. Simplicissimus marries, and he can be said eventually to have "settled down." But the two do not go together. Many novels, indeed, derive their conclusions from matrimony, but the only finality in Grimmelshausen is death. When Simplicissimus describes himself as living "unter einer Botmäßigkeit," he is referring to the marriage contracted in Lippstadt and to the loss of what he calls "meine edle Freyheit" (278). Grimmelshausen generally reserves the word "edel" (noble) for the spiritually positive and constructive things in life. It is the state of freedom, of course, rather than his hero's previous behaviour in that state, that he is celebrating here, and no doubt he would have been wary, even assuming he had wanted to do so, of attacking the institution of marriage. But he does not seem impressed by the settled state and it is noteworthy that he leaves Simplicissimus a widower, as he puts it: in his "erste Freyheit" (original freedom: 404). Not dissimilarly, the "Merodebrüder" are subjected to fierce criticism (IV: chapter 13), but one cannot but note a tinge of envy, a sense of what David Copperfield calls "something gipsy-like and agreeable" in Grimmelshausen's description of their freedom from the strict discipline that the regular soldier has to endure.[44]

Henry James speaks of the "queer elements of the accidental and the arbitrary" in the kind of novel that lacks "composition," though it may have "life."[45] He is clearly no apostle of freedom. Grimmelshausen does not want to create, in James's elegant phrase, a "fluid pudding." His aim, and his achievement, is a structural principle that gives unity with freedom, that allows constant themes to emerge and recur, but which also allows freedom of movement. At the same time, there can be no suggestion that he desires anything approaching the subversively "carnevalesque" effect associated with Mikhail Bakhtin. Even Anne Leblans, who brings the two together in her essay "Grimmelshausen and the Carnevalesque," and sees the German writer as "inverting hierarchies," has to admit that he is "no revolutionary." In fact, his depiction of a "verkehrte Welt" is anything but a rejection of order.[46]

Style

Style (in the narrower sense of the writer's handling of language) is not the whole of what we mean by manner, but it is obviously an important constituent part of it and indeed, in much that we have already said, we have found ourselves trespassing in that province. A brief concluding section on this topic may not come amiss.

Quite apart from the fact that Grimmelshausen wrote a separate treatise on the subject (the *Teutscher Michel*), there is evidence in the narrative work itself to suggest that he had a special sensitivity to and interest in language. Hayens has said that he was "no stylist."[47] This may be true in the sense that he lacked the formal rhetorical training of the typical baroque author, but he had read enough, and had a sufficient innate sensitivity to prose structures and rhythms and the resonances of words, to be able to manage as much stylistic formality as he needed for his purposes, whether serious or parodistic. Even when he abstracted material from his sources to serve his own ends, as in the fine piece of sustained "high" baroque prose in which the *Simplicissimus* ends, he does not merely copy, but carries out subtle adaptations of detail, as Weydt has shown in the case mentioned.[48] Weydt's commentary is not exhaustive, and in one of the sections that he does not treat specifically there is an example that illustrates our point very well.

The source is Ägidius Albertinus's version of a text by the Spanish writer Antonio de Guevara (*Menosprecio de la Corte*), a characteristic piece of epideictic rhetoric in which the age-old theme of "rus" (country) versus "aula" (court) is expounded. Grimmelshausen uses it to signal his hero's rejection of the world and return to the hermit's life. Albertinus renders the eighth section, which deals with the untrustworthiness of the world, as follows:

> Behüt dich Gott Welt / dann in deinem Pallast findet weder die Warheit noch Trew kein Herberg. Wer mit dir redt / der wird verschambt / wer dir trawt / der wird betrogen / wer dir folgt / der wird verführt / wer dich fürchtet / der wird am aller übelsten gehalten / wer dich liebet / der wird übel belohnt / und wer sich auff dich am allermeisten verlest / der wird am meisten zu schanden gemacht. (Weydt, 221–2)

In the *Simplicissimus*, the passage reads:

> Adjeu Welt / dann in deinem Pallast findet weder Warheit noch Treu ihre Herberg! Wer mit dir redet wird verschamt / wer dir traut wird betrogen / wer dir folgt wird verführt / wer dich förchtet wird am aller-übelsten gehalten / wer dich liebt wird übel belohnt / und wer sich am allermeisten auff dich verläst / wird auch am allermeisten zu schanden gemacht. (458)

Of the numerous alterations carried out by Grimmelshausen here with the general effect of producing a smoother, more flowing and literary piece of prose, that to the final clause is the most striking. The re-positioning of "am allermeisten" in the first half, and its substitution for "am meisten" in the second, transform the balance and rhetorical effect of the sentence.

We have already quoted in chapter 1, in the process of comparing and contrasting Grimmelshausen with Moscherosch, the opening paragraph of the whole work, pointing to the livelier, more entertaining and generally Simplician qualities that it has. It is worth adding here that the passage is at the same time, and without any loss of these qualities, a controlled and structured piece of writing. Much the same could be said of the description of the assault on the farm in book I: chapter 4, also quoted earlier, of the gluttonous orgy (I: 30), the picture of the gamblers (II: 20), the Battle of Wittstock (II: 27), the avarice of the notary of Cologne (III: 24), and other "set pieces." In many of these Grimmelshausen shows a sure hand in the control of devices like accumulation and antithesis, and an equally sure instinct for the detail that enlivens and loosens the style, so that formality and informality hold the balance with each other. The language of the book is, indeed, in true Simplician spirit, a rich and varied tapestry, spiced, at times, with authentic-sounding dialect.

Flashes of baroque wit and intellectual linguistic playfulness (e.g. puns, such as the formation of the concept "katzenübel" by analogy with the familiar "hundsübel" in the story of Olivier and the cat) are not infrequent. When the old woman who is leading Simplicissimus into temptation in the Paris episode is met with his scruples as a married man, she indulges in a style of metaphorical argument that would not have disgraced a Lohenstein play. In France, she says, they are "not so curmudgeonly as to forbid a man to drink the water when there is an abundance of it" and even if he is, as he claims, married, she "cannot imagine that the gentleman would be so silly as to die of thirst rather than drink from someone else's well" (304).

Even in passages where it is possible to speak of a baroque intellectuality, though, there is a tendency towards the idiomatic and what might be called, in a broad sense, the proverbial. In developing his description of the moment when Simplicissimus, as "Huntsman of Soest," sees the ham, sausages and bacon curing in the priest's fireplace, Grimmelshausen employs as a metaphor the familiar expression for the man for whom everything in the garden is lovely: "Der Himmel hängt ihm voller Geigen" (literally, he sees the sky full of violins):

> da sahe ich / daß der schwartze Himmel auch schwartz voller Lauten Flöten und Geigen hienge / ich vermeyne aber die Schincken / Knackwürst und Speckseiten / die sich im Kamin befanden; diese blickte ich trostmüthig an / weil mich bedünckte / als ob sie mit mir lachten / und wünschte sie / aber vergeblich / meinen Cameraden in Wald / dann sie waren so hartnäckig / daß sie mir zu Trotz hangen blieben.... (190–1)

[And then I saw the dark sky darkly filled with lutes, flutes and violins, by which I mean the hams, sausages and sides of bacon which were there in the fireplace. I gave them a look of hopeful anticipation, because it seemed to me that they were smiling at me invitingly; I conceived the desire to carry them off into the forest to join my comrades, but it was all in vain, for they remained stonily indifferent to my advances and stayed where they were, hanging from the ceiling.]

We can feel the intellectuality of the baroque style in this passage, even catch a hint of a baroque conceit, perhaps. But just as it is a property of the familiar idiom, proverb or saying, however figurative its meaning, to retain a great deal of concreteness in its impact, so here it is the presence of solid material objects that dominates.

The great frequency of figures taken from, or clearly modelled on popular speech, in the context of what is still recognisably a baroque style by no means lacking in a sense of rhythm and even rhetorical elegance, maintains contact not only with the concreteness, but also with the sounds and smells and living creatures, the vigour and movement of actual and immediate life. In the third chapter of book I, the young Simplicius makes a racket with his bagpipes "bad enough to poison all the toads in the herb-garden" ("daß man die Krotten im Krautgarten hätte vergeben mögen": 14). In chapter 14 of book III, when he is describing the worries stirred up in Simplicissimus's mind by Springinsfeld's warning that his prosperity will make him enemies, Grimmelshausen has his hero say: "Spring-ins-feld hatte mir einen unruhigen Floh ins Ohr gesetzt" (247: literally, "Springinsfeld had placed a restless flea in my ear"; i.e. unsettled me). The meaning is abstract; the stylistic effect is concrete and dynamic and entirely appropriate for the present work, whereas in the *Keuscher Joseph*, the same idiom betrays an uncertainty on Grimmelshausen's part in handling the required register for the "polite" novel.[49] The same effect can be noted over and over again. One further example can stand for many more: in chapter 24 of book III, in which he is depicting the meanness of the notary of Cologne, Simplicissimus writes: "Unser Brod war gemeiniglich schwartz und altbachen / der Tranck aber ein dinn saur Bier / das mir die Darm hätte zerschneiden mögen" (The bread we were given was usually black and stale, and our drink was a thin beer, sour enough to slice through my guts like a knife: 284–5).

Themes that stood out in our examination of what may be called the content of the book, its dynamic polarity and its quality of variegation, have recurred in the discussion of its more technical aspects. The style, as is only to be expected, is no exception. This must already be clear as far as the global picture is concerned, and the same applies within individual chapters, and indeed paragraphs. In book V, chapter 8, for example, when the author is contrasting Simplicissimus's second experience of marriage with his high hopes beforehand, we are given a baroque play on words: what he had expected to be a voyage to England lands him, unexpectedly, in Holland. He expected a full, and has acquired a hollow ("hohl") vessel. The basis of this formulation is a play on the meanings of "eng" (narrow, tight-packed) and "hohl" (with a possible further reference to "Engel" [angels] and "Hölle" [hell]). The first part of the sentence quoted, however, has put the point in a different style: "Aber die Pfeiff fiel mir bald in Dreck" (But my pipe very soon fell into the muck: 397). The burden of the sentence is consistent throughout, but it contains a marked stylistic shift. In book II, chapter 28, an earthy enough subject, namely Simplicissimus's attempts to get rid of the lice that are plaguing him under the cuirass that he has to bear for his master, is rendered, with a parodistic irony of which Grimmelshausen is a master, into a rhetorical *allegoria*. It is described, in *extenso*, in terms of a military campaign (179–80), the basis, of course, being not realism, but baroque wit. At the same time, we never forget the reality of what is being described, especially when we are shown the thumbnails ("the swords on my thumbs") dripping with blood and dead bodies. A similar movement occurs in book I, chapter 12, in the description of the death of Simplicissimus's hermit father. The death itself is rendered in a moving and serious style: the boy's uncomprehending reaction (narrated, we should remember, by the older and wiser Simplicissimus) breaks with solemnity:

> Er ... begab sich in das Grab / gleichsam wie einer / der sich sonst schlaffen legen will / sprechende: Ach grosser GOtt / nun nim wieder hin die Seele / die du mir gegeben / HERR / in deine Hände befehl ich meinen Geist etc. Hierauff beschloß er seine Lippen und Augen sänfftiglich / ich aber stund da wie ein Stockfisch. . . . (36)
>
> [He ... went down into the grave, just like someone laying himself down to sleep in the normal way, saying: "Great God, take back now the soul which thou gavest me. Lord, into thy hands I commend my spirit ... Whereupon he gently closed his eyes and lips, while I stood there gaping like a dried codfish. . . .]

It is as if the brute force of life is asserting itself at a moment of high spirituality, and it is not inappropriate that that should be the case, for as we have repeatedly observed, the world of *Der abentheurliche Simplicissimus* is one in which both elements exist concurrently. It is indeed the admittedly imperfect but always vital and interesting place that we call "this world," and Grimmelshausen, for all his criticism of its imperfections, ultimately accepts it.

Notes

[1] Cf. Günther Weydt, "Das Problem Simplicissimus," in *Nachahmung und Schöpfung im Barock*, 12–13. See also Gersch, preface to *Geheimpoetik*, ix-x, on the "romantisch inspiriertes Grimmelshausenbild" that he aims to counteract.

[2] Kenneth Hayens, *Grimmelshausen* (Oxford: Oxford U. P., 1932). Hayens recognises a moral intention, but denies Grimmelshausen compositional talent (see especially 104–5). His summation is that "Grimmelshausen presents us with a picture of struggling humanity."

[3] Kenneth Negus (*Grimmelshausen* [New York 1974]) considers the concept of *vanitas* as a thematic "key," but fixes eventually on a "life" that "teems and moves in all directions." He proposes the abandonment of "the chase after the hobgoblin of formal and thematic consistency" (95).

[4] See Weydt, "Das Problem Simplicissimus."

[5] For example, (anonymous), *Vida de Lazarillo de Tormes y de sus fortunas y adversidades* (1554) or Quevedo, *Historia de la vida del buscón* (1608).

[6] On linearity, cf. R. Scholes and R. Kellogg: *The Nature of Narrative* (New York 1966), 209: the ground plan of the picaresque is "the linear simplicity of primitive epic." A more "thematic" approach is taken by Northrop Frye, who describes the genre as "satirical" in the sense that it is a pragmatic "counterblast" to — one assumes, Romantic — "escape." (*Anatomy of Criticism* [Princeton: Princeton U. P., 1957] 229).

[7] Eberhard Lämmert, *Bauformen des Erzählens*, 3d ed. (Stuttgart 1968), 47.

[8] Harsdörffer, *Jämmerliche Mordgeschichte*, 720.

[9] Simplicissimus is born soon after the Battle of Höchst (1622). His "Knan" dates the plundering of the farm from the Battle of Nördlingen (1634) but from the evidence of book I (52, 63) it must have occurred two years earlier.

[10] See *ST* 383 (V:4). The theme is a frequently recurring one: book III chapter 8 (224): "So wunderlich ist das Glück / und so veränderlich die Zeit" and book IV, chapter 7 (311): "O schnelle und unglückselige Veränderung . . . ."

[11] The *vanitas* theme rises to a crescendo in the final two chapters, where the "Know thyself" formula, first articulated by the hermit in book I (34–5) is developed with high baroque rhetoric, to be followed by an elaborate and stately "farewell to the World." Weydt ("Das Problem Simplicissimus," 235) sees this as a "peak," a pair of "mighty final chords," but is it, in fact, the end? The final paragraph of the last chapter shifts into a much more matter-of-fact key and the actual conclusion is the non-committal "stehet dahin" (it remains an open question). The actual word "Ende" is reached by a trick: the author expresses the wish that in death, he will enjoy a "seliges Ende."

[12] "Abentheurlich" is specifically linked to "adventure" in *Das wunderbarliche Vogelnest* (book I, 89): King Arthur's knights are "abentheurliche Irr-Ritter." The word indicates a spectrum which includes the idea "strange" in the sense of "eerie,

dangerous." (Cf. book III: chapter 12, 243: the ruin in which Simplicissimus discovers a hidden treasure is "so abentheuerlich beschaffen" that no one will go near it.) That the word can be interchangeable with "seltzam" is instanced by the ending of *Der seltzame Springinsfeld*: " . . . nahm also dieser abentheuerliche Springinsfeld auff des eben so seltzamen *Simplicissimi* Bauerhoff . . . sein letztes Ende (132).

[13] Cf. *Rathstübel Plutonis*, 89: "mein redlicher teutscher Simplice" and *ST* 246: "auß einem Teutschen auffrichtigen Hertzen." The Egyptian Selicha even says to Joseph: "Warum hast du dann neulichen meinen austrücklichen teutschen Worten im Garten nicht vertraut?" (*Keuscher Joseph*, 44). See also chapter 1 above.

[14] See W. E. Schäfer, "Der Satyr und die Satire. Zu Titelkupfern Grimmelshausens und Moscheroschs" in *Festschrift Weydt*, ed. W. Rasch et al. Text and illustration facing page 204.

[15] There are several references to the soul, e.g. book II, ch. 20 (153), where the old Herzbruder says that gambling can lead a man to the loss of "so gar seiner Seelen Seligkeit"; IV: 10 (319): "Seelengefahr"; V: 1 (377): Herzbruder's concern over his friend's salvation; and — a highly Simplician example — I: 30 (84), where the naive young Simplicissimus asks how the "edle Seelen" of the banqueters can survive in men who are stuffing their bodies "as if they were fattening a pig for market."

[16] Sybille Penkert, "Grimmelshausens Titelkupfer-Fiktionen" in *Internationaler Arbeitskreis für deutsche Barockliteratur. Erstes Jahrestreffen, Vorträge und Berichte* (Wolfenbüttel 1973), 64 ff. The final message is that Grimmelshausen's primary purpose is didactic.

[17] They are living in "godless times in which the world is full of treachery" (381).

[18] Feldges, *Grimmelshausens "Landstörtzerin Courasche,"* 65.

[19] Gisela Noehles, "Das Titelkupfer zum Simplicissimus Teutsch" in *Simplicius Simplicissimus, Grimmelshausen und seine Zeit*. Catalogue (Münster, 1976), 111–12.

[20] Juvenal, *Satires*, trans. William Gifford, ed. John Warrington (London/New York: Everyman, 1954), 5.

[21] *ST* 383: "Es gehet wol seltzam in der veränderlichen Welt her!"

[22] Negus, *Grimmelshausen*, 72.

[23] *ST* 358: "heillos" can be read as "hopeless" or as "un-saved" (heil-los). Cf. *ST* 338: "Mein lieber Simplici, du hast den *Macchiavellum* noch nicht gelesen."

[24] The name is given by H. Kulick as "Leutkircherheide" (near Villigen?): see notes to *Simplicissimus* (Reclam: Stuttgart 1961), 740.

[25] See *ST* 310 (IV: 7): "Womit einer sündiget . . ."

[26] M. Kremer, "Wirklichkeitsnähe in der Barockliteratur," 148.

[27] Cf. my comments on the *Bartkrieg* above, chapter 2.

[28] See Clemens Lugowski. "Literarische Formen und lebendiger Gehalt im 'Simplicissimus'" (1934), reprinted in *Der Simplicissimusdichter und sein Werk*, G. Weydt, ed. (Darmstadt: Wissenschaftliche Buchgesellschaft, 1969), 163.

[29] H. Geulen, "Wirklichkeitsbegriff und Realismus in Grimmelshausens *Simplicissimus Teutsch*," *Argenis* 1 (1977), 34.

[30] Ibid., 31–2.

[31] See also the discussion of the realism question, above, chapter 2.

[32] Weydt, "Das Problem Simplicissimus," 13–18.

[33] Valentin, "Du rire au plus haut savoir," 105–6. Valentin, however, still insists on the subordination ("assujetissement") of the comic, which, he rightly remarks, ties us to the world ("enferme dans la temporalité," 104), to the serious. Grimmelshausen, he argues, is trying, with Sorel's help, to emancipate the writer from the total domination of the "theologian," but also trying to steer some kind of middle course between the two.

[34] Recurrences of the "Einsiedel" theme are found at the following places in *Simplicissimus*: book I: chapters 18 (51–2); 22 (61ff.); and 25 (73); book II: chapters 2 (99); 16 (141); 13 (131); 20 (150: "erwachte umb Mitternacht..."); and 29 (182); book III: chapter 1 (203); book IV: chapters 7 (311); 10 (321); and 17 (343); book V: chapter 1 (377) and, of course, the conclusion.

[35] For "story," "discourse," and "closure," see Bruce Robbins, "Death and Vocation. Narrativizing Narrative Theory," *PMLA* 107 (1992), 43. Kermode's view is quoted on page 48. See also Menhennet, "Grimmelshausen, the Picaresque and the Large Loose Baggy Monster."

[36] Weydt, "Das Problem Simplicissimus," 147–8.

[37] Cervantes, *Don Quixote*, trans. J. M. Cohen, (Harmondsworth 1950), 426.

[38] Cf. *ST* III:23 : "Viel Lachen [ist] kein Anzeichen eines vernüngftigen Mannes" (283: To laugh a great deal is not the mark of a man of reason). Cf. also *Continuatio*, chapter 1 and *Springinsfeld*, chapter 3. The phrasing, as we have already noted in chapter 2, is borrowed from Moscherosch, but Grimmelshausen is no doubt sincere.

[39] E.g. *Courasche*, 21: "Aber wo komm ich hin? Ich muß meine Histori erzehlen."

[40] A. A. Mendilow, *Time and the Novel* (1952; reprint, New York, 1965), 203.

[41] Meid, *Grimmelshausen: Epoche-Werk-Wirkung*, 150.

[42] Ägidius Albertinus, for example, separates body and mind: "Ob schon wir mit dem Leib in der Welt wohnen / so können wir mit dem Gemüt im Himmel seyn" (*Hirnschleiffer*, 304). The world is a "Babylonian captivity" (306).

[43] I hope to consider this theme at more length on another occasion.

[44] "Wenn sie aber Gesellen-weis marchiren... so haben sie keinen Wachtmeister / der sie commandirt / keinen Feldwaibel oder Schergianten / der ihnen das Wambs außklopfft... sondern leben vielmehr wie die Frey-Herren" (*ST* 331-2). Cf. the

description of dinner with the Micawbers in the debtors' prison, *David Copperfield*, chapter 11.

[45] Henry James, *The Art of the Novel*, R. P. Blackmur, ed. (London, 1935), 84. On the "shapelessness" of life, cf. Ivy Compton Burnett's remark: "I think it is better for a novel to have a plot. Otherwise it has no shape . . . As regards plot, I find real life no help at all. Real life seems to have no plots." (Reported by Miriam Allott in M. A., ed., *Novelists on the Novel*, [1959; reprint, London, 1965], 249.) These compositional principles have, of course, kept a tighter hold on the novel in Britain than in some other countries!

[46] Anne Leblans, "Grimmelshausen and the Carnevalesque: The Polarisation of Courtly and Popular Carnival in Grimmelshausen's *Der abentheurliche Simplicissimus*," *MLN*, 105 (1990), 494–511, esp. 496 and 507.

[47] Hayens, *Grimmelshausen*, 119.

[48] Weydt, "Weltklage und Lebensrückblick. Guevara, Albertinus und Grimmelshausen," in Weydt, *Nachahmung und Schöpfung*, 216–40.

[49] *Keuscher Joseph*, 71. ("Durch diese dunckele zweydeutige Sprach setzte Asaneth dem Potiphar ein Flohe ins Ohr.")

4: Reaction: The *Continuatio*

HOT ON THE heels of *Simplicissimus* came the *Continuatio des abentheurlichen Simplicissimi oder Der Schluß desselben* (1669), which appeared both as a separate publication and bound together with the original five-book novel, but in either case set apart by the fact that it has a title page, a *pictura* — the winged horse with the motto "Ad astra volandum" — and a *subscriptio* of its own. The general view is that it was written at speed: one of the principal sources, Henry Neville's *Isle of Pines*, became available to Grimmelshausen only in 1668, and another likely source, Rochefort's *Histoire naturelle des îles Antilles*, did not appear in German translation until July of that year.[1]

Whether the *Continuatio* should be regarded as the sixth book of a unified *Simplicissimus* or assessed separately has long been, as Gersch demonstrates, a bone of contention. Gersch himself sees it as an integral part of one whole, but with a special function.[2] We will attempt a more systematic presentation of our own view a little later. That there is a decided change of mood and style, a shift away from entertainment and towards didacticism, can hardly be disputed. Grimmelshausen is still himself, but the moralist exerts a stronger inhibiting influence on the storyteller than was previously the case. The possible causes and implications are matters for later examination.

Story and Allegory

This work could be seen as a kind of reprise of and variation on *Der abentheurliche Simplicissimus*. After a series of poetological remarks, in which seriousness of intent and content are emphasized, the first chapter returns to Simplicissimus as a hermit, withdrawn from, or at most on the fringe of the world. He lacks, however, the discipline required if he is to live up to such a high ideal. A dream-vision (chapters 2–5) shows him first a conclave in hell, in which Lucifer calls his henchmen together to consider the implications of the restoration of peace on earth. The allegorical tendency which all critics have observed asserts itself in a dispute over precedence between the vices of Extravagance and Avarice, which is carried over to the earthly plane when the two attach themselves respectively to a rich English youth, Julus, and his servant, Avarus, to the eventual destruction of both. Shortly after awaking from his dream, Simplicissimus meets Baldanders, a figure derived from Hans Sachs,[3] but developed into a baroque allegory of the mutability of this world.

This section corresponds broadly in its structural function to the sequence in *Simplicissimus* that precedes the hero's entry "into the world." It also echoes and contrasts with the state of "Rhue" (rest) and "Verachtung der Welt" (disdain for the world) in which he at least claims, at the end of that book, to have left it. Another model now replaces the Einsiedel, at least temporarily. Impressed by the "Verachtung der Ruhe" (disdain for rest: *Continuatio* 508) of St. Alexius, Simplicissimus reflects that the appearance of Baldanders was perhaps a sign that he should accept the inconstancy of this world (509), rather than flee into a state of rest which can easily become idleness, mere absence of movement. He returns, then, to "this world," to undertake a pilgrimage to the Holy Places. And while he is a more or less pious pilgrim during his travels, he is also *abentheurlich* in both senses: adventurous and odd. He is also not above playing on the taste for curiosities of those he meets, and from whom he begs food and shelter. He wanders through Switzerland, experiencing a number of encounters, including the conversation with the "Schermesser"[4] and an interesting confrontation with some ghosts (to which we shall return), reaches Egypt and is enslaved by a band of robbers, who are inspired by his odd appearance to exhibit him as a kind of fairground freak, is eventually rescued and embarks on a voyage that ends in shipwreck. He is marooned, together with the ship's carpenter and an Abyssinian maid, on an uninhabited island. The maid is in fact an emissary of the devil, who tempts the carpenter into planning Simplicissimus's murder, but when the latter crosses himself, she disappears in a puff of smoke, leaving behind nothing but a suitably evil smell.

At this point (the end of chapter 21), the orientation of the book changes radically, though the setting remains the same. The island has already been portrayed as fruitful. Now, Simplicissimus and the repentant carpenter live "like the first humans in the Golden Age" (564) in what is later described as "an earthly Paradise"(572). After the death of the carpenter, Simplicissimus resumes the life of the hermit ("fieng widerumb ein Einsidlerisches Leben an": 566), but this time with an exemplary piety and firmness of purpose. He writes his life story down on the leaves of a kind of palm that is suitable for the purpose, at which point the first-person narrative concludes with the wish that the writer may enjoy a "seliges Ende." The book itself is brought back to Europe by a Dutch sea captain, Jan Cornelissen, who has put in at the island in search of provisions and refreshment for his sick seamen. Cornelissen's account of the island and of his meeting with Simplicissimus, who has refused point-blank to be rescued, concludes the narrative, to which Grimmelshausen, in his own name (or at least, initials) adds a postscript, in which he identifies himself as the editor of the posthumous papers of Samuel Greifnson von Hirschfeld, the ex-musketeer and "author" of the *Satyrischer Pilgram*, and holds out the prospect of further "satyrical" works from the deceased's prolific pen.

The pattern of the first novel, in which the hero moves into the world and out of it again, is, then, repeated here, and the same duality of positive and negative interest is apparent. There is, however, a tilting of the balance between the "realistic" (insofar as the term can be applied to Grimmelshausen) and the "spiritualistic" attitudes to the world. This could well be said to be prefigured in the vignette used on the *Continuatio's* separate title page, which shows Pegasus aspiring to fly free of the world and up to the stars. It is clearly an emblematic indication, masquerading as a printer's device, of the thrust of the book.[5] The "Island of the Crosses," as the Dutchmen call it, is more than merely exotic. It is not literally "out of this world," though it seems to be so for Simplicissimus. He describes himself, in his own narrative, as living "so zu sagen / nit mehr in der Welt" (so to speak, no longer in the world: 568). In conversation with Cornelissen, he says that his only companion on the island is God: he refuses to return to his former state among men in the world ("bey den Menschen in der Welt": 585).

For the seamen, it is a place of concrete, if curious, interest, and some of this genuine interest is communicated to us. The strange lights with the aid of which they find their way out of the hermit's cave are designated by Cornelissen as "wunderbarlich" (strange), a word cognate, at least, with Simplicissimus's own apellation, "abentheurlich," as we can see from his description of the behaviour of the men suffering from what we might call "plum-madness" as a "wunderbarliches abentheurlichs Wesen" (strange, odd behaviour: 581). Cornelissen is not content simply to identify these light sources as beetles, but gives a description that enhances the sense of oddness and concretises them to a considerable extent. They are in fact "black beetles, the size of a German stag-beetle, with white spots as big as a pfennig at the bottom of the neck which glowed in the dark much more brightly than a candle" (580). Yet the sense of reality is under a certain strain. Cornelissen, himself a realist but one whose mind is not closed to the spiritual, says that the episode had the feel, "more of a dream than a true story"(580). There is a partial allegorisation here: the beetles are actual beetles, based, in all probability, on detail from Rochefort's account of the Antilles, but they are associated with the "dark light" of Divine Enlightenment referred to in the inscription discussed below.[6]

The strangeness here still contains elements of the "seltzam," but there is also a degree of estrangement. The "madness" that overtakes some of the seamen when they eat plums and begin to hallucinate causes odd and sometimes comic behaviour ("sonderbare Anfechtungen... Grillen": 575), which is described with some relish. There is a tinge of individual and idiosyncratic oddness, for example, in the description of the man who thinks he is a sow and crawls about grunting and shouting: "Malt! Malt!" (582). But the fact that this sickness can be cured by eating the kernels of the selfsame fruit that caused it gives us pause. We begin to sense an abstract meaning behind the ostensibly concrete image. To envisage the men eating real, hard plum-stones is not impossible, perhaps, but creates a sense of inappropriateness, a kind of disjunction. We find ourselves nudged towards an allegorisation of the episode: could it be a fable, perhaps, about the difference between physical appearance and spiritual reality?[7]

The point — the alienation from physical reality — is emphasized by the inscription that Simplicissimus has attached to the trees in question: "Ich mach es wie Circe die zaubrische Hur" (I act like that whorish enchantress, Circe: 577). Circe was for Grimmelshausen, who no doubt derived his information from Garzoni, a figure representative of deception and the temptations of the world and the flesh: sex, of course, but also the excessive indulgence in food and drink that can turn men into swine and is so graphically portrayed in *Der abentheurliche Simplicissimus* (I:30). When he refers to Circe in that case, though (*ST* 82) the spiritual stands alongside the physical world as a parallel and alternative perspective. We are made aware of the status of the gluttony as sin, but this does not inhibit our parallel awareness of the busy activity and solid material reality of the scene itself. Here, in the *Continuatio*, the very nature of the ostensibly physical object is being spiritualised.

One cannot but think of the famous analogy of the world as a book in which one can see spiritual meanings in physical things, which is referred to by Simplicissimus (*Continuatio* 568) and cited by so many writers on baroque allegory and emblematics as opening up, "in continuation," as Dietrich Jöns puts it, "of the allegorical tradition of the Christian Middle Ages,"[8] the prospect of a total allegorisation of the physical world by positing a *sensus allegoricus* under every *sensus literalis*. Simplicissimus himself, in his communion with God, is said by the chaplain of the Dutch ship to have reached the highest level of spiritual insight of which man is capable in one of his inscriptions on the island's trees, which has more than a modicum of mysticism in it: "Ach allerhöchstes Gut! du wohnest so im Finstern Liecht! Daß man vor Klarheit groß / den grossen Glantz kan sehen nicht." (O highest Good! Thou dwellest so in the dark light that because the clarity is so great, thy great brilliance cannot be seen: 573).

The eventual source of the thought is 1 Tim. 6: 16. The common view is that Grimmelshausen received it from Vittoria Colonna, via Garzoni, who used it to support the argument that the poet is a "complete theologian."[9] Gersch wishes to push further his parallel with medieval "Lichtmetaphysik."[10] When we return to Grimmelshausen, though, and to his actual words, this could be seen as an example of learned and ingenious scholarship taken too far. Although it seems clear that Grimmelshausen wishes to define Simplicissimus's life on the island as a spiritual peak, and although it can certainly be argued that a generally religious orientation is characteristic of the book as a whole, that is not the whole story, and this is not the whole Simplicissimus. That a man in this state of mind should look back on his previous life in repentance for his misdeeds, and wonder at the fact that God has spared him to repent and save his soul, is not too surprising.[11] But this does not necessarily mean that we are being asked, as Gersch maintains that we are, to read "the whole Simplician life story" in a spiritualistic sense.[12] And even if we were, the tone and style of *Der abentheurliche Simplicissimus* would prevent us from doing so. It is possible that, as he wrote these sections of the *Continuatio*, Grimmelshausen indeed devoutly wished to be read in a medieval spirit. It is possible also that when he has Simplicissimus beg the reader to disregard those parts of what he has written that should not emanate from the mouth or the pen of a repentant sinner, and to bear in mind that "the narration of frivolous matters and tales demands words suitable to the purpose" ("da die Erzehlung leichter Händel und Geschichten auch bequeme Wort erfordern solche an Tag zugeben": 569)[13] he is trying to protect himself against accusations that in the *Simplicissimus* at any rate, he has failed to observe the requirement for didacticism that was statutory in baroque literary theory. But this is no more a definitive recantation than is the use of the same argument in part 1 of *Das wunderbarliche Vogelnest* (37) to assuage the imaginary anger of the "reader who loves honour and decency" at the story he has just told of the peasant-woman who "moistens her cheese with warm water." Narrator and reader are well aware that it was not for that reader that the story was told; or alternatively, that he has been able to suspend his morality in order to enjoy the broad humour.

Even within this final part of the *Continuatio*, there are whole sections for which the application of Gersch's "allegorische Texttheorie" would be inappropriate. In the case of the palm wine, for example, our labour would produce at best a mouse of a commonplace. There is nothing magical or diabolical about this beverage. Many of the references to it are purely factual, and in describing the first occasion on which the carpenter becomes intoxicated on it, our pious narrator even falls back into the brisk and colloquial style of book I, chapter 30 of *Simplicissimus:* "Hernach soffe er sich so voll darin / daß er dorckelte" (*Continuatio* 564 : afterwards, he knocked back so much of the stuff that he could hardly stand). The wine in fact kills the carpenter eventually, but it is not a Circe-esque enchantment, but human immoderation that is the cause. Simplicissimus sums it up in a *Grabschrifft* (epitaph), an epigrammatic form in which many a baroque poet exercised his sharp wit. The carpenter has escaped the fury of the ocean and, through God's grace, the temptations of the devil ... but the palm wine has got him in the end (565). It is all thoroughly mundane. Nor does Simplicissimus sign the pledge: we still find that he has kept a store of it, which is looted by the Dutch seamen (583). The meaning, or rather the simple moral of the story, is that one should indulge in intoxicating drink only in moderation. One does not construct allegories to make points of this kind.

At earlier stages of the *Continuatio*, there are clearly allegorical (or at least, non-realistic) passages that nevertheless show much of the Simplician spirit as we have earlier defined it. The Schermesser episode is one such. Another is the encounter with Baldanders. That this figure is an allegory of change and inconstancy is made indisputably clear by Grimmelshausen himself. (It also serves, in a subordinate capacity, to represent the role of imagination in poetry — and perhaps a debt to Hans Sachs, the "Lehrer der

Dichtung" [teacher of poetry] from whom the figure is derived[14] — through the "art" that Baldanders teaches to Simplicissimus, and which the latter uses to "talk" to the Schermesser.) But in some ways at least, this figure corresponds to the monster in the *Simplicissimus* frontispiece, in that it combines the emblematically significant with factors suggestive of the concrete physicality and odd variegation of earthly actuality. Baldanders represents an absolute and eternal principle, and indeed, his origin lies beyond this world "gleich wie mein Ursprung auß dem Paradeiß ist / und mein Thun und Wesen bestehet so lang die Welt bleibt" (as my origin is from Paradise and my activity and business will not cease as long as the world endures: 506). But as, indeed, the end of that phrase indicates, and as we saw in discussing the theme of change in the previous chapter,[15] his nature is also that of the world itself. The changes described give a strong impression of earthly life and movement:

> Alß er diß geschriben / wurde er zu einem grossen Aichbaum / bald darauff zu einer Sau / geschwind zu einer Bratwurst / und unversehens zu einen grossen Baurentreck (mit Gunst) er machte sich zu einem schönen Kleewasen / und ehe ich mich versahe / zu einem Kuhefladen; item zu einer schönen Blum oder Zweig / zu einem Maulbeerbaum / und darauff in einen schönen seidenen Teppich etc. biß er sich endlich wider in menschliche Gestalten verändert...(507)

> [When he had written these words, he turned into a big oak-tree and soon after that into a sow; changed rapidly into a fried sausage and suddenly into a great big rustic turd (begging your pardon); made himself into a pretty meadow full of clover and then, quicker than the eye could see, into a cowpat, and furthermore into a pretty flower or twig, a mulberry tree and following that, a beautiful silken rug until finally, he resumed human shape...].

There is change and inconstancy here, certainly, but there is also an epitome of life which is more than just an allegory of the life process, seen from a transcendental perspective. There is a discernible sequence — from acorn to silkworm, etc. — but also a sense of stylistic variegation such as we can see also in the vision of hell, to be treated later. And Grimmelshausen communicates not just the changing nature of life in this world, but also its vigour and solid reality. The rapidity of change is frequently used by baroque authors to emphasize the vanity of worldly things: "Was dieser heute bawt" writes Gryphius for example, "reißt jener morgen ein"[16] (What this man builds today, that man pulls down tomorrow). In theory, Grimmelshausen could simply be making a similar point (and no doubt, there is something of the feeling of *vanitas* here as well). But he has also deliberately infringed the dignity and alloyed the abstraction of the allegorical mode: the sausage, for example, and the peasant who eats it and through whose digestive tract it wends its way, are no mere metaphors.

Baldanders, then, is an allegory, but a Simplician one and that means also that the episode has an element of oddness about it. The Simplician *Seltzamkeit* has not disappeared, though the general shift of emphasis towards the transcendental has dulled its impact somewhat. Simplicissimus the wanderer is still a figure who stands out in the crowd for his appearance and manner, and excites curiosity. His curious listeners in chapter 14 are attracted by his "Seltzamkeit" (527); the young gentleman's wife, in chapter 15, comes down to look at him "vielleicht meine Seltzamkeit zu sehen" (perhaps to have a look at this odd fellow: 533), and the landowner in the same chapter is struck by his odd appearance, his "seltzamer Auffzug" (534), as well as by the patience with which he endures bad weather. He certainly no longer has much, if anything, of the *picaro* about him, but he remains the curious outsider. He has retained his unusual "Künste" (the "natural magic" arts that are demonstrated in the ghost chapter that we shall discuss later, and appear also in *Springinsfeld*) and is in general a kind of catalyst for the strange and exotic, which Grimmelshausen includes, surely, not only to satirise the often credulous curiosity of the mass of men, but also to colour and enliven the book. The parade of peculiarities in chapter 14 is presented as a set of fantastic traveller's tales whose "oddness" is stressed in the chapter heading. Simplicissimus the narrator dissociates himself from them to some extent, but the attraction of the curious, something of the Münchhausen effect, still adheres to them and therefore also to him. His own direct response to *Seltzamkeit* comes to the fore in Cairo. He is struck by the exotic variety of "all kinds of nations," and by the fact that there are "as many strange plants as there are people" ("eben so villerley seltzame Gewächs als Leute"); what seems oddest of all ("am allerseltzsambsten") is the custom of hatching out, in special ovens, "many hundreds of young chickens, from which even the hens had been kept away as soon as they laid them," a job supervised by the old women (546).

If there is a meaning here, it is so well-hidden as to be hermetic. What is communicated is primarily the fascination of "being," of curious fact. The world is still (indeed more so than before) a place that provokes moral and religious reflection, but it is also still a place full of odd surprises. Grimmelshausen has not lost his earthly roots because he is, in this work, adopting a more definitively, even aggressively moral stance. We saw that oddness, with more than a tinge of the comic, subsists even in the island "paradise"; the same is true of his vision of the infernal regions. Lucifer is more peculiar, more comic even, than terrifying. He is supposed to be the prince of the infernal court, but at the news of peace on earth, his behaviour is anything but Miltonic. He flies into a temper ("grießgrammet") and the terrible sound that reverberates through all hell loses its terror when we learn that it is the grinding of his teeth. His rage makes him bang his head against the rock wall in a way unbecoming, as Belial remarks, signalling the comic mix of styles, of his "unvergleichliche Hoheit" (incomparable eminence: 476) as a mighty ruler. In their "friendly conversation" (478), the two create such a din that "the whole hellish army" comes running to find out what all the noise is about. It is a less than impressive sight: an unprepossessing, but also a comically variegated ("unterschiedlich") and odd ("seltzam") crew with a strong sense of earthiness about them. Some are "as fat and corpulent as a Bacchus" and others "as yellow-skinned and thin as a dessicated old farm horse"(478).

Eventually, Avarice makes his entry, "a very pale fellow riding on a scabby old wolf": an allegory, obviously, but one that also, as we can see, stimulates the comic narrative artist as well as the moralist in Grimmelshausen. Rider and steed are almost a Don Quixote and Rocinante: "Roß und Mann sahe so verhungert / mager / matt und hinfällig auß / als wann beydes schon ein lange Zeit in einem Grab oder auff der Schintgruben gelegen wäre!"(Both horse and rider looked as starved, thin, weak and decrepit as if they had both of them spent a long time lying in a grave or a flaying-pit at the skinner's yard: 479). And while the debate that follows between the two vices, Avarice and Extravagance, is clearly moral satire in a traditional allegorical form, it strays stylistically, at times coming close to the realm of realist narrative dialogue, as when Extravagance calls her grandfather an old fool ("alter Narr": 481) or a "Pfetzpfenning" (pinchpenny: 482). The story of Julus and Avarus that follows is, of course, primarily a morality, but by the same token, not an allegory. Julus and Avarus are *beset* by allegorical figures, but they are not themselves "allegorische Gestalten," as G. Mayer maintains;[17] rather, they are real people in a real world. If they were not, the moral-satirical point would be lost. And yet the (in itself necessary) reality is conveyed more graphically than is necessary for that purpose.

The moralist, then, has not entirely suppressed the storyteller, but he has imposed limits on his freedom. In chapter 15, for example, we are told the story of the man who expects to be given an important appointment but on his return home, says to his wife, when she asks "what they had made him," that "I've been made a bloody skivvy." His children proudly tell their friends: "Our Dad's been made a bloody skivvy," and Simplicissimus, who is standing by, "has to laugh" (534). Even Simplicissimus the narrator on the Isle of Crosses clearly feels the same way and encourages the reader to laugh also. A little cameo of marital infidelity emerges in the middle of an allegory when the Schermesser relates the sights it saw during its incarnation as the shift belonging to the chambermaid of a nobleman's wife (519). Such moments of pure narrative pleasure are outnumbered, however, by stories which, while they retain narrative interest, fulfil a more "serious" purpose, such as the ghost story told in chapters 15 and 16. It takes place within the framework of the theme of sin and its expiation.

At the outset, this is not immediately or unequivocally apparent. The scene is set, initially, in graphic and "realistic" narrative style. On his Swiss wanderings, Simplicissimus attracts the attention of a nobleman as he is walking towards the latter's country house with the mud (and we can really feel this mud!) up to his ankles and the rain descending "as if somebody were pouring it down in bucketfuls" ("als wann mans mit Kübeln herunter gegossen hätte": 534). The lord of the manor takes him in and invites him to stay the night. Simplicissimus finds out that he is not being entertained on account of his "devout" appearance and manner when his host, in saying Good Night, addresses him by his correct name and refers to a previous meeting at the spa in Griesbach, after the death of the younger Herzbruder (*ST:* V), at which he had asserted to some Swiss visitors that only a lily-livered fool could believe in ghosts. One of the Swiss, who claimed that he really did have a haunted room in his castle, had tried to take revenge by invading Simplicissimus's bedroom and playing ghost, but had been driven off with a drubbing (recounted here for the first time: 536). Unable to escape from the room, Simplicissimus goes to bed "in fear and anxiety," expecting an unpleasant visitation, either of the spectral or the human variety.

In the atmosphere of *Der abentheurliche Simplicissimus*, we would have been inclined, on balance, to expect the latter, with the comic discomfiture either of the victim, or of the would-be perpetrator. But even though the reference to earlier times has laid the foundation for a possible *Schwank*, the general tone of the *Continuatio* makes us feel that we are quite possibly going to meet some genuine spirits. And so it proves. This is an example, on the smaller scale, of the "reprise and variation" pattern to which we referred earlier. At midnight, the door (which has been bolted on the inside) opens, and four figures walk in, from whom an unnatural light seems to emanate. The atmosphere created by their manner and appearance is one of solemnity and there is no doubt of the real fear felt by Simplicissimus:

> ... ich steckte die Schnauppe unter die Decke und behielte nichts haussen als die Augen / wie ein erschrockenes und forchtsambs Meußlein das da in seiner Höle sitzet und auff passet / zu sehen ob es plasy sey oder nicht / hervor zu kommen; sie hingegen tratten vor mein Bette und beschaueten mich wol und ich sie hingegen auch / als solches ein gar kleine weil gewäret hatte / tratten sie mit einander in ein Eck deß Zimmers / huben eine steinene Platten auff / damit der Ort besetzt war / und langten dort alle Zugehör herauß / die ein Barbierer zu brauchen Pflegt / wann er jemand den Bart butzet; mit solchen Instrumenten kamen sie wider zu mir / setzten ein Stul in die Mitte deß Zimmers / und gaben mit wincken und deuten zu verstehen / daß ich mich auß dem Bethe begeben; auff dem Stul sitzen: und mich von ihnen parbieren lassen solte; weil ich aber still ligen blieb / griffe der Vornehmste selbst an das Deckbeth / solches auffzuheben und mich mit Gewalt auff den Stul zu setzen; da kan jeder wol dencken wie mir die Katz den Rücken hinauff geloffen.... (537)

> [I stuck my snout under the blanket, leaving nothing outside but my eyes, just as a frightened, timorous little mouse sits there in its hole, looking out to see whether it is alright to come out or not. They, on the other hand, came and stood at the foot of my bed; they stared at me, and I stared back and when this had gone on for just a little while, they walked over together

to a corner of the room, lifted out the stone slab that covered the spot and drew out from it all the tools a barber customarily uses to trim someone's beard. They came back to me with these instruments, placed a chair in the middle of the room and indicated to me by signing and pointing that I was to get out of the bed, sit on the chair and allow them to ply the barber's trade on me. But because I continued to lie there without moving, the principal figure among them himself grasped the bed-cover, intending to lift it up and move me on to the chair by force. As you can well imagine, I felt fingers running up my spine. . . .)

There is a momentary switch into Grimmelshausen's more entertaining narrative style at the beginning of this passage. Indeed, the passage as a whole is an effective piece of narrative, but the mood changes in its latter stages from the almost comic fright of Simplicissimus at the beginning to a fear of the uncanny which affects the reader as well. The barbering motif, which may have seemed rather curious at first glance, has a quasi-allegorical force: the visitants are an ancestor of the present lord of the manor and those who helped him steal from their rightful owners a couple of villages, whose inhabitants were then mercilessly "cropped and shorn." The pile of gold accumulated through this unjust action in the past is the source of present torment, from which Simplicissimus can release the unquiet spirits by helping to redistribute these ill-gotten gains. When he has promised to do so, they wish to seal the compact with a clasp of hands.

Next day, he fulfils his pledge to the restless spirits and Grimmelshausen's taste for the curious asserts itself yet again. The money has become sand, and has to be transmuted back into metal by an art which Simplicissimus has learned from his reading of "that odd fellow, Theophrastus Paracelsus" (540). But this is contained within a moral framework; the tone is serious and the outcome is the restoration of the moral order. The haunting ceases and the house is brought back to its proper order ("in richtigen Stand gesetzt": 541).

The Simplician style has here adapted itself well to a more serious moral context. The story is still an effective ghost story and has many of the virtues of good narrative: movement, precise and graphic detail (for example the burning of the corner of the coverlet) and a sense of atmosphere (as in the slow, measured rhythm of the process in which the spirits silently restore the room to its former condition, and take their leave). But there is a muted quality to the narrative in this case.

The Moral Tone

It is not primarily the greater prominence of the religious points of reference that makes the difference in tone between the present work and *Der abentheurliche Simplicissimus*. Certainly, the narrator here is more inclined to heartfelt pious outpourings than was even the hermit we met at the beginning of the other novel. We cannot, somehow, imagine that the original Einsiedel would have decorated all the trees in *his* forest with "schöne Sprüche." This, as we shall be discussing later, does not necessarily mean that the hermit on the island is closer to God and more truly at peace than is the one in the forest, who, after all, does not need to insulate himself totally from human contact.[18]

It is, we would suggest, the practical application of piety to human behaviour that interests Grimmelshausen most. We have seen some of the effects of this preoccupation in the ghost story treated in the previous section, and it is surely the driving force behind the Julus-Avarus story (to which, interestingly enough, Gersch devotes very little attention). It is true that this story is, formally speaking, framed in an allegorical contest between two vices, but this in turn is progressively absorbed into a merely human psychological process in which a man can proceed, through the "Staffeln deß Verderbens" (stages of corruption: 490), from virtue to vice. The temptations of Avarice and Extravagance become "inner voices," attempting to drown out the "innerliches zusprechen" (inward admonition: 495) of reason and conscience. The author's moral preoccupations certainly make the narrative less redolent of the vitality of actual life than is the case elsewhere in the Simplician corpus, but the world of actuality — and the importance within it of money and goods[19] — is still real enough, even in this "Vision oder Traum" (489), to be of interest for its own sake, especially when the two youths reach Paris (chapter 6).

We noticed how the spirit of freedom was more or less unquenchable in *Der abentheurliche Simplicissimus*. That spirit has not been completely quenched, even here, but there has been a shift across the scale: a reactive movement from humour towards seriousness, from freedom towards discipline. We can see this in the "poetological" reflections in chapter 1, and we see it more clearly still when, in introducing his account of the doings of Julus and Avarus on the continent, our narrator remarks:

> ... wie das junge Viehe / wann es wol außgewintert ist / und im Früling auß dem vertrüßlichen Stall auff die lustige Waydt gelassen wird / anfahet zu gumpen / und solte es auch zu seinem Verderben in einen Spalt: oder Zaunstecken springen / also machts auch die unbesonnene Jugend / wann sie sich nicht mehr unter der Ruthen vätterlicher Zucht: sonder auß der Eltern Augen in der lang erwünschten Freyheit befindet; Als deren gemeiniglich Erfahrenheit und Vorsichtigkeit manglet. (490)

> [For just as the young animals on the farm, having come safely through the winter and being now let out of the wearisome stall into the pleasant pasture, begin to hop and skip about, even if it be to their own harm, by jumping into a crack in the ground or against a stake in the fence, so does heedless youth behave when it no longer has to live under the rod of fatherly discipline but finds itself beyond the reach of the parental eye, in the freedom after which it yearned for so long, since it is commonly lacking in experience and prudence.]

Grimmelshausen shows an awareness of the freshness and attraction of freedom here, just as he was aware of its dangers in the earlier novel. But there has been a clear shift of emphasis in the *Continuatio,* and throughout the latter work, we are continually catching a note of sternness, even asperity that we did not hear so clearly before. It is undoubtedly the Simplicissimus of the island, who in his "heartfelt repentance" (569) castigates the sins of his youth with what one is tempted to call a one-sided and un-Simplician severity, who has written the *Continuatio,* though fortunately not always in such a near-Calvinistic mood. It is this perspective on human frailty that makes him attribute the failure of his first attempt at the eremitical life to "freedom," that is, to the lack of the discipline of a cleric who could have supervised him and kept him up to the moral mark (473–4). Such a figure (the "Pater" of book II of *Das wunderbarliche Vogelnest*) does appear at the end of the whole Simplician corpus, when it seems that Grimmelshausen wishes to achieve the definitive and final one of his many "ends." But that end is not yet, and it was certainly not a man in this frame of mind who wrote *Der abentheurliche Simplicissimus.*

And while it is possible to see the *Continuatio* as to some extent a corrective, an attempt to rectify the balance vis-à-vis the earlier novel, it is questionable whether, even at the time, Grimmelshausen saw this as the last word on the subject. That he felt he had formerly dispensed the spice of life very freely, perhaps a little too freely, is fairly clear, and the moral mood rarely relaxes its grip sufficiently to allow him to indulge his sense of fun here with full freedom. When Simplicissimus, in chapter 13, gives in to the temptation to enjoy a joke at his curious host's expense, by leaving behind a mysterious message in Baldanders's code to the effect that the best way to avoid being shot is to stand in a position that is not being shot at, his sense of responsibility asserts itself and he adds a corrective codicil in the tone of Herzbruder: God alone protects those whom He decides to protect (526). But just as Grimmelshausen does not condemn the palm wine because of the evil effects of overindulgence (after all, he had been an innkeeper!), so his conclusion to the story of Julus and Avarus is less ascetic than we might perhaps have expected: " . . .daß die Freygiebigkeit leichtlich zu einer verschwendung: und die gesparsamkeit leichtlich zum geitz werden könne / wann die weißheit nit vorhanden / welche freygiebigkeit und gesparsamkeit durch mässigkeit regiere und im Zaum halte" (that generosity can easily become extravagance, and thrift avarice, if that wisdom is not present that can govern generosity and thrift through moderation: 505). He advocates control and discipline, certainly, but not a total renunciation of the world.

Such a renunciation is, however, rather assertively proclaimed by the Simplicissimus whom we see towards the end of the book, indeed, at the conclusion of the book that he himself has written:

> . . . ein ehrlich gesinnter Christlicher Leser / wird sich vilmehr verwundern und die Göttliche Barmhertzigkeit preysen / wann er findet / daß ein so

schlimer Gesell wie ich gewesen / dannoch die Gnad von GOtt gehabt / der Welt zu resignirn, und in einem solchen Standt zuleben / darinnen er zur ewigen Glory zukommen / und die seelige Ewigkeit nechst dem heiligen Leyden deß Erlösers zu erlangen verhofft / durch ein seeligs ENDE. (569–70)

[... the reader who is of an honest Christian mind will rather (i.e. rather than be corrupted by the naughty things that the book contains) be amazed and praise the Divine Mercy when he finds that such a bad lot as I have been has yet been given the grace from God to forswear the World and live his life in a condition in which he has hopes of coming to the eternal glory and attaining eternal bliss by dint (after the sacred Passion of Our Saviour) of achieving a blessed END.]

This tone, and the reference to salvation, is echoed at the end of the cycle. But we have not at this point reached the very end; not even the end of the *Continuatio*, which is after all only partly Simplicissimus's book. This "end" is followed by the narrative of Captain Cornelissen, in which we learn of Simplicissimus's reaction when the prospect of returning to Europe arises. In the fear and uncertainty caused by the spread of the "plum-madness," the Captain's party resolves to seek out Simplicissimus. We learn for the first time of a cave in the cliffs that is an impregnable fortress: Simplicissimus himself calls it his "Sicherheit" (secure place: 576). He emerges from it only because without his help, both ship and crew will perish. When all are sane and safe once more, Cornelissen invites him to come back to Europe with them, whereupon it becomes clear that for him, security rests in isolation, freedom (from sin) in the imprisonment of being marooned on the island. Even here, he has had to guard against the threat of his own unreliable ("variabel": 567) thoughts by imposing a spiritual discipline on himself through meditation (for lack of devotional literature) on the "book of the world." As he taps the palm tree for its wine, for example, he meditates on the blood shed by the crucified Christ (568). Now, they want him to go back to Europe: his reply is almost aggressive. He knows, of course, that the Thirty Years' War is over, but the world of men is still a battlefield. "Hier ist Fried" he says, "dort ist Krieg" (here, there is peace, there, there is war):

... hier ist eine stille Einsame ohne Zorn / Hader und Zanck; eine Sicherheit vor eiteln Begierden / ein Vestung wider alles unordentliche verlangen; ein Schutz wider die vielfältige Strick der Welt und ein stille Ruhe / darinnen man dem Allerhöchsten allein dienen: seine Wunder betrachten / und ihm loben und preysen kan.(584)

[Here, there is a quiet solitude with no wrath, no arguing, no quarrelling; a secure refuge against all vain lusts, a fortress against all disorderly desires, a protection against the many and various snares of the world and a quiet place where I can find rest, serve the All-highest God alone, consider His wonders and praise and magnify Him.]

In interpreting Simplicissimus's rejection of the world here, we must distinguish between the theological and the merely human levels of meaning. The spiritual ideal of a complete devotion to God is not in itself devalued by the fact that Simplicissimus is patently not confident that he can maintain it outside the "refuge" and "fortress" of his present isolation. Aylett is justified in speaking of a "defensive" attitude here, but not of the "sterility, futility and fragility" of the island "Utopia."[20] Spiritual peaks cannot, in the long run, be lived on by the great mass of men, but they serve a real moral purpose in that they can be looked up to ("ad astra volandum"?). We are given a passionate expression of theological *contemptus mundi* here, just as we were at the end of the original novel. The eschatological overtones are, if anything, more pronounced in the *Continuatio*. But we have not reached the "Last Things" as far as Simplicissimus is concerned. He has achieved a greater spiritual maturity. But with all respect to Melitta Gerhard, this is not a "letzte Reife" (final maturity).[21] "Man lebt doch in der Welt," as Grimmelshausen puts it in the *Gauckel-Tasche*.[22] It is on earth, among men, that fulfilment is to be found, in a world that is dangerous, it is true, but which is also the world where true freedom is achieved. If it is true that we can visualise a polarity between the winged horse of the *Continuatio* and the fantastic, but earthbound monster of *Der abentheurliche Simplicissimus*, it is in the long run not the case that, as Ashcroft puts it, "Pegasus overcomes the chimaera."[23]

Continuation or Conclusion?

Grimmelshausen describes this work on its title page as "the continuation or conclusion" of *Der abentheurliche Simplicissimus*. Which is it? Or can it possibly be both? Like a good baroque author, he enjoys a game and sometimes seems to invite the reader to play the game with him. Reader awareness and involvement are a part of his Simplician manner. The issue, however, is a serious one: the question of the relation between the two books. Some, such as Scholte and Julius Petersen, who see the first book as a symmetrically designed whole in five parts, insist on separation.[24] Others argue for a greater or lesser degree of integration, as for example Gersch, or Walter Ernst Schäfer, who sees the *Continuatio* as truly a "sixth book" of *Simplicissimus* by virtue of the fact that it takes up and answers the question of sloth which was raised, but not resolved, in the original novel.[25] This can be seen as necessary if, like Peter Trieffenbach, one sees "the meaning of the whole story" as lying in the restoration of a "fallen" Simplicissimus to true humanity, the Biblical figure for which process of salvation is Nebuchadnezzar.[26]

This is in many ways an attractive idea, for the *Continuatio* does certainly complement its predecessor by completing the pattern of war and peace. And while virtue can often shine all the more brightly in times of tribulation, as Belial points out to Lucifer, "ein geruhiger Fried / welcher den Wollust auff dem Rücken mit sich bringt" (a restful peace which brings voluptuousness on its back: 477) can be more destructive, morally, than war. Simplicissimus, in rejecting the opportunity to return to Europe, cites above all the "Laster des Wollusts" and "laue Andacht" (lukewarm observance) which came with the peace as his reasons for staying where he is (584). But unless one accepts as a final solution the exceptional condition in which Simplicissimus finds himself and in which he has not so much defeated vice as walled himself up in a fortress to keep it out, the addition of peace to the equation has, rather than bringing the process to an end, opened up a new field which it will be for future works to investigate. And it is indeed investigated: in the two parts of *Das wunderbarliche Vogelnest* and to some extent, in *Springinsfeld*, and in non-narrative form in the *Rathstübel Plutonis*. The transition between the first two Simplician books may even represent the point at which Grimmelshausen, who quite possibly did originally conceive *Simplicissimus* as a single, self-contained work, began to feel, if not perhaps yet to think, in terms of wider horizons.

A full consideration of the question of the Simplician cycle must be reserved for our final chapter. What brings the subject to mind here in a preliminary way is the fact that we are faced with the issue of conclusiveness, or the lack of it, in Grimmelshausen the Simplician writer.[27] We seem to be witnessing the emergence of a conscious or instinctive awareness of a principle — which seems to be linked with the tendency to seek the "plurality of perspective" that we have already glimpsed in our discussion of the *Simplicissimus*[28] — of almost infinite extendability. In every conclusion there are loose ends that afford potential new beginnings. Both *Courasche* and *Springinsfeld* develop figures who pass only fleetingly before our eyes in the *Simplicissimus*, and there is a sense, at least, in which the "sequel" novels could be described as extensions of the original one. When he "Simplicianised" his *Keuscher Joseph* (first version 1665), Grimmelshausen did so by an additive process: he tacked on the life story of Musai, which has picaresque traits. There are signs of the same procedure in the *Ratio Status*, first published in 1670, but generally agreed to be an early work.[29]

That the first Simplician novel is open-ended, and that the *Continuatio* picks up the thread at the point where book V of *Simplicissimus* left it, may be agreed without great difficulty. As we saw earlier, the latter draws to a close without having brought the hero convincingly to a point of rest. This leaves the possibility that the present book might have been designed to provide a satisfyingly conclusive conclusion. Instead, Grimmelshausen (once again the ironist!) plays a game with us, unravelling the idea of conclusiveness and investing the word "end" itself with a deliberate ambiguity. The work "ends" three times, and with an ever-decreasing sense of finality. Firstly, Simplicissimus finishes his own narrative (570) and though this is done with the same trick as is used to reach the "Ende" of *Der abentheurliche Simplicissimus*, namely the anticipation of the end of the speaker's life, which opens a vista into the future, this *is* a true conclusion in one sense. It is the end, not of Simplicissimus's life, but of his "life history" as narrated by himself. It is at this point, and in this sense, that the word "Schluß," as used on the title page, and the word "beschließen," and the reference to a "sixth book" in the heading of the relevant chapter (23), are valid. Simplicissimus is never again to function as his own biographer; the figure survives, but as a character in the narratives of others. As a reformed, and even more importantly, a settled person, he is no longer the best vehicle for the Simplician manner, which sets out to hold up the mirror to the whole variety of life.

And so the concept of authorship, within the fictional Simplician world created by Grimmelshausen the writer, becomes more complex and multifaceted. Simplicissimus lives on as a figure, but *qua* author, he is dead; long live the "Simplician author," to use the designation employed in the preface to part 2 of *Das wunderbarliche Vogelnest*. The Dutch captain takes the former's story further in what is an annexe to *his* book, but an integral part of Grimmelshausen's. The "Ende" of Cornelissen's "Relation" is simply that, not the end of the book as a whole. Grimmelshausen then takes up the reins in his own right and adds his own *Beschluß*, introducing his favourite "alter ego," Samuel Greifnson — the ex-musketeer with a penchant for disguising himself under anagrams — as the true "author," then killing Greifnson off and announcing himself as the editor of his posthumous papers. He then brings in the word "conclusion" yet again, saying that "I could not withhold this conclusion, since he had already published the first five parts during his lifetime."

There are, then, two "continuations," Greifnson's and the editor Grimmelshausen's. We know already, from the title page, that "Greifnson" calls his *Continuatio* a "Schluß" (conclusion).[30] Should we take this to mean that Grimmelshausen himself regards it as the genuine conclusion of a rounded and self-contained work, which answers the questions it has asked? Gersch certainly seems to think so.[31] This would endow the decision to remain on the island with a greater measure of finality than we have been prepared to allow it. We cannot, of course, adduce our knowledge of Simplicissimus's later reappearance in European society as conclusive evidence in this case, hard as it is to wipe that knowledge out of our minds. But while we may not be able to bring forward definitive proof, the balance of probabilities seems to be against Gersch's view. He wishes to see the *Continuatio* as the consciously defined final stage of an integral six-book *Simplicissimus*, because he considers this sixth book to be a *Nachwort* (postscript) in epic form, whose function is to dissuade the reader from merely enjoying the whole work, and disregarding its hidden meaning or meanings.[32] It seems an odd strategy: why not a preface to the new, complete edition (assuming, that is, that the sixth book is still necessary)? And the scornful reaction of Christian Weise, for one, in the preface to *Die drey ärgsten Erznarren*, would seem to indicate that if that was the intention, the strategy did not work. A more feasible hypothesis might be that Grimmelshausen had come to realise that *Der aben-*

theurliche Simplicissimus could be, perhaps was being read as a work of predominantly worldly and entertaining orientation. He could not rewrite it now, and probably did not want to, but he could well have felt the urge to redress the balance somewhat.

It is perfectly possible that, in his role as "literary executor," he is referring simply to the work as the deceased "author" left it, with Simplicissimus's "autobiography" having been brought to an end. Greifnson himself, whom we must surely assume as the originator of the chapter headings, has designated Cornelissen's report as an appendage and chapter 23 as a conclusion. But for Grimmelshausen, Greifnson's "conclusions" are not final, but provisional, for only a little earlier, he has used the formula that — as Gersch himself has pointed out in another context — is the standard format for a "Vorausdeutung," the indication of a continuation still to come. Greifnson, he says, has left behind "noch mehr seine *Satyrische* Gedichte welche / wann diß Werck beliebt wird / wol auch durch den Druck an Tag gegeben werden köndten" (still more tales of the satyric kind which, if this work finds favour, may well also be offered in public print). No further details of these works are given, and the name of Greifnson does not appear on any subsequent title pages (unless one counts the second edition of the *Keuscher Joseph*), but likely candidates are surely the *Courasche* and *Springinsfeld*, both of which appeared in 1670, and both of which are expressly linked on their title pages with Simplicissimus, the book or the person, and purport to have been written down by yet another of the anagrammatic Simplician *personae*.[33] The other major publications of that year, *Dietwalt und Amelinde* and *Simplicianischer Zweyköpffiger Ratio Status* both bear Grimmelshausen's own name as author. *Dietwalt und Amelinde*, whose dedication (by Grimmelshausen) bears the date 3 March 1669, contains a mention of "alte Courage," and the "Zuruff" at the end of the same volume looks forward "eagerly" to news of both Courage and Springinsfeld.

As we have already indicated, there are a number of correspondences between the *Continuatio* and *Der abentheurliche Simplicissimus*, which suggest that from time to time at any rate, Grimmelshausen wished to juxtapose the two and direct our attention to the parallels and contrasts. We have pointed already to a broad structural similarity (the movement into and out of the world, the more radical movement being in the second work). To this, we could add the incidence of eschatological reminders, emphasizing the themes of damnation and salvation, temporality and eternity. Just as *Simplicissimus* begins with a reference to the Last Days and returns to the theme of Judgement in its final chapter (albeit indirectly, through the quotation from Guevara: *ST* 463), so in the *Continuatio*, Lucifer refers pointedly to the approaching end of the world (477), and Simplicissimus's account of his life on the island is replete with references to God and His mercy, to the Fall (561), the Elect (557), Judgement (567), eternal Glory, and blessed Eternity (570). Again, the weight of emphasis on eternal things is greater in the second work. Even more striking, perhaps, is the duality of the juxtaposition in chapter 15 of a "Poß" (536) resurrected from the earlier days and recounted here with a fair degree of *brio* and no sense of awe of the supernatural, in which Simplicissimus drives off a "ghost" whose flesh is all too solid, with the real ghost story, with an underlying moral theme, that we have already discussed.

We should reemphasize that we do not in any way accept that this change of tone is meant to reflect back on our interpretation of the *Simplicissimus*, but it does seem to us that (planned or not), it gives the *Continuatio* a particular role and justification within the strategy (if such there be) of a wider Simplician whole. It is hard to see how it could be satisfactorily "integrated" with its predecessor. But as we have seen, juxtaposition, not integration, is Grimmelshausen's preferred structural technique, and structurally, the *Continuatio* can be seen as a typically Simplician sideways movement. It is at this point that it seems most appropriate to return to the prefatory remarks in its opening chapter.

The first fifty-one lines (in Tarot's edition) of chapter 1 of the *Continuatio* are devoted to self-defence and protestation of good intent. Whether he had already been the object of criticism or was simply trying to forestall it is not important: Grimmelshausen claims that he is writing within the framework of the Horatian concept— standard for any literary work of the baroque that had ambitions to be taken seriously— namely, that the writer should both improve and entertain. That he wishes to be taken seriously (and probably fears that he may not be, or perhaps even has evidence that this is already happening) is clear from his statement that he regards himself as being a cut above ("umb etwas zugut") the profession of fool and prankster ("Schalcks-Narr und Possen-Reisser"). By the time that he came to compose (as it is generally assumed he did) the congratulatory "Zuruff" for *Dietwalt und Amelinde*, it is clear that such criticisms had been made, and that they rankled: "Der den *Simplicem* gemachet ist fürwahr ein kluger Kopff Obs im Obenhin-Betrachten gleich nicht merkt manch tummer Tropff (*DA* 100: The man who created *Simplicissimus* was truly a man of no mean intelligence, even if many a stupid idiot fails to see it on a superficial reading). He justifies the fact that he sometimes adopts a manner that could be described as "possierlich" (472, line 17) with the traditional argument of the satirist, which is based on the analogy of the gilded or sugared pill.

He adopts this manner, he says, rather than the "theologische[r] Stylus" because he wishes to reach the wider audience of what might now be called the "ordinary reader" and because wholesome and therapeutic messages need to be made thus superficially palatable, if they are to be generally absorbed. Some readers, he admits, may read him for amusement alone, but the reader that he really desires is the one who is not distracted by the painted shell from the kernel, "what I really wanted to say to him" (473, lines 18–19). On the basis of the use of the shell and kernel metaphor,

Gersch argues that Grimmelshausen is here going beyond a claim to merely satirical status, and must be read in the spirit of the "allegorical text-theory," which constantly looks for the "spiritual sense" under the surface, and which survived, as he is able to show, from the Middle Ages into the seventeenth century.[34] The chain of proof is not conclusive: Gersch himself can say only that "we will be justified in assuming" that this is what he later calls a "Leseanweisung": an instruction on how the book is to be read.[35] It is quite possible that the image has a dual function: as a support for the argument that has gone before (self-defence against a charge of mere frivolity), and as a reference to the fact that the work before us makes extensive use of allegory, though it does not necessarily allegorise everything in sight.

Whatever the rights and wrongs of that argument, the emphasis is clearly on the serious, at the expense of the entertaining elements. As a description of the novel that has gone before, it seems inappropriate, and it is hardly conceivable that an artist of Grimmelshausen's calibre could have been unaware of the kind of book he had written. In any case, the tenses ("ich erzehle," "wird nicht erlangen") suggest that the writer is pointing forward, into the book that is now beginning, rather than back, though no doubt with the consciousness of what he wrote earlier, and of actual or possible reactions to it, in his mind. In *Der abentheurliche Simplicissimus*, Grimmelshausen had introduced "so manchen lächerlichen schwang" (that is, *Schwänke*), as another of Grimmelshausen's several narrative voices, Philarchus, is to say in the *Springinsfeld* (18). At this point, Grimmelshausen is considering the process of writing (and reading) from the point of view of the hermit on the island, whose mind is firmly set on the ultimate, eternal destination of the human soul, and inclined to set little store by its temporal refreshment:

> ... dann viel lachen ist mir selbst ein Eckel / und wer die edle ohnwiederbringliche Zeit vergeblich hinstreichen läst / der verschwendet die jenige Göttliche Gaab ohnnützlich / die uns verliehen wird / unserer Seelen Hail in: und vermittelst derselben zuwürcken. (*Continuatio* 472)

> [... for frequent laughter is repellent to me, and any man who allows the noble, irrecoverable treasure of time to slip by to no good purpose is wasting for no return that gift which was given us by God so that in it and through it, we might work the salvation of our souls.]

It is not, of course, that the *idea* of the precedence of man's eternal over his temporal welfare is absent from *Der abentheurliche Simplicissimus*. But it is usually voiced without the almost ascetically religious tone that we detect in the words just quoted, the clerical tone of the sermon, the catechism, or the Prayer Book. How different is the style in which the Einsiedel of the earlier novel conveys his equally serious religious message in chapter 12 of book I! Admittedly, he is speaking to a young and naïve boy at this point, but the narrator — an adult — does add that a message delivered in this style, if it has "Safft und Nachdruck" (vigour — literally, sap — and emphasis: *ST* 35), can be more effective than "a long sermon, of which you have understood every word and which is soon forgotten once again." It is not insignificant that the long, often vituperative (and genuinely impressive) farewell to the world at the end of book V is explicitly presented as a quotation from a book that Simplicissimus has been studying. The ideas are accepted, but by virtue of its heavy formal rhetoric, it is still a foreign body in the Simplician context, and quite deliberately so. It would be less so in the *Continuatio*, though fortunately for us, while the general tone remains relatively dark, the sternness of attitude that the prospective narrator has adopted in his introduction is relaxed somewhat as the story gets under way.

In the *Continuatio* as a whole, as very probably in the section we have just examined, Grimmelshausen can be seen as carrying out a shift of perspective that is essentially reactive. He does take the serious issues seriously, and he does wish to be taken seriously as a writer. He is not attempting to disown what he must have recognised were his major literary achievements by the use of anagrams:[36] he identifies himself, after all, in the *Continuatio* by signing his own initials with an easily deciphered realignment of the letters of his place of residence ("Rheinnec" and "Cernhein": anagrams of Renchen with an added "i"), and links himself with the Simplician corpus on the title page of *Ratio Status* and in the dedicatory material[37] of *Dietwalt und Amelinde*. In his own immediate area, at least, he must have been known as the Simplician "satyricus." The fact that he did not gain wider recognition in his own lifetime is more likely attributable to the fact that in spite of his protests, he was not judged to have fulfilled the poetic requirements of the age than to his use of a technique — satire — with which it was very familiar.

He had been carried away by his own talent to write a book that was too entertaining for the good of his reputation and in which (as he saw it at the time) the balance between the temporal and eternal, the comic and serious, had been towards the former in each case, even though, as we saw, the two sides of the duality had both been represented. But although he could not go back, he now, in all probability, was at least beginning to see a way forward, and within the larger unity of what was to become a cycle of works, he was able to carry out a shift, not so much of philosophy, as of tone and style: a shift which redressed the balance somewhat without destroying the unity of the larger whole. In the novels that follow and which are all, in their way, "continuations," we shall be able to observe the polarity between awareness of eternity and solemnity on the one hand, and worldliness and an often outrageously derisive comic vision on the other.

Notes

[1] Cf. Weydt, *Nachahmung und Schöpfung im Barock*, 406. For Rochefort, see J. B. Dallett, "Grimmelshausen und die neue Welt," *Argenis* 1 (1977), note 65.

[2] See Gersch's "Forschungsbericht," in his *Geheimpoetik*, 162–84.

[3] This is pointed out by Grimmelshausen himself (506). Cf. also Tarot, "Simplicissimus und Baldanders," 108.

[4] See above, chapter 2.

[5] See J. Ashcroft, "Emblems and Imagery in Grimmelshausen's "Simplicissimus," *MLR* 68 (1973), 853–61.

[6] Cf. Gersch, *Geheimpoetik*, 152 ff. (poetological interpretation); Dallett, "Grimmelshausen," 172 ff., Ashcroft, "Emblems and Imagery, 848 ff. Ashcroft sees the beetles as "applied emblems," which "convince" because they are integrated into the narrative. The meaning of the word "convince" is not immediately clear. How much of their material and curious reality do they retain as applied emblems?

[7] Gersch (*Geheimpoetik*, 145) sees it as a parable on the morally damaging effect of "falsches Lesen," and links the motif with "allegorische Texttheorie" (146). Beer, however, uses the same motif in the preface to the *Winter-Nächte* in a deployment of the orthodox satirist's self-defence against the criticisms of the moralist. The reader who can "distinguish between good and evil" and who peruses the book "mit genauer Obsicht und gutem Fleiß" will be "lachend unterrichtet," will be led to love virtue and abhor vice and will draw from his reading the "Nutzen, der demjenigen daraus entspringen wird, der nicht nach der bloßen Schale, sondern nach dem Kern schnappet."(8–9) There is no hint of allegory here, or in the text. Grimmelshausen could well be arguing in the same way.

[8] Dietrich Jöns, "Emblematisches bei Grimmelshausen," *Euphorion* 62 (1968), 385: "In der Fortführung christlich-mittelalterlicher Allegorese." The metaphor of the book is dealt with on the same page: see also Praz, *Studies in Seventeenth-Century Imagery*, 18; Gersch, *Geheimpoetik*, 118 ff.

[9] Cf. Feldges, *Grimmelshausens "Landstörtzerin Courasche,"* 30.

[10] Gersch, *Geheimpoetik*, 126 ff.

[11] See *Continuatio*, 569.

[12] For instance Gersch, *Geheimpoetik*, 160: "die verborgenen Sinndimensionen des ganzen "Simplicissimus"-Romans."

[13] An argument that smacks of Sorel: cf. *Francion* I: 120: "la naifveté de la comedie veut cela."

[14] Cf. Paul Gutzwiller, *Der Narr bei Grimmelshausen* (Berne 1959), 60.

[15] See above, chapter 3. For Baldanders, see also W. Wiethölter, "Baldanderst Lehr und Kunst. Zur Allegorie des Allegorischen in Grimmelshausens Simplicissimus Teutsch," *Deutsche Vierteljahrsschrift* 62 (1994), 45–65. Wiethölter, who argues (not implausibly) against the "eschatological" interpretation of the work, sees this

figure as a symbol of the fact that there are no fixed meanings in the world. It could, more simply, be just an image of mutability.

[16] Andreas Gryphius, *Gesamtausgabe der deutschsprachigen Werke*, vol. 1, ed. M. Szyrocki, (Tübingen: Niemeyer, 1963), 33.

[17] See G. Mayer, "Die Personalität des Simplicius Simplicissimus," *Zeitschrift für Deutsche Philologie* 88 (1969), 501.

[18] Rolf Tarot maintains that Simplicius, the hermit on the island, "[hat] jenen Stand erreicht, den sein Vater im Spessart erreicht hatte" ("Grimmelshausens *Simplicissimus* und die Form autobiographischen Erzählens," *Études Germaniques* 46, 72–3). In terms of theological "Einfalt" as defined by Tarot (devotion to God), this is certainly defensible, but there is a significant change of tone: the sense of ease and spontaneity that one associates with simplicity in practical life is much more an attribute of the Spessart- than of the island-hermit.

[19] Cf. I. M. Battafarano, "Hexenwahn und Teufelsglaube im Simplicissimus," *Argenis* 1 (1977), 367 ff. Whether an awareness of the coming of the "Geld-Ware-Gesellschaft" means that the ethical problems of the postwar period are now given a "weltimmanente Begründung" in Grimmelshausen's counsel of moderation (*Continuatio* 505) is debatable. The temptation to excessive "Freygiebigkeit" still comes from an external, spiritual source.

[20] R. P. T. Aylett, *The Nature of Realism in Grimmelshausen's "Simplicissimus" Cycle of Novels*, (Berne/Frankfurt 1982), 47–8.

[21] Quoted by Aylett (46) from Melitta Gerhard, *Der deutsche Entwicklungsroman bis zu Goethes "Wilhelm Meister,"* (Halle 1926).

[22] See Grimmelshausen, *Kleinere Schriften*, 28.

[23] Ashcroft, "Emblems and Imagery," 861.

[24] Cf. Tarot, Introduction to *Simplicissimus* (xxxix), and Gersch, *Geheimpoetik*, 9–10.

[25] W. E. Schäfer, "Laster und Lastersystem bei Grimmelshausen," *Germanisch Romanische Monatsschrift* 12 (1962), 233–43

[26] P. Trieffenbach, *Der Lebenslauf des Simplicius Simplicissimus. Figur-Initiation-Satire*, (Stuttgart 1979), 39.

[27] Cf. also Menhennet, "Baggy Monster," 116.

[28] Cf. chapter 3.

[29] The Sabud story (which represents a marked shift of tone) is said to be written to fill the blank paper which the author has left.

[30] Cf. also the heading for chapter 23.

[31] Gersch, *Geheimpoetik*, 9.

[32] Ibid., 279

[33] Ibid., 11–12.

[34] Wiethölter, in "Baldanderst Lehr und Kunst," presents Grimmelshausen's "Vexierspiel" with anagrams as a series of "identitätsauflösende Effekte" (61), attributing to him a degree of semiotic sophistication that seems inherently unlikely.

The basic principle, surely, is that "Simplician" identity can be transferred from one authorial persona to another.

[35] Cf. Gersch, *Geheimpoetik*, 75–79.

[36] For Grimmelshausen's use of anagrams, see Weydt, *Nachahmung*, 191–6. Weydt sees Grimmelshausen as "hiding" behind anagrams (196).

[37] See the "Sonnet" of Sylvander (7) and the "Zuruff," 100ff.

5: Vice and Vitality: The *Ertzbetrügerin Courasche*

IT IS "ASTOUNDING," says Feldges of the *Courasche*, that a portrait which was "doubtless" conceived and executed as an exemplary warning should have lost nothing thereby of its "delightful vitality."[1] Meid talks of a "contradiction" between didactic intention and artistic realisation, which "also allows Courage to appear as a victim"[2] (that is, we become aware of her also as a real individual with a point of view). The paradox at the centre of the book is noted also by Streller, who speaks of a "secret admiration" on Grimmelshausen's part for the devilish woman ("Teufelweib") he has created.[3] Some have even gone so far as to see in the "heroine" of this novel a triumph of vitality over morality, a view which Herbert Arnold rightly rejects as anachronistic ("modernistisch"),[4] insofar as that triumph is conceived as taking place in the writer's mind. Streller's formulation does not resolve the paradox, nor does Feldges's suggestion that Courage achieves an existence that makes her "independent" of her creator and his moral intentions:[5] this, surely, merely asserts that Grimmelshausen was an incompetent allegorist.

In an attempt to resolve the apparent contradiction, Arnold falls back on the idea of a duality of levels: a level of depiction ("Schilderungsebene") and one of significance ("Bedeutungsebene"),[6] and while we cannot accept the implied separation of manner from meaning in Grimmelshausen, this does at least bring us face to face with the distinctive central problem of the *Courasche*. It is the only one in which a clear moral corrective is not built into the narrative structure and style. We feel sure that Grimmelshausen cannot be endorsing Courage's immorality, yet he seems deliberately to have blocked off all the routes through which his moral disapproval might have found expression. He has used the standard form, familiar from his reading of Ägidius Albertinus, of the autobiography, retrospectively narrated as the confession of a sinner,[7] but he has omitted to make his rogue repentant. He has resisted the temptation of permitting his nominal author, Philarchus, an adequate counterblast and allowing the book to split, as does Hogg's *Confessions of a Justified Sinner*, into discrete parts. He has embarked on a form of narrative that is not unique, but relatively rare; the novel whose deep structure, if we may appropriate the term, is ironic, one in which the reader is aware of the coexistence of two "truths."

Courage knows that her life has been sinful: she flaunts the fact, indeed, in an attempt to undermine Simplicissimus's respectable social standing, as revenge for his slighting reference to her in his own life history (*ST* 391). But in insisting on her own sinfulness, she shows no sign of feeling moral guilt, or of a practical appreciation of the fact that sin might have transcendental consequences. Lack of repentance and lack of an organ for the Eternal go together. Her reaction to the knowledge that her beauty is transitory, which she accepts as simply a fact of life, has been to profit, not spiritually but materially, as a prostitute while the rosebuds were still available for gathering. Looking back, she is so far from repenting that she says: "I would have to regret it to this very hour if I had done any less"(34). There is an ambivalence, not in her meaning, but in the expression she uses ("reuen," which contains the idea of repentance as well as that of regret), that enables us to make a distinction here. She has, so to speak, been using her talents to get on in the world, as she does on other occasions to survive in it, while at the same time satisfying the needs and desires of what she calls her "nature." For her, as for Agathe in Sorel's *Francion*, it is "une gloire d'avoir suivi la bonne nature,"[8] and as with Agathe, the frankness with which she speaks is potentially disturbing from the moral perspective, but also engaging, and self-validating as an expression of the life force that still runs through her veins.

She is aware, though, that according to the moral code of society, her sexual activities are reprehensible and her appetites excessive, a point which she makes on various occasions. She does not endorse that code as the older Simplicissimus does. He has found his way back into society: she, as the title page indicates, has slid (sometimes pushed, it is true, but going willingly) into the position of moral and social outsider, from which she has no desire to be "saved." But she does not challenge the moral code of society: indeed, she is invoking it against Simplicissimus. She has an objective, but not a subjective conviction of sin. The ambivalence of "reuen," however, allows another perspective to appear alongside hers, and allows our attention to alternate between the two. From the moral point of view, she ought to repent. To her, the thought of eternal damnation is something external, something that "is said" to her (wie mir gesagt wird: 15); we see her life both from the internal and the external perspective.

This implies a structural polarity in the work. Courage is sole narrator of the story, which is dictated to Philarchus, not reported by him (as indeed, he is dominated by her while in her presence, and able to assert himself only when she is away). Grimmelshausen is her literary author and begetter. There is a need for a duality in the authorial voice which cannot be registered by the standard terminology of allegory or satire. Streller maintains that Courage's "Weltverfallenheit," the limitation of her horizon exclusively to things earthly, means that the novel becomes completely satirical.[9] But since, with her lack of true values, she cannot be the voice of satire, this must imply that her own narrative should be consistently undermined with an irony similar to that of Fielding's *Jonathan Wild*, and lose its savour, which it manifestly does not. Nothing is surer than that she is allowed her point of view, and allowed to speak with her own voice, which is the voice of vitality. That it is simultaneously that of vice is made apparent by the other half of the authorial polarity. By the device of having her expose her sins (whose true sinfulness she does not understand) in order to shame Simplicissimus socially, Grimmelshausen enables her to tell the truth at two levels; to be herself and express herself without inhibition, and at the same time to serve as a negative example. Her insistence on confession can hardly be "obsession with the truth," as Weydt calls it,[10] for she is incapable of seeing the real truth. If she could, she would repent. Through authorial irony, the coexistence of two parallel but totally un-integrated perspectives is assured in this case also.

Courage has an intellectual knowledge of God; she sees Him as a power in the world, something in the order of a superior Fate or Fortune. He is the "lumen" that renders some people immune to the influence of her *spiritus familiaris* (100); it is He, she feels, who in all probability, foiled her attempt to rob a credulous young lady.[11] She can even call on Him to save her from her tormentors (62) and be so frightened by the avalanche of pears descending on her head that she thinks He has sent an earthquake to punish her in the here and now for her "shameful sins" (132–3: it is important to her, of course, that they be seen as such because the shame rubs off on her enemy; at the same time, and with the same word, Grimmelshausen engages our moral sense). But she does not feel shame, for she has no knowledge of God in her heart. "Gewissenhafte Leut" (people with a conscience) may, she says, think that God was calling her to repentance in the "pearquake" episode of chapter 25. She, however, is a model of what it is to be "leichtfertig" and have no capacity for repentance. Although Hogg's Robert Wringhim may feel at one point that "the grace of repentance" is "withheld," there is a spiritual force within him, which we may call conscience, that makes him regret the fact, and he does, in the end, "dare to repent."[12] Here too, Grimmelshausen makes use of ironic ambivalence: the reader may draw inferences for Courage's state of mind that she does not draw for herself.

There is, then, at times a double irony in this book: that of the narrator and that of the author. Courage is intellectually aware, but spiritually unaware, of the religious context of what she says. Her "general Beicht" (general confession: 14) is in fact a kind of blasphemy; an ironic parody, as J.-M. Valentin has shown, of the standard Catholic forms of confession and contrition.[13] In her educational background, she has enjoyed advantages denied to Simplicissimus and Springinsfeld and these have clearly included religious instruction; she knows the terms and conditions of confession and is aware that repentance is in the orthodox doctrine, a "gift of heaven" (15: "die himmlische Gabe der Reue"). She states quite baldly, without any indication of regret (*Reue*), that she is incapable of receiving it. She tells the priests who might want to convert her that the present state of her humours renders her less amenable to moral persuasion than she might have been in her sanguine youth, but it is they, not she, who see her as pitiable ("die arme Courage" 16). It is unthinkable that she could exclaim, as does Gusman in Ägidius Albertinus's version of Alemán: "O Mensch / o religios, der du dises lisest /

nimb ein exempel an mir armseligen."[14] She is certainly, in a sense, a "negative example";[15] a consciously "miserable sinner" she is not. Her total lack of self-pity can, admittedly, be said to derive from a lack of moral self-awareness. By having her deploy the serious terminology of sin and repentance, the author ensures that the reader will be able to judge her from that perspective as well. But her acceptance of reality, a limitation of her horizon, admittedly, makes her a suitable channel both for the satirical exposure of hypocrisy and for the spontaneous enjoyment of the humour and vitality of life. The "Trutz" (spite) with which she pursues Simplicissimus, announced in the subtitle and the opening chapter and continued through the text, and which shows her to be driven by pride and wrath, continues to provide a transcendental vantage point, a (serious) parallel irony to her own.

In the same chapter in which she reveals herself, and is revealed, as a hardened sinner, she teases the no doubt staid and eminently respectable "Herren" who might credit her with a conscience (14: hers, she says later, is "a wide one": 51) with an ironic urbanity that we also savour, and there are many other such touches in the narrative, as when she regales us with a speech full of gallant conceits and compliments in the heroic baroque manner, intended by her lovesick swain "to persuade me to that course of action on which I was just as keen as he was" (67), or when she refers to a newborn calf, falsely suspected by superstitious peasants of being a man-eater, as "this common enemy of the human race"(139). She takes a genuine delight in the irony of the fact that the "fette Lügen" (barefaced lies) of the passport issued to her by the Colonel himself, in which she is described as a thoroughly respectable woman, are "mit eigenhändiger Subscription und beygedrucktem Sigill in bester Form bekräfftigt" (he has attested [these outright lies] in all solemn form by appending his signature in his own hand and affixing his seal: 50–1).

Sinful though she may be, Courage is a lively and intelligent character: as knowledgeable and resourceful, and as much in control of the Simplician narrative style as was Simplicissimus himself. The point is made on the very title page. The book, we are told, will be as "useful," (or morally beneficial) to its readers as was *Simplicissimus*. (This makes it unlikely that Courage herself is the origin of these remarks, which, like the chapter headings, are probably best seen as stemming from the editor who contributed the concluding "Wahrhafftige Ursach" [true cause].) We learn further, though, that it is at the same time as amusing and enjoyable to read as was the earlier novel. The fact that in the absence of a repentant narrator there is no corrective voice in this book makes the role of the style even more important than usual in the Simplician scheme of things. We have seen that by introducing into her "confession" terminology and phrasing that demand to be taken seriously (though to her, perhaps, they are mere remembered formalities), Grimmelshausen is able to carve out a contrasting parallel path to that laid down by her impenetrable "Leichtfertigkeit," in essence, lack of moral awareness. It is not enough to say, as Feldges does, attributing to Grimmelshausen a Socratic "maieutic" technique: "Die Darstellung der lebendigen Wirklichkeit ist bereits ohne moralischen Kommentar heilsam"[16] (The depiction of living reality is therapeutic in itself, without a moral commentary). It is the manner of depiction that is crucial, and that can cause a sideways shift of perspective.

Correspondingly, Courage can be both a target and a vehicle for satire, and amusing as well as spiteful. When she refers to the "unzüchtig Gegrabel" (improper gropings: 25) of the captain of horse who eventually becomes her first husband, which contrast sharply with his honourable promises ("ehrlichs Versprechen"), the repeated formula of noun and adjective sharpens the antithesis ("unzüchtig-ehrlich") through which she drives the satirical dart firmly home. The fact that Courage openly parades her own impropriety, taking more delight in his pawing hands than in his persuasive words, and states that she resisted his advances not to repel his assault, but to spur him on to further attacks, may well awaken our moral displeasure against her, but does not weaken the satire directed against the captain, or lessen our enjoyment of her superior wit. He is the gallant captain, the "Ritter" (knight), whose duty is to protect; the irony of his lack of the chivalrous virtues is highlighted by Courage's ironic description of her own "resistance" as gallant ("ritterlich").

The Simplician manner certainly manages to create a polarity in our judgement of one of Courage's most prominent characteristics, her sexuality. Nowhere in the Simplician corpus is the demonic aspect of sex, its power to ensnare the soul, made more obvious. Courage's power over men, her barrenness, and her more than normally insatiable desires set her apart, not as an allegory, but certainly as a representative figure for the sin of fornication. But she is also a channel for the vitality of the world as well as for its viciousness. It makes a noticeable difference whether she uses the signpost-word "schändlich" (shameful) in referring to her activities as a prostitute ("schändlicher Gewinn": 54), or speaks of "earning my diurnal bread by practising my nocturnal trade" ("Mein täglich Maulfutter mit meiner nächtlichen Handarbeit zu gewinnen": 71). The first phrase presents us with the ugliness of earthly sin, as an abstraction from the specific reality, which is measured purely in terms of "eternal" criteria. Courage herself is no doubt thinking only of spiting Simplicissimus. Grimmelshausen points us towards what she can see, but not feel. But he is not in a mood to preach a sermon over her, as he almost does in the case of the peasant lass in part 1 of *Das wunderbarliche Vogelnest* who attempts to lure her companion into the bushes. There, the woman is simply an exemplar, a "frail vessel" in whom reason is rendered impotent by the "sickness" of love.[17] Courage is a vital individual who lives in a real world, and the second phrase we have quoted allows her to interpose her present individuality as a lively and ironic narrator and locate her past activities firmly in the life of this world, with its real needs. Style, again, plays an important role: the wit with which "täglich" and "nächtlich," "Maulfutter" and "Handarbeit" are balanced and contrasted disarm any inclination we might have had to neutralize the character, as it were, and allegorize it as an embodiment of the whore of Babylon. That is how Philarchus, in the *Springinsfeld*, sees her, when she is safely out of the way. But that is, in both senses of the word, another story.

Courage, the narrator, speaks as a gypsy, a self-exiled outsider who has, as the editor's final note, the "Wahrhafftige Ursach" (true cause), puts it, forsworn all honour and virtue ("aller Ehr und Tugend selbst abgesagt"). "Ehre" and "ehrlich" stand, in Courage's vocabulary as often in Springinsfeld's, for social respectability and repute. She has not simply lost these things, she has also lost all respect for them, but she is still aware of their practical importance. It is interesting to note how often the word "Ehre" (honour, repute) comes to her mind. She herself is the natural daughter of a count and of a mother who was poor, but "von ehrlichen Geschlecht"(of reputable family: 54) and her life has been a more or less uninterrupted descent down the social ladder, until finally, she has stepped off the bottom rung. She is anything but devoid of pride, and, as we shall see, well aware of the social importance of "Ehr und Tugend" (honour and virtue) not only for women, but for men too, in the world in which she lives. It is at that level that *she* recognizes the importance and validity of chastity and the other virtues (while *we* can make the transfer to the moral dimension). And it is at that level that she is attacking Simplicissimus: her dishonour dishonours him. It is no doubt with this purpose in mind that she seems to endorse the conventional view of the gypsies as a "Lumpen-Gesind" (low rabble), as the socially conventional Harsdörffer calls them,[18] and confesses herself, in very much the same language as that used by Philarchus in *Springinsfeld*,[19] amazed that the lands through which they wander tolerate their presence (147).

But the relish with which she narrates her exploits makes it clear that she is a gypsy at heart. Her nature and origins impel her towards the fringes of "correct" society. She is, it is true, the daughter of a count, but of a rebel count from the rebel Bohemian nation. And "Bohemian" here means Czech. Her real name is Libuschka, the capital city of her "Vatterland" is Prague (123), and German is not her native language: she can speak it pretty well, but she conceals the fact from the German cavalryman who has carried her off (19). Even when it would pay her, socially, to live a respectable ("ehrlich") life, her "nature" pushes her in the opposite direction. Her exclusion from reputable society is not something that she plans or wishes, for her material welfare and security are always on her mind, but when it comes, in chapter 25, it is not uncongenial to her, and seems, indeed, a natural development, in that her inner alienation from the values of that society, with its concern for propriety, becomes apparent. Tricked into believing that her partner in crime has confessed, she reacts with the obscenity (and the verve) of a low-life character: "So schlag ihm der Hagel ins Maul / weils der alte Scheusser nicht hat halten können" (Can't he keep his mouth shut, the old shitbag? Then I hope Old Nick will shove his teeth down his throat!: 134). She escapes the torture and death that, under the full force of the law, she says she would have deserved (this, no doubt, for Simplicissimus's benefit on her part and for the reader's, on that of Grimmelshausen the ironic writer!), because as she says, "many who were held to be reputable citizens would have [had] to come to the funeral with me." She has as much of the gift of the gab as any lawyer ("Ich könnte schwätzen wie ein Rechtsgelehrter") and soon convinces the more intelligent of the council members that justice should, in this case, be tempered with discretion. In all this, we must disapprove of her, but we cannot but feel a certain pleasure at her partial victory over respectability, just as we feel a distance between ourselves and the gypsies, but at the same time take pleasure in the narrative of their free, wandering life and their ingenious roguery.

True Bohemian (as Grimmelshausen sees it) as she is in all senses of the word, Courage has a propensity and talent for roguery. She is not only a "Landstörtzerin" (vagrant), but also an "Ertzbetrügerin" (arch-deceiver). It is in this context, perhaps, that the novel succeeds most spectacularly in being both deadly serious and comic. As a deceiver Courage is at once the successor of Till Eulenspiegel and the handmaid of the devil. It is not so much in the tit-for-tat revenge that she takes on Simplicissimus as in her treatment of Springinsfeld (which she is also able to relate, in her narrative, to her revenge) that this latter aspect becomes apparent. As a spirited and inventive trickster, she can afford us amusement and earn at least a measure of respect, even in playing the sex game with the lustful potential clients who buzz round her like bees round a honeypot in Vienna (32). We can understand her need to satisfy her own bodily desires, and sympathise when she becomes the victim of male brutality. At the very least, all these things can be accepted as part of life, and the vitality of real life in her narration enjoyed without debilitating thoughts of allegory. But in her ruthless exploitation of the power bestowed on her by her sexual attractiveness, which is the greatest of all deceptions for Grimmelshausen in that it blinds men both to their temporal and to their eternal welfare, she arouses a different reaction and seems at times to assume almost a devilish status. It is in the long Springinsfeld episode (chapters 15 to 22) that this tendency forces its way to the surface. Courage shows us the face of malice more openly here than anywhere else in the book. The vengefulness that is built into the whole structure comes spitting forth, at times, without the saving grace of irony or wit, in the way in which she rejoices at the degradation of Simplicissimus's former comrade and right-hand-man, who is her nominal husband. We need not go as far as the men whom she has bested and humiliated, Springinsfeld and Philarchus, as they fulminate against her in the successor novel. Grimmelshausen's presentation of their view is, indeed, by no means entirely sympathetic. At the same time, there can be little doubt that he saw Courage's behaviour here as a perversion of God's ordinance.

It is no accident that the devil makes one of his relatively rare personal appearances at this point, for it is here that the transcendental dimension truly impinges on the ironic format. The fact that, as the critics have rightly noted, hers is a "verkehrte Welt," a radical reversal of the God-given world-order in the deepest religious sense, now comes to us directly, with Courage's own commitment behind it, even though she may not herself be fully aware of the fact. She is aware that she is flouting the social order in denying Springinsfeld the "billiche Oberherrlichkeit" (due or proper authority: 87) of husband over wife. But the word "Gewalt" (violence, or power, and the exercise thereof), which she herself has used before of her relations with men, and which has gained her some sympathy and understanding when we saw her suffering or circumventing the imposition of such power on her, does not seem to occur to her now, when she is exerting it herself. Men have called her "witch" and associated her with the devil before, as for example the major to whose bestial ("viehisch") violence she is subjected in chapter 12, but in a spirit of vengeance, because she has bested them. Now, she is inflicting violence on simplicity and (relative) innocence.

Courage has assimilated the concept of the devil into her mental cosmos, together with that of God and other Christian orthodoxies, even though they mean nothing to her morally or emotionally. So when Springinsfeld's words and behaviour make it clear to her that she has "a fool on the end of [her] string," she decides to take advantage of the situation to set herself up as a sutler-woman, using him as a necessary front, a pro-forma sutler, as he is a pro-forma husband. In what seems at first glance almost a direct intervention into the ironic narrative, Grimmelshausen has her draw a parallel between herself and the devil, and seems to make her his mouthpiece in warning the good Christian not to emulate her:

Ich verfolgte das / was ich angefangen / und unterstunde zu fischen / dieweil das Wasser trüb war; und warum wolte ichs nicht gethan haben / da doch der Teuffel selbst die jenige die er in solchem Stand findet / wie sich mein Leffler befande / vollends in seine Netze zu bringen unterstehet? Ich sage dies nicht / daß ein ehrlicher Christen-Mensch / den Wercken dieses seines abgefaimten bösen Feindes zu folgen / an mir ein Exempel nehmen soll / weil ich ihm damahls nachahmte.... (81)

[I continued what I had started and made bold to fish while the water was muddied ... and why shouldn't I have done so, since the Devil himself, when he comes upon people in the condition in which my amorous swain found himself, makes bold to draw them right into his nets? I am not saying this to persuade honest Christian folk to take me as their model and follow in the path of their most hardened and evil enemy because I imitated him then....]

She has not formally identified herself with the devil. As an arch-deceiver, proud of her ability, she has simply followed the path of the greatest deceiver of all. She accepts, as we have seen, the idea of sin in this world, and the devil represents that idea to the highest potency. But she has used terminology (which to her perhaps is merely formulaic) that brings thoughts of the next world into our minds. The irony that in this book enables readers to detach themselves from the "authorial" perspective must come into play: we can see what she cannot, namely that she has an immortal soul and that she has imperilled it. Indeed, it is hard not to feel that at this point, Grimmelshausen has felt the need to go beyond irony and pronounce the anathema direct on Courage's behaviour, to get her not just to condemn, but to damn herself out of her own mouth. If the "Verteufelung" of which Feldges speaks[20] occurs anywhere in the book, it is here rather than in her joining of the gypsy band.

She gets her "Galan" to sign a marriage contract in which there is no marriage, and in which he has the title, but she the authority ("Meisterschafft") of the husband, and even after she has trained him up in roguery, he remains her fool and her "obedient" slave. His very name is acquired (in accordance with the marriage contract) as a result of the first command she gives him. The episode is a mixture of positive and negative: on the one hand, it is an amusingly narrated *Schwank*, on the other, it stamps on Springinsfeld the mark of shame. The name he receives (on the surface harmless enough) is not only the badge of cuckoldry; but his real subordination, hidden under a mask of apparent authority, is also emphasised. A young ensign of noble origin, to whom she has taken a fancy (which is reciprocated), turns up at the sutler's cart. The "husband," having put up the tent and turned the horses out to pasture, is busying himself about the cart. "Have you got any money on you?" she asks the young officer, and when he answers in the affirmative, she turns to her (pro forma) sutler ("mein Marquetender") and tells him:

> Spring-ins-felt / und fange unsern Schecken / der Herr Fendrich wolte ihn gern bereuten / und uns demselben abhandlen / und gleich paar bezahlen; Indessen nun mein guter Marquetender gehorsamlich hingieng / meinen ersten Befelch zu vollbringen / hielte die alte Schildwacht / dieweil wir den Kauff miteinander machten / und auch einander ritterlich bezahlten; demnach sich aber das Pferd nicht von meinem Marquetender so leichtlich / wie seine Marquetenderin vom Fendrich fangen lassen wolte / kam er gantz ermüthet widerum zum Zelt / eben so ungedultig / als sich der Fendrich wegen seines langen Wartens stellet . . . (84–5).

> [Hop into the field and catch our dapple: the young gentleman, the ensign here, would like to take a ride on him and buy him from us, and he's paying cash. And while this honest sutler-man of mine went obediently off to carry out the first order I had given him, my foster-mother stood outside on sentry while the two of us clinched a sale in which each remunerated the

other with chivalrous generosity. Now, since my sutler-husband did not find it as easy to catch the horse as the ensign had found it to catch his sutler-wife, he came back to the tent exhausted and as much out of patience as the ensign pretended to be because he had been made to wait so long. . . .]

One cannot but feel a quickening of the style and a fresh touch of humour here, as Grimmelshausen responds to the narrative possibilities of a real comic situation. But the references to "mein Marquetender" reveal a streak of derisive cruelty. And while there are certainly other lively and comic moments in the Springinsfeld sequence, there are also those in which something perhaps not approaching formal allegory, but rather the abstract framework of a representative, even potentially transcendental vision of Courage begin to appear. The style is at times more analytical than narrative: the formal statement of the marriage contract, for example, and the constant reiteration of the fact that Springinsfeld is reduced to a state of servitude emphasize that this is an extraordinary and extreme situation. He acquires and practises roguish skills, which inevitably gives rise to narrative opportunities that Grimmelshausen exploits with relish, but the fact that this is a process of corruption is emphasized by the fact that Courage uses of him a word ("abgefaimbt": hardened [85]) that she previously used to describe the devil. Even after she has narrated a couple of lively and amusing tales of comic pranks in which Springinsfeld has acted as her able lieutenant, Courage reduces him to the ranks once more: "I doubt if I could have found a better slave in the whole world" (110).

It is in this sequence also that Grimmelshausen gives the most overt symbolic indications of direct associations with the devil on Courage's part, certainly in Springinsfeld's dream of her as "Frau Welt," to which Feldges refers (and which we have already discussed in chapter 2) but most significantly in chapter 18, when he shows her acquiring the *spiritus familiaris*, even though the narration here also shows a due recognition of the vitality and narrative potential of material reality. The old soldier who sells Courage the dangerous and devilish glass is both a sinister and a curious figure. He is given a sense of mystery by the fact that he has "carried a musket a long time before the Bohemian troubles [that triggered the Thirty Years' War] began." He seems to wander into the story out of another world, and then to depart once more. At the same time, he is visualised, in the racy soldier's slang, as "ein alter Hünerfanger" (literally, old chicken-catcher: 95), as a "Kracher" (creaker? . . . Simplicius describes himself as such in the *Rathstübel Plutonis*), a "Weinbeisser"(96), and as "der alte Lauer"(the old crook: 97).[21] The effects of the glass smack of the black arts, and the reference in the chapter heading (94) to Courage's "godlessness," and her own remark that God protects some prospective victims from the glass's magic power (100) elevate this object to a dark symbolic status. But the physical description also invests the object with an air of curious vitality: Courage sees something that is "not quite a spider and not quite a scorpion" and is "incessantly scrabbling about" in a sealed glass and might be taken for "some kind of representation of perpetual motion" (95).

Courage is markedly a representative figure, perhaps by virtue of what makes her unique within the Simplician cycle: namely, the fact that she is a woman who is also the central and dominant character of a complete novel (the "Leirerin" [hurdy-gurdy player] in *Springinsfeld* is a more peripheral figure and her status as a woman is hardly an issue). As Weydt has pointed out, Grimmelshausen will have known the German version of Andrea Perez's *Picara Justina,* but his book is much more than a simple attempt to exploit the exotic possibilities of a woman picaro.[22] Here, we are presented with a sustained account of the career of a woman in a man's world, written by a man who shares the conventional attitudes of his time, but whose responsiveness to his characters as living beings in a real environment makes him capable of presenting her, too, as a person with a point of view.

There was a positive image of woman in the seventeenth century. Even Grimmelshausen, in works like *Proximus und Lympida,* shows us heroines who are intelligent, courageous, chaste and virtuous, and we can point (quite apart from the paragons of the Petrarchistic lyric) to Gryphius's Catharina von Georgien, Anton Ulrich's Aramena, Ziegler's Banise, and others of the same ilk. But in the period of the baroque, the "überirdisch" (superterrestrial) woman is the heroic, idealised exception; "natural" woman is far more often seen negatively, as the fragile vessel that is all too prone to sin, the cunning and recalcitrant creature that needs to be kept in a position of inferiority, the daughter of Eve who, as an *occasio luxuriae,* can all too easily lure a man into the nets of the devil, as we have already seen Courage remark. There can be little doubt that Grimmelshausen shared this view, as Feldges, among others, has shown,[23] and that his portrait of Courage reflects it. Cunning, malice, lack of conscience, pride, unchastity, desire to dominate — that is, to usurp the man's role — the possible link with witchcraft;[24] she has all the standard vices — as Grimmelshausen would have seen them — at least some of the time. She glories, for example, in the deceptions she has practised and in her "Leichtfertigkeit," she dismisses her virginity as "nicht dreier Heller wert" (not worth a farthing: 25), and worst of all, perhaps, not only can she reduce men to folly, even a kind of slavery by the use of the ultimate woman's weapon, but she is more of a man than most of the men in the book. She prefers to wear men's clothes (or at least the nether garment), rides into battle and reverses the normal order by defeating men in battle and even taking them prisoner.

And yet, while she could be seen as "unwomanly," she is a real woman, as well as a demonic image, since, like any Simplician character, she lives in a real rather than an allegorical world. And she is, in this book, the channel for the spirit of reality; the humour and the vital force of life. Her sexual powers and appetites are not only aspects of a traditional negative image of woman, but are actual physical energies — and indeed needs — and are recognised as such. Again, we can trace the earthly-transcendental dualism in the style. The word *Begierde* (desire, appetite), for example, brings lust to mind, and when Courage speaks of her "unmässige Begierden" (excessive desires: 46), her "unersättliche Natur" (insatiable nature: 113), her mouth "watering for new food" after she forgets her captain (31), or — using the traditional metaphor of the unbridled horse — of giving free rein to the desires she had held in check up to now ("meinen bisher bezwungenen Begierden den Zaum einmal schiessen zu lassen": 33), we are clearly in the world of lustful appetites, of the negative view of women as "inherently weak and lascivious creatures."[25] Here, Courage is giving the conventional description of a male-dominated society, no doubt with her attack on Simplicissimus's reputation in mind, and Grimmelshausen is inviting us to consider her behaviour from a slightly different angle. When, however, she tells us that her virginity had been a burden too heavy to bear ("ein schwerer unträglicher Last": 26), or in describing a period of celibacy, that it was very hard for her to bear it any longer, and entirely against her nature (52), the tone is more neutral: while we still see her as unchaste and disreputable (since she is not an "ehrliche Jungfrau," she cannot get the kind of husband she would like), a real physical need and force of nature is conveyed to us. And when she remarks that "I have never been so squeamish as to deny an honest fellow a ride if he has been gripped by necessity" ("einem guten Kerl eine Fahrt abzuschlagen / wann ihn die Noth begriffen": 74), the writer and the figure who speaks are at one. The appreciation of the salty humour and verve of popular speech — as clear in this book as in the *Simplicissimus* itself — and the acceptance of a natural energy that takes its course are here blended in one phrase.

The context in which Courage makes this remark is significant. She is being ambushed, having been unfairly sent away in disgrace from the regiment, by "zween Haluncken . . . [die] . . . eben das jenige von mir mit Gewalt begehrten / wessentwegen ich verjagt: und mein Auserwehlter tod geschossen worden" (two scurvy knaves [who] wanted to take from me by force that for which I had been cast out and my chosen mate had been shot: 74). And so she opposes violence with violence, their swords with her two knives. And her mannishness does not, on this occasion, attract condemnation. Rather, it is an opportunity for narrative development, which Grimmelshausen seizes with alacrity. She kills one of her attackers, and while the other does call her "a whore, a baggage, a witch and even a devil" (75), this is mere abuse, motivated, no doubt, by the frustration of a man who cannot subdue a woman. She replies in kind and the duel even assumes a comic note as they circle round making curious leaps ("seltzame Sprüng") and so much noise that Springinsfeld is attracted to the scene and puts the man to flight "at a speed which was enough to make the soles fall off his shoes." Ironically, Courage is soon to assume the role of tyrant, but in this sequence, her function is closer to that of victim — of male *Gewalt*, that is.

She is completely the victim in the sequence (chapter 12) in which she falls into the hands of the major whom she previously humiliated by taking him prisoner in battle, and is subjected to multiple rape and other forms of bestial maltreatment. This is not, it should be stressed, a simple black-and-white portrayal. The chapter heading (which we feel must have been written by a man)[26] presents it as a kind of evening of the sexual score, which is mirrored in the double use of "Courage" as a proper name and as a euphemism for the sexual organs. She herself — or Grimmelshausen, through her — seems to acknowledge this ("ich hatte es hiebevor verschuldet"),[27] up to the point at which she is forced to allow the servants to enjoy her in the presence of their masters, and she emphasizes the bestial ("viehisch") nature of the men's behaviour. It is at this point, for the only time, that Grimmelshausen allows her to call on God for help and to label the actions of her oppressors as unchristian (62–3). For the moment, her function has changed, as can quite easily happen with a figure in baroque drama or narrative.[28] No longer the aggressor, she has become here almost a representative figure for the vulnerability of women, and the atrocities which could be inflicted on them, in the Thirty Years' War.

In society in general, it was woman's function, in the seventeenth century, not to dominate men, but to accept their authority. Under the emblem of a woman riding on a man's back, Ägidius Albertinus, in his *Hirnschleiffer* (1618), asserts: "Nichts kan unbillicher und ungereimbter seyn / weder wann der Mann sich vom Weib regiren und beherrschen . . . lest" (Nothing can be more unreasonable and absurd than a man allowing himself to be governed and dominated by a woman).[29] Courage would have agreed: if she had married Springinsfeld, she says, he would have had rightful authority ("billiche Oberherrlichkeit": 87) over her. She wonders, indeed, whether tame husbands ("fromme Männer": 101) are men at all. But if she is no social revolutionary, neither is Courage a passively submissive spirit. It is, after all, "meines gleichen lose Weiber" (wanton women like myself: 101 [another example of the book's double irony?]) who bend the "fromme Männer" to their will. She is willing, as is made clear in chapter 7 when her lieutenant-husband challenges her to a duel for supremacy, to accept the rightful authority — or at least the outward authority[30] — of a husband in the established order, but not one which grinds the woman under the heel of the man. And though she makes no claim ("Anspruch") to dominance, she accepts with alacrity the chance to achieve it. Grimmelshausen (seduced, perhaps, by the opportunity for comic narrative offered by the scene), casts the lieutenant in the role of "Tropf" (fool, ninny) and allows her to fetch him a blow which sends him reeling out of the tent "wie ein Ochs dem ein Streich worden" (like an ox that had been stunned with a poleaxe: 42). The narrative has for the moment wooed the writer (and the reader) on to the side of the "strong woman."

Grimmelshausen endorses the patriarchal view of male authority in general, but while he does not reject the stereotypes, he can go beyond them in feeling his way into the position of a living character that he has created. Courage belongs to the genus "woman," but she is also an intelligent individual with a free (if rebelliously flawed) spirit, and he can appreciate and give expression to her feelings when the particular perspective allows. When Springinsfeld appears, not as the innocent who is being corrupted, or the "husband" whose rightful authority is flouted, but as a foolish boaster who believes that that no woman can outsmart him, Courage proceeds to establish an ascendency — which we feel is in this case legitimate — by replying to his foolish boast ("er entblödete sich zu rühmen": 85) with a demonstration of her superior wit: a vindication of "meiner und aller verständigen Weiber dexterität" (my quick-wittedness and that of all intelligent women: 86). This is not primarily a piece of satirical sniping against female cunning: Springinsfeld has been identified in this instance as a comic figure, and the story is told mainly for comedy. Grimmelshausen is thinking in terms of individual human reality, not of satirical stereotypes. And in chapter 4, when he is describing her life "in sin" with the captain of horse, he certainly does not present her as the wronged innocent, but allows her to describe, with some spirit, the imbalance in such a relationship. The man feels entitled to humiliate her by public use of her ambivalent nickname, which, in its sexual meaning, is a badge of social shame, and there is nothing that she, as a woman without reputation, can do but "swallow what she finds hard to digest." But her sense of intrinsic dignity and freedom of spirit, at least, is not crushed. She speaks for herself, but also, for a moment, as a woman for all women and to all young women. An important principle, that of freedom, is at stake. "Don't let your virginity be stolen in such a sordid way [as mine was]," she warns, "for with it, your freedom goes down the drain" ("mit derselbigen gehet zugleich euere Freiheit in Duckas": 27). She goes on to warn thieving men that women can take revenge, and states coolly that if her "Rittmeister" had not kept on holding out the hope of an honourable marriage, she would have "put a bullet in him in some skirmish, when he was least expecting it" (27). Again, there is nothing in the tone to suggest that Grimmelshausen is primarily concerned with condemning her here. He would not, of course, condone a murderous vengefulness, but neither would he advocate a spiritless resignation to the status of a mere chattel.

Though she can be a shrewd social observer and hence a reliable vehicle for social satire, there is, as we have seen, a serious limitation in Courage's mental and moral make-up that prevents her from feeling the eternal dimension of her experiences. A particularly striking example occurs in chapter 26, after her expulsion from the spa town Griesbach, when she turns back (as ever) to the army and looks for another husband: "Aber ach! die erste Blüte meiner ohnvergleichlichen Schönheit war fort / und wie eine Frühlingsblum verwelcket" (But ah, the first blossom of my incomparable beauty was gone;

withered away like a spring flower: 135). The phrase reminds us irresistibly of the great baroque master of *vanitas,* Andreas Gryphius,[31] who in his turn is echoing the Biblical "flower of the field" image. One suspects that it was from the latter source that Grimmelshausen took it, but he doubtless wished, like Gryphius, to evoke with it the thought of "what is eternal." But not with reference to Courage herself. The *memento mori* is conveyed to us, not to her. She simply accepts the transitoriness of beauty as a fact, scrapes together as much money as she can from her remaining possessions, and sets out to seek her fortune wherever it might be found (136). For her, all facts are facts of this life, for there is nothing else. It is, as we have said, a limitation that she should be such a complete realist, but there is also a certain strength in this limitation, and one, perhaps, that helps to explain the vitality that so "astounds" Feldges and the "secret admiration" that surprises Streller. She is reprehensible; she is, ultimately, in her "Leichtfertigkeit" — her lack of a conscience and a sense of the eternal reality — guilty of a worse folly than any of her dupes, but she is an ideal channel for that essence of earthly reality, the vitality of life, which retains an irresistible charm for Grimmelshausen and which he cannot suppress, even if it means that the figure gains a certain attractiveness in consequence.

Courage is, in this sense, the most vital of all his creations. The sense of movement in this book is even stronger than in the *Simplicissimus.* There does not seem to be a quiet fibre in her body. She knows the value of reputation and of stability, and she is well aware that the world of war is dominated by instability and Fortune.[32] But the basic principle of her life is movement rather than rest. Not even the best-fortified town, she says, can protect her and her goods " ... against the military power of those who lodge in huts and tents in the open field and move around from one place to another" (124). She seeks her safety among the soldiers, just as at the end, she finally takes refuge ("nahm ... endlich ... Zuflucht": 141) among the gypsies. There is no presence of the Divine in her life, no calm centre of constancy, no Einsiedel to provide a standard and a reminder or to turn the knowledge of God she has acquired from conventional instruction into a real experience. She plunges into the flux of the world when, in the guise of war, it confronts her. This is not inexperience, but her "nature." She is the most willing victim imaginable of the war and the world, for she is full of a dangerous curiosity ("Fürwitz": 17: a warning to us, of course) that fills her head with "Grillen und Dauben" (cranks and caprices). She enjoys the disruption that the war brings. Her heart "leaps up" (20) when she hears the sound of fife and drum, cannon and trumpet. When she lives "an honest, pious, quiet and withdrawn life," it is "against [her] will" (52), and at a crucial moment, at the beginning of chapter 15, when "honour," "wisdom," and "reason" speak in favour of withdrawing from the ambit of the war to a comfortable and quiet life, " ... liese [sie ihrer] unbesonnenen Jugend weder Weißheit noch Vernunft einreden / sondern je toller das Bier gebrauet wurde / je besser es [ihr] schmeckte" ([her] heedless youth would listen to neither wisdom nor reason; rather, the headier the brew, the better [she] liked it: 77). She may see the practical unwisdom of her former behaviour, but there is no indication that she is looking back with regret, whatever thought the terminology she uses may evoke in *our* minds. The vicissitudes and movement of the war constitute the element in which she can most easily shine: it is as an Amazon that she comes closest to being the "etwas ehrliches" (something honest: 57) that she feels her second husband, the only one she may have truly loved, deserved to have.

It is hardly surprising that the brutal and occasionally even comic events of the war are conveyed, if anything, even more graphically in this book than in *Simplicissimus*, where it often tends to occur in a more generalised, stylised, or even allegorical form. The famous description of the Battle of Wittstock contains detail that is in itself gruesome, but makes a less sharp impact by virtue of the fact that the whole is a formal accumulative set piece. Nothing in it has quite the force of the moment in *Courasche* when an enemy soldier tries to rescue Courage's prisoner and fires off his pistol: "daß mir Hut und Federn darvon stobe . . . [ich] bezahlte ihn dergestalt mit meinem Sebel / daß er noch etliche Schritte ohne Kopff mit mir ritte / welches verwunderlich und abscheulich anzusehen war" (. . . so that my hat flew off, feathers and all. I paid him out so thoroughly with my sabre that for a few strides, he was riding headless alongside me; a sight both strange and gruesome: 45). The viciousness of the war is not disguised ("most people become worse, rather than better in wartime": 48), but neither is its vitality. Courage can even describe the Battle of Wimpfen as "lustig" (jolly: 40). It is in this dynamic and disorderly environment that she is truly active and alive and her continued existence in the gypsy community, outside the social order, is a natural extension of it.

War per se is not a vehicle for didacticism. It is a location of death, and — at the same time — of vivid life, even comedy. Its ambivalence, and the naturally realistic tendency of this book, are well exemplified by chapter 26, the last in which Courage still retains a formal connection with army life. Having been expelled from Offenburg, she is on the move again, hoping to find (what else?) another husband and an improvement in her fortunes. But she is set upon by a party of musketeers. Yet again the woman (admittedly herself a predator), seems fated to become the victim of violence and violation. She is saved, on this occasion, from gang-rape by the fact that one of the musketeers is attracted to her and so, in unexpected fashion, she does acquire another husband. It is not much of a bargain, but, as she says, " . . . what else could or should I have done? Better to let this one have his way with a good grace than find myself compelled by force to give the whole party what he was asking for out of love" (136). There is nothing lively or attractive about this description, but nothing remotely emotional or moral either. Both narrator and author are simply concerned with registering the plain facts of a bleak life.

Courage starts on the way back by setting up a small trade in tobacco and brandy. And Grimmelshausen conveys to us the effort, the pain and the strength of will involved:

> Es kam mich blutsauer an / so zu Fuß daher zu marchiren / und noch darzu einen schweren Pack zu tragen / neben dem / daß es auch zu Zeiten schmal essen und trincken setzte / welches unangenehmlichen Dings ich mein Lebtag nicht versucht / viel weniger gewohnet hatte. . . .
> (136–7)

> [It was a terrible grind for me, having to march along on foot and carry a heavy pack into the bargain, in addition to which food and drink were in short supply at times; an uncongenial state of affairs I had never tasted in my life before, much less been used to. . . .]

There is no didactic or allegorical purpose here, just the graphic realisation of a character setting out once again, in fulfilment of the law of life, to climb a steep hill from the very bottom. And she does begin to make progress, symbolised by the acquisition of a good, fast-running mule (an asset which will stand her in good stead in the sequel). But then the war, or her "fatum" as she calls it, brings it all to an end at the Battle of Herbsthausen. This is the point at which she leaves the military world, and becomes a gypsy.

But the musketeer has one more function to fulfil. Grimmelshausen makes another of the deliberate sideways steps in his narrative technique to which we have already referred, and moves into the mode of storytelling for its own sake. We have been prepared for this to some extent by the chapter heading (by Greifnson-Grimmelshausen?), which announces "ein recht lächerlicher Poß" (135). In the text itself, Courage demonstratively breaks off the thread of her "Histori" and addresses not Simplicissimus, with whom she has kept up a running dialogue (which, incidentally, helps us in our mental orientation), but the reader directly, using the noun "Stückel" (that is, *Stücklein*), in combination with the adjective "artlich," an indication of a narrative that will be lively and amusing: "Ehe ich aber fortfahre / solchen meinen Lebens-Lauf weiters hinaus zu erzehlen / so wil ich dem Leser zuvor ein artliches Stückel eröffnen (But before I go on to relate the further story of my life, I would like to regale the reader with a jolly little anecdote: 137).

It is a story that contains both the solidly real, bleak brutality of the war and the element of cussed, in its way glorious humour that is part of the principle of life, and is called forth here by a combination of the stupidity of the musketeer with that of the peasants: the military and the civil in comic concert. The dualism of cold and warmth provides a neat counterpoint. In a winter frost in which the world is as hard as iron, the musketeer is sent on a secret mission disguised as a carpenter. On his way back, taking a byway through the wilderness, he stumbles on a dead body so richly apparelled that it must be that of an officer, perhaps dead of the cold, perhaps murdered by the denizens of the Black Forest. Nothing could be more anonymous and desolate. Who the man was, how he died, it is all the same to him ("doch galte das ihm gleich": 138). The body is just a body ("Cörper"): all the musketeer cares about is the clothes. He strips off the upper garment and wants to take the scarlet breeches as well. But after he has taken the boots off, a problem arises:

> Als er aber die Hosen herab streiffte / wolten solche nicht hotten / weil die Feuchtigkeit des allbereit verwesenden Cörpers sich unter den Knien herum / allwo man dazumal die Hosenbändel zu binden pflegte / sich beydes in das Futter und den Überzug gesetzt hatte / und dannenhero Schenckel und Hosen wie ein Stein zusammen gefroren waren. (138)

> [But when he came to pull off the breeches, they wouldn't budge, because all round the legs under the knees, where it was then the custom to tie the knee-bands, the fluids of the already decomposing body had got into both the lining and the outer cloth, and so breeches and thighs were frozen together as hard as stone.]

The detail of the body is grim, but specific and substantial. This is neither an allegorical shell to be cracked nor a mere example from which we are to abstract some general truth, but an unsentimental statement of the raw, bare facts of death. It can certainly be said to embody the brutality of war, but it is as individually real as anything in *War and Peace*. And alongside it stands the living musketeer, untroubled by thoughts of mortality, greedy for the dead man's rich clothes and rather stupid. He can think of nothing better than to chop off the corpse's lower half, pack it into a bundle and carry it off with him. Life is beginning to show its grotesque and curious, and even comic side. The man takes refuge in a building belonging to a farmer, where he is allowed to bed down behind the warm stove.

With the introduction of the motif of warmth, the inscrutably comic conjunctions of our earthly existence begin to make themselves felt. The farmer's cow has just calved and the frail little creature is placed in the warmth, beside the "carpenter," for the night. Events unfold with an almost Sophoclean inevitability. The frozen legs thaw out, the musketeer removes the breeches, turns them inside out and puts them on and decamps through the window, leaving behind his rags, an innocent new-born calf, and the lower half of a human being. When the cow-maid comes upon this scene in the morning, a rich comic chaos ensues, described in a passage which is unfortunately too long to be quoted in full. What should be done with this monstrous little animal? With a self-irony in which he indulges on more than one occasion in the cycle, Grimmelshausen brings in the village *Schultheiss* (mayor or magistrate), who is as much at a loss as the others:

der liesse alsobald der Gemein zusammen leuten / um das Hauß gesamter hand zu stürmen / und diesen gemeinen Feind des menschlichen Geschlechts / ehe er gar zu einer Kuhe aufwüchse / bey zeiten auszureuten. . . . (139)

[And he had the bells rung to call the whole parish together, so that they might storm the house in a body and extirpate this common enemy of the human race betimes, before it could grow up to become a veritable cow.]

Heroes, however, are in short supply, and the final solution adopted is to burn the building down and compensate the farmer from the common chest. This leads Courage to think that if he can be so fortunate by accident, her new husband might, with a little tuition from her, become a new Springinsfeld. But the man lacks the necessary talents and in any case, is soon brusquely despatched at the Battle of Herbsthausen.

While the chapter does offer, in its opening, an opportunity for moral reflection in the reminder of *vanitas* when the fading of Courage's beauty is mentioned, it is the immanent power of life, hard and comic, cold and warm, that has been dominant. There is nothing here that obviously furthers the narrator's aim of bathing Simplicissimus in reflected ignominy, or the author's ironic purpose of underpinning a moral theme. We see Courage first as the survivor, then as the realistic and relaxed, indeed thoroughly Simplician narrator of a comic "Posse."

She goes on to tell of her escape from Herbsthausen and her career as a gypsy, cutting the account short and leaving it open-ended, after a further two chapters, with a final re-iteration of the "Spite-Simplex" motif. It is true that in doing this, she makes a series of negative comments about the gypsy life, and that by referring to her initial change of complexion as the adoption of "what people call the Devil's colour" (141), she opens the path of moral reflection once more, but the fact that she even laughs at the radical change in her appearance and circumstances, and finds the gypsy life so attractive that she "wouldn't have changed places with a Colonel's wife" (141: recalling the insouciance of the book's opening chapter) prevents us from remaining exclusively tied to that path. We cannot brush aside the presence and personality of Courage the narrator. In similar fashion, the thunderous condemnation of prostitution in the scribe's "Zugab," or supplementary remarks (copied from Garzoni), is balanced by the recrudescence, in the editor's concluding paragraph, of that lively, mischievous tone of which we cannot entirely approve, but from which we find it impossible entirely to dissociate ourselves: "Reibet ihm darneben trefflich ein / wie meisterlich sie ihn hingegen bezahlt / und betrogen habe" (At the same time, she makes him thoroughly aware of the masterly fashion in which she has paid him out and taken him in: 149).

In the *Springinsfeld* (where, of course, she is not able to stand up for herself), it is revealed that in thinking that she had deceived Simplicissimus, she was deceiving herself. Springinsfeld, who has a score to settle, is allowed to abuse her in choice terms, Philarchus (whom she has also bested and duped) is none too complimentary, and Simplicissimus describes her as being in imminent danger of damnation. None of this should be allowed to reflect back on her own book, which is, from a viewpoint that takes the next world into account, the dark self-revelation of a vicious and hardened sinner, and at the same time, a splendidly lively reflection of the vitality of life in this one. The ironic technique enables the reader to savour the latter, without being drawn into complicity with the former.

Notes

[1] M. Feldges, *Grimmelshausens "Landstörtzerin Courasche,"* 189. She is seen as a "Beispiel der verkehrten Welt" (105). For the theme of "Verkehrte Welt" see also H. A. Arnold, "Moralisch-didaktische Elemente und ihre Darstellung in Grimmelshausens Roman 'Courasche,'" *Zeitschrift für Deutsche Philologie* 88 (1969), 521–60.

[2] Cf. Meid, *Grimmelshausen: Epoche-Werk-Wirkung*, 160.

[3] Siegfried Streller, *Grimmelshausens Simplicianische Schriften: Allegorie, Zahl und Wirklichkeitsdarstellung* (Berlin 1957), 203. She is the "Frauenbild des personifizierten Sündenfalls."

[4] See particularly H. M. Enzensberger's "Nachwort" to the DTV edition of *Courasche* (Munich, 1963) and Arnold, "Moralisch-didaktische Elemente," 522, n. 2. Meid (*Grimmelshausen*) sees Enzensberger's view as "nicht unbegründet," but only for the character, not the novel as a whole (161).

[5] Feldges, 189.

[6] Arnold, "Moralisch-didaktische Elemente," 559.

[7] The book is in fact dictated to a scribe, Philarchus Grossus von Trommerheim (Grimmelshausen as a "Schreiber"!), who is allowed to add only a brief, if vituperative "Zugab"(addendum), but this is too little, too late, and its rhetorical vehemence suggests a lack of objectivity. This is in turn followed by an editor's postscript in which the point of view from which the main text is written is reasserted.

[8] *Francion*, I: 62. Agathe is "consoled," she says, by the thought that she has used her charms (when she had them) "to good effect" ("Je les ay assez bien employez": 70). To live without a man for a whole year, says Courage, is for her "gar schwer und gantz wider die Natur" (very hard and entirely against nature). Koschlig (*Das Ingenium Grimmelshausens*, 72), makes it seem likely that the figure of Agathe influenced the portrayal of the old procuress in the Paris episode of *Simplicissimus*. It is not unthinkable that this influence could have stretched to the *Courasche*.

[9] Cf. S. Streller, "'Ob gienge ich zuviel Satyricè drein.' Traditionslinien und Wandlungen in Grimmelshausens Satireauffassung," *Simpliciana* 15 (1993), 41.

[10] "Zur Wahrheitsbesessenheit emanzipiert": Cf. "Nachwort" to *Courasche* (Ed. Weydt [Stuttgart: Reclam, 1971], 170). We have tried to show that Courage is a

vehicle for human vitality, but in no way "emancipated." She can appreciate freedom in the social sphere, but is spiritually as un-free as it is possible to be!

[11] Ibid., 143 "... vom gütigen Himmel beschützt." The word "gütig" (benevolent) here could well be a hint from Grimmelshausen that we should be aware of a point of view other than Courage's.

[12] James Hogg: *Confessions of a Justified Sinner* (reprint, London: Everyman, 1992), 94, 198.

[13] J.-M. Valentin, "Théologie et esthétique, sur le chapitre premier de la *Landstörtzerin Courasche*," *Études Germaniques* 42 (1987), 286 ff. Valentin's main concern is the "deconfessionalisation" of the picaresque novel.

[14] See Ägidius Albertinus, *Gusman von Alfarche* (1615; reprint, Hildesheim 1975), 448.

[15] For example, J. H. Petersen, "Formen der Icherzählung," 504. Petersen, however, seems to wish that we see Courage too exclusively from the negative (sinful) perspective.

[16] Feldges, 155.

[17] *Vogelnest*, 109: "ein schwaches Weibsbilde ... das mit dieser unsichtbaren Kranckheit der Liebe behafftet / und dardurch ... aller Sinn und rechthafften Gebrauch ihrer Vernunfft beraubt ist."

[18] G. P. Harsdörffer, *Grosser Schau-Platz jämmerlicher Mordgeschichte*, 20.

[19] Cf. *Springinsfeld*, 30, where the word "Lumpen-Gesindel" is also used. Grimmelshausen uses it again, this time with reference to the tribe of beggars, in part 1 of *Das wunderbarliche Vogelnest* (24).

[20] Feldges, 88.

[21] *Courasche*, 95. For the "spiritus familiaris," cf. also my article: "Narrative and Satire in Grimmelshausen and Beer," *MLR* 70 (1975), especially 811. For Simplicius as "alter Kracher," see *Rathstübel Plutonis*, 74.

[22] Weydt, *Nachahmung*, 81. Weydt wishes to promote a story by Harsdörffer (which Grimmelshausen certainly knew and used in the *Ewigwährender Kalender*) as a source, but it can have at best little more than a scene-setting significance. The development of the theme of a woman in a man's world is entirely Grimmelshausen's.

[23] Feldges, 44–77. Cf. also H. A. Arnold, "Die Rollen der Courasche," in *Die Frau von der Reformation zur Romantik*, ed. B. Becker-Cantarino (Bonn 1980), 86–111, and Streller, *Grimmelshausens Simplicianische Schriften*, 52, 193.

[24] For this theme, cf. A. Solbach, "Macht und Sexualität der Hexenfigur in Grimmelshausen's *Courasche*," *Simpliciana* 8 (1986), 72.

[25] "An sich selbst schwache und geile Creaturen": *Vogelnest*, 46.

[26] "Der Courage wird ihre treffliche Courage auch trefflich eingetränckt."

[27] "I had deserved it by my previous behaviour": Grimmelshausen may be trying to imply that she had made herself fair game, to a certain extent, by her activities as a

prostitute. There is no question of *condoning* what has gone on, on his part or anyone else's (62).

[28] Cf. my article "The three functions of Hugo Peter in Gryphius's *Carolus Stuardus*," MLR 68 (1973), 839–42.

[29] Ägidius Albertinus, *Hirnschleiffer*, ed. L. S. Larsen, Bibliothek des Literaturvereins in Stuttgart 299, (Stuttgart: Hiersemann, 1977), 113. The work was known to Grimmelshausen (cf. Weydt, *Nachahmung*, 414).

[30] Grimmelshausen seems to have accepted that it was the ambition of wives to rule their husbands. Abisag, in *Ratio Status*, is described as being "ohne das geneigt / wie andere Weiber vel clam, vel vi, vel precario das Regiment zuführen" (59).

[31] E.g. "Ach was ist alles dis was wir vor köstlich achten / ... Als eine wiesen blum / die man nicht wiederfindt" [Oh, what is all this that we esteem to be so precious ... but a flower of the field, which we shall never find again?]. (Andreas Gryphius, *Sonette*, ed. M. Szyrocki [Tübingen 1963], 34). Biblical references include Ps. 103:15, James 1, 10–11, and several others.

[32] Cf. *Courasche* 103: "Glücks- und Unglücks-Fäll (deren es unterschiedliche im Kriege abgibt)."

6: The Soldier's Tale: *Der seltzame Springinsfeld*

THE OPENING NINE chapters of *Der seltzame Springinsfeld* introduce an important new note into the Simplician sequence, namely the everyday, relatively settled reality of the peacetime world. There has been peace before, of course, in the later stages of the *Simplicissimus* and during the *Continuatio*, but in neither case was the major figure of the story truly integrated into that world. And while we knew intellectually that the narrator's present was part of the equation, the main orientation was towards life beyond, rather than within it. Actuality was the unsettled world of war: the sense of time and place in the peacetime episodes is at best vague and the sense of abstraction — indeed alienation — from the everyday world correspondingly strong (for example the "Mummelsee," "Baldanders," and "Schermesser" episodes, Simplicius as vagrant, the Isle of the Crosses). Now, we are in a very specific place and time: Strasbourg, Christmastide 1669–70, a time when the appearance of the *Courasche*, already published in fact and presumably known to the reader, can be referred to in the story as imminent. The social theme, which still, of course, has a moral and religious content, has acquired more prominence and is underpinned by the polarity of the motifs of warmth (inside) and cold (outside the circle). War and the past still impinge through the narrator Springinsfeld, but the ex-musketeer Greifnson is no longer with us, and the scribe, together with other figures whom we shall meet, belongs to a generation with a future.

Simplicius has returned from the island and settled as a farmer and head of a household that includes his "Knan" and "Meuder" and the Young Simplicius, his adopted natural son. The two poles in the novel, the rich man's household in chapter 1, in which the "scribe" of the novel, Philarchus, vainly and mistakenly seeks a niche, and the inn in chapter 2 where he finds warmth and at least a degree of integration, are both rendered graphically and concretely and provide a solid social framework. Simplicius is no longer a soldier or a *picaro*, though still "seltzam" (it is his "seltzamer Auffzug," [odd appearance] indeed, that first attracts Philarchus's attention [13] and this quality is evoked in the "Gaukeltasche" episode in chapter 7, without in any way inhibiting, or being inhibited by the undeniable symbolic poetological significance). The only figure left entirely in the cold is the gypsy Courage; Philarchus enters the inn in search of physical warmth, as does Springinsfeld himself, though he is still at that point mentally and physically a vagrant. The issue in this, the present part of the action, is whether he will stay, whether he will at last become integrated and join the peace. Peace is not a solution to all problems, of course, and in particular not to that of the search for constancy, and it is not a theme for treatment in the present book, but rather in the two *Vogelnest* novels. Here, we are brought just to the brink. This helps to explain the apparent paradox that though we have talked much of peace and of warmth, the bulk of the *Springinsfeld* is dominated by war, and by the cold of winter. At the centre stands the soldier, not the Christian, but the seventeenth-century mercenary soldier, both young and old.

The title sequence[1] shows Springinsfeld simultaneously carrying the beggar's fiddle and wearing the soldier's sword, and the one, as we shall argue, is in his case the logical continuation of the other. The novel falls into two parts, in each of which Springinsfeld features as the focus of attention. As an itinerant beggar, he is introduced to Simplicius's domestic circle and way of life (chapters 1–9) — a sequence narrated by Philarchus who, it turns out, has perforce been Courage's scribe — and then he tells the company his own life history ("Lebenslauff") as they lie snug in their communal bedroom at the inn through the cold winter's night, arriving back at the present in the final chapter for the winding-up of the story. Springinsfeld, we learn in a postscript, is eventually persuaded to go and live on Simplicissimus's farm, where he soon dies, after his former comrade has managed to effect the conversion that he failed to achieve in the story proper.

It is common practice to apply the terminology of the *Rahmenerzahlung* (frame-story),[2] a structure often employed in the German *Novelle*, to the *Springinsfeld*, and there clearly is a similarity, but this does not exhaust the function of the novel's opening sequence. There have been moments previously at which it has been possible to suggest that Grimmelshausen was beginning to think in terms of a wider Simplician unity that could embrace all the multifarious activity and the multiplicity of agents that he was deploying. Here, it seems that we can discern the emergence of a network of characters and events; a simultaneous awareness of strands that may be distinct and may run along different lines, but are also interconnected and interrelated. They are not brought together, but we are made aware of their simultaneity within a wider context.

In this novel, clearly, Springinsfeld stands at the centre, in explicit or implicit dialogue with Simplicius. The latter is a major player in the action of the first nine chapters, and the last one. It is he who causes the story to be told (and written down, as the title page informs us) and he is the chief listener. Courage (who may not be far away) is brought in through Philarchus, who was her unwilling guest while he wrote down her life history (the impending publication of which hangs like a cloud over the heads of the assembled company). He gives a detailed account of her present appearance and way of life. With the development of Springinsfeld, who, like Courage, appeared briefly in the original novel, the point has been reached where the past can be said to have "caught up" with the present. We seem to be at a crossroads. A younger generation, including the Young Simplicius and (later in the book) the halberdier and the Leirerin, whose influence survives her through the magic bird's nest, point towards the future.

The Soldier and the Beggar

The soldier-beggar theme, a traditional, indeed proverbial one which has already appeared in the *Simplicissimus* (e.g. *ST* 266: "Junge Soldaten / alte Bettler"), is present in all the elements of the title sequence of *Der seltzame Springinsfeld*, and Simplicius brings it to the fore again when he gives up, for the moment, the attempt to draw Springinsfeld into the social fold and invites him instead to relate his life story. How did he become a soldier, and how did he degenerate into "such a miserable hobbling cripple"? ("zu einem solchen elenden Steltzer": 56).

The change from soldier to beggar is put here in very stark terms, more so than in the aforementioned title sequence, for if the Springinsfeld shown in the engraving is perhaps down on his luck, he is most clearly not down and out, and while the title page describes him as raddled and emaciated, it then lightens the mood by telling us that he is a "really crafty" old so-and-so. He is not ready to lie down to be pitied or derided. From the moment (in chapter 2) when he jokes about the loss of his leg and welcomes the reunion with his old comrade in arms with a soldierly expletive,[3] we can see that the spirit that saw him through sundry wars, with their privations, illnesses, and injuries of which he bears the outward and visible signs, is still alive and able and willing to kick. He demonstrates in the same chapter that he is by no means destitute, and, as Simplicius points out in reproving his hotheaded behaviour, he behaves in the inn exactly as if he were back in Soest, where he was Simplicius's right-hand man in many an escapade (cf. *Simplicissimus* books II and III), and as if the Thirty Years' War were still in progress.[4] He still thinks as a soldier in his altercation with Simplicius's "Meuder" (chapter 13), and when he is commenting on the reluctance of soldiers to quit the martial profession, in spite of its miseries and vicissitudes, he exclaims: "nicht weiß ich was vor eine Art einer sonderbaren unbesonnenen Unsinnigkeit *uns* behafftet"(I don't know what kind of crazy, heedless madness it is that afflicts *us:* 79) The actual soldier in him is still very much alive, just as, through his birth and early experience, the "Gaukler," the itinerant juggler, was part of him *before* he became a soldier. It may well be that, as the the verses appended to the title put it, "young soldiers [become] old beggars," but the opposition between "young" and "old" is greater than that between "soldier" and "beggar." The duality, we begin to see, is a Simplician one. The figure is both representative — of the world of war and the life of the soldier, which in turn represents man cut off from God and at the mercy of Fortune — and at the same time individual and real.

Without in any way implying that the role played by war in the lives of Simplicissimus and Courage is not an important one, it is possible to argue that it is more of a real presence in that of Springinsfeld, who comes closest of all among Grimmelshausen's major figures to embodying the mercenary soldier of the period. The essentially cold brutality of war is reflected in the novel's imagery and mood, prefigured, perhaps, in the episode in *Courasche* discussed in our last chapter, in which Courage's last husband discovers the frozen corpse.[5] But even there, the brutality of the man's death is incidental and the whole is strongly tinged with comedy. When Springinsfeld "puts an end to the bitter remnant of pleading life" in a wounded officer whom he finds while scavenging on the battlefield at Nördlingen (83) there is no such relief, and the figure of Springinsfeld becomes the epitome of the mercenary. He is without a horse and in very low water financially, and the army takes no notice of him and gives him nothing to do. His instincts are still soldierly, but not regimental, "demnach mirs gleich golte / ob Kayser oder Schwed siegen würde / wann ich nur mein Theil auch darvon kriegte" (so that it made no difference to me who won, the emperor or the Swede, as long as I could make something out of it for myself: 82).

This chapter, indeed, belongs to a clear sequence in which the themes of war and soldiering are concentrated on, not allegorically, since there is an insufficient degree of alienation from reality for this, but in representative form. Chapter 14 contains an heroic set piece (the Battle of Lützen) in which the spirit of the "two valiant heroes" Pappenheim and Gustavus Adolphus infects the whole armies (78). It is followed, after a typically sudden transition in Springinsfeld's fortunes from prosperity to misery, by the account of his ironically described "heroic behaviour" (81) at Nördlingen and in chapter 16 by the episode (to be discussed in detail later) in which our hero is besieged by a pack of wolves. It is no accident, surely, that this latter chapter is introduced with a description of the plagues of war (84), which makes us think of the Four Horsemen of the Apocalypse.

Soldiering as an ethos and a condition has entered into Springinsfeld's bones. He speaks of the army and of war as an insider. This is anything but an idealisation of the soldier's life, but there is a sense of a soldierly ethos to which Springinsfeld, though he is no systematic thinker, in his way subscribes. Together with the Leirerin (whose position we shall consider later), he is the main vehicle in the book, not of social criticism in a systematic sense, but of Grimmelshausen's appreciation that the underdog and the excluded have their own individual reality and perspective on life, and of his inability to give his full emotional commitment to a class structure which, in preference to disorder, he endorsed intellectually and within which he himself was attempting to climb. Haberkamm, indeed, sees the astrological references (particularly those of the heading of chapter 2, which characterises Philarchus as Mercury, Simplicius as Saturn, and Springinsfeld as Mars) as intended to "functionalise" the elements of rebelliousness in the book and remove some of its immediate political sting.[6] But while his attitude to civil order is ambivalent, Springinsfeld certainly endorses order in the military field. When there is a mutiny (chapter 20), he stands apart from it and clearly does not approve of the removal of proper authority ("billiche Gewalt") from the officers.[7] The whole episode is treated, in fact, as a baroque comedy ("ein artliches Spiel": 102) in which incompetents attempt to play the roles allotted to their betters. Springinsfeld is critical, certainly, of the almost insuperable obstacles placed in the way of the common soldier who seeks promotion, but appreciates, as his praise of the general, Mercy, at the beginning of chapter 18 shows, the merits of an army run with the proper "Ordre."

Springinsfeld's is very much the perspective of the common fighting soldier: crude, not to say brutal at times, often amoral, but also with a kind of honour within his own lights. He sees nothing wrong in stripping a dead body, or in stealing from peasants, but he uses without irony words like "ehrlich" (honourable, though not in the sense of middle-class respectability!), "redlich" (honest), "rechtschaffen" (upright) and even "ritterlich" (chivalrous, valiant) to describe the soldier who, whatever the conditions, simply does his job as best he can, and accepts that this may mean the loss of his own life, though certainly not in a sacrificial sense.[8] He speaks, for example, of the general, Melander, who failed to achieve victory, but gave his all, even his life, as a "rechtschaffener Soldat" (an upright soldier: 101). Even when he has been tricked into joining the Venetian army, he fights like "ein ehrlicher Landsknecht"(122) to defend "our miserable pile of stones" (121). When he loses his leg, what saves him from being abandoned by the Venetians (who, he says scathingly, tend to throw away their soldiers as they do their brooms, when they have worn them out) is that he is known as the epitome of a good soldier ("ein Ausbund von einem guten Soldaten": 123). On the other hand, he is no idealistic *miles Christianus*, touches of whom we have seen in Simplicissimus's friend Herzbruder, but very much the real seventeeth-century mercenary, a man who, as we have seen, may have a certain soldierly ethos, but whose highest priority is to look after himself. Herzbruder makes the pilgrimage to Einsiedeln on hard, dry peas: Springinsfeld would have followed Simplicissimus's example and boiled his: that is, if the idea of going on a pilgrimage with a friend — assuming that he had one — could have come into his head at all.

In Springinsfeld's world, then — and this is Springinsfeld's book, after all — we are not in the world of allegory, and if war is a "negatives Exempel", to use Volker Meid's expression,[9] it is not so in the sense of a medieval *exemplum*. In what we have called its representative role, it is an image of instability, the world of men without God and dominated by Fortune. Fortune and the soldier have a special relationship, as emerges in the "spendthrift" chapter (11), which can be said to have been lifted out of the narrative mainstream sufficiently to acquire a representative function, in particular in the Lumpus story.

Fortune as the whimsical goddess, the directing hand of mere worldly history for great and small alike, certainly exists in the *Springinsfeld*. It is evoked, in more or less allegorical form, in the verses that serve as *subscriptio* to the frontispiece. But for the most part, it appears as the soldier sees it, as the good, or — more frequently — bad luck enjoyed or suffered by our hero in his efforts to make progress if possible, or at least to survive on ground that is never still and firm beneath his feet. Springinsfeld's perspective is predominantly that of the outsider, but although he shares Courage's fatalism, he is not, as we have seen, a total rebel, like her or his "second and much worse Courage" (119), the Leirerin, both of whom are presented as patterns of *Leichtfertigkeit*. (That Springinsfeld is capable of seeing them as such distinguishes his situation from theirs). He has some concept of honour as a soldier, and periodically entertains hopes of achieving officer status and becoming a "Kerl von aestimation" (a man of some standing: 92), hopes that are, of course, comprehensively dashed. Money is the key to advancement, and only Fortune, by sending him good luck in the search for booty (the soldier's first thought as soon as bare survival is assured) can give him that key. But even when he gets his hands on wealth momentarily, he can never hang on to it, and this is the theme of the eleventh chapter, to which the Lumpus episode belongs.

This chapter is detached from the main flow of the story in a marked manner. It is placed between Springinsfeld's account of his campaigns in Spinola's army, when all went well for him, and his entry into the "German War," the Thirty Years' War proper. It is, as Simplicius points out at the beginning of chapter 12, a blatant digression from the thread of Springinsfeld's life history, and takes the ostensible form of the narration of stories with a distinctly curious twist; anecdotes, as the heading has it, "concerning three remarkable spendthrifts" ("Von dreyen merckwürdigen Verschwendern"). But there is a strong hint of its representative function in the introduction, which is a general reflection on the soldier's life and his inability, unless favoured with the aid of "der gütige Himmel" (kind heaven: 60), to take advantage of the "great good fortune" of a rich booty to break loose from that life. This is a rare flash of transcendental awareness within Springinsfeld's narrative, though whether it reflects insight on the part of the narrator, for whom such kindness might well be just another kind of luck, is another matter. There is no clear evidence, even in the final conversation of the book, that Springinsfeld could say, with the Simplicius of the *Rathstübel Plutonis*, "I am now no longer as silly and heedless as I was when I took everything as it came, as good or bad luck."[10]

After two brief anecdotes concerning soldiers who found and gambled away a fortune, we come to the Lumpus story, which occupies four-fifths of the chapter. Its basic format is that of the exemplary tale, though it develops the element of eccentricity implicit in the word "merkwürdig" (remarkable) into an individual portrait with a much stronger sense of reality than Harsdörffer, in his collections of novellas, does his "merckwürdige" or "denkwürdige Erzehlungen." Lumpus is no pale stereotype, but a colourful figure embodying characteristics of the actual mercenary soldier and his life. He is a fool, and his final condition is one of misery, but he has his own essentially fatalistic soldier's insight. He feels instinctively that he stands no chance of breaking out of his social environment, so he resolves to take a holiday from the grind of servitude and spend every penny of the money he has found on an eight-week spree — as if he were a "great Lord" who never has to worry about not having enough money — simply because he has "always wanted to know what it felt like" (65). He knows that he can have this experience only for a short time, and takes measures, indeed, to ensure that he will escape punishment for desertion when eventually he returns to the ranks. Luxury is a dream, but why not enjoy the dream briefly? It is significant that our final impression of Lumpus is not the picture of misery seen by Springinsfeld at the end of the war (with which the narrative is prefaced) but the image of a man who may fall short of wisdom, but who has some spirit and imagination: Lumpus as survivor, rather than merely as a pitiable or contemptible failure.

The feeling, then, is of a hard life, punctuated by flashes of luck, but exposed to "erbärmliche Zufäll" (miserable mischances: 79) and above all, plagued by instability and inconstancy. The hard historical facts and grand strategies of the Thirty Years' War itself, the to-and-fro of the armies, the successes and failures of generals, the litanies of towns taken or lost rattling past so quickly that we can hardly register them individually, are obviously all things that have an impact on Springinsfeld's life, but one feels that they go on at a remove from him, above his head, so to speak. This impression is strengthened by the matter-of-fact, almost expressionless prose — Meid calls it "holzschnittartig": like a woodcut; Streller refers to its "dürre Trockenheit" (arid dryness)[11] — in which much of this material is narrated. Individual episodes can have animation and profile, but war as a general phenomenon is like an impersonal tide of constant inconstancy and movement, sweeping the hero hither and thither.

The episode that stands out most of all and contrasts, in its method and manner, most vividly with that low-key general narrative style, is the one in chapter 16 in which Springinsfeld, on a lone secret mission, enters a deserted village and is driven by a pack of wolves onto the roof of a house, on which precarious perch he spends a most uncomfortable and fearful time in the cold of a November night. The main reason given for telling this story, which is characterised as "ein Poß" (a comic episode), is that it is "so seltzam / verwunderlich und mir eine so schlechte Kurtzweil gewesen / daß ich ihn erzehlen muß" (87: So curious and amazing and such an uncomfortable experience for me that I have to tell it). An important part of the motivation is that it is simply a good story, with the inherent potential to amaze and amuse. This function it certainly fulfils, and the stylistic animation and graphic quality that it arouses create a strong sense of a narrative reality, which militates against that degree of alienation that allegory requires. And while it presents an extreme case, it is not far removed from the actuality of the Thirty Years' War. In Renchen itself, as Bechtold reports, a mere seventeen out of a hundred and eighty inhabitants remained in 1649: "Um die menschenleeren Wohnstätten und Gehöfte strichen nächtlicherweile hungernde Wölfe aus den umliegenden Wäldern."[12] At the same time, it is undoubtedly a piece of what we have called representative writing. Grimmelshausen takes care to mark it off from the surrounding narrative by emphasising its digressive nature. It is "von keiner Importanz," as it makes no real contribution to the life history, but the writer *must* break off the thread of his main "Histori" to tell it. He then hints at a representative function: "in spite of the fact that there are many (among my readers) who, being unaware of the miserable state of ruination to which Germany was then reduced, are not going to believe me." (87)

This is, then, at one and the same time a vivid tale of a man in a predicament at once comic and dangerous, and an image of the war, an even more powerful one than the account of the pillaging of the farm in *Simplicissimus*, which we discussed in chapter 2. War is the cause of much individual suffering and death; beyond that, it is a general breakdown of order, a "verkehrte Welt." Confronted by a wolf, advancing (like an enemy army) upon him with gaping jaws, Springinsfeld conducts a "retreat" into what should be a safe redoubt: a house meant for human habitation. The distinction between savagery and civilisation has, however, been lost, and Grimmelshausen presents this in a characteristically Simplician fashion, in which the coexistence of the strands of the comic and real and the serious and symbolic is apparent:

> Ich gedachte wohl nit / daß mir der Wolff in das Haus nachfolgen würde / aber er war so unverschämt / daß er den Orth nicht respectirte, der zur menschlichen Wohnung gewidmet worden / sonder zottelte in einem reputirlichen Wolffgang fein allgemach hernach. . . . (87–8)

> [It did not enter my head that the wolf would follow me into the house, but with a brazen lack of respect for the dignity of a place designated for human habitation, he came ambling in after me with the leisurely gait of a well-bred wolf.]

Springinsfeld goes upstairs, but the wolf shows that "he too can climb a staircase," and our hero is reduced to scrambling through a skylight and bombarding his adversary, who has now been joined by his "comrades" (the whole process is narrated in terms of a military action), with roof tiles. It is a beautifully controlled piece of Simplician storytelling, in which humour and seriousness (indeed actual and potential tragedy) run smoothly side by side on parallel tracks.

In spite of all Springinsfeld's efforts, the wolves set up and maintain a "siege or blockade"(88). From this point on, the tale takes a sinister turn, and our thoughts move from the war proper to the idea of isolation: Springinsfeld literally and perhaps also spiritually out in the cold. The exposed and dangerous nature of his situation is highlighted: the "pitch-black night," "sharp, cutting winds with intermingled flakes of snow," and the harsh ("grausam" — literally, cruel) howling of the wolves which seems almost to have the power to draw him down from the roof have a spiritual as well as a physical impact and drive him to the point where, in extremis, the thought of the torments of the damned in hell enters his mind. The introduction of this theme, rendered in a sombre, rhetorically pointed prose that contrasts noticeably with what has gone before, cannot but raise thoughts in the reader's mind of the "Holy War" (as Bunyan might have seen it) that has been fought over Springinsfeld's soul,[13] and continues in Simplicius's attempts, in the earlier and later chapters, to convert him. There is no suggestion in the text of any stirring of conscience, or of true transcendental awareness, in the narrator himself. He has just been reminded of one of the pieces of conventional Christian teaching he has picked up along the way. But there is an existential resonance in the words he uses, in particular in his repetition of the word "ewig," the feeling that "day would never dawn again" (89) and the depth of the silence that matches the blackness of the night ("I heard neither the cock crow, nor the clock strike": 89) which makes the reader, at least, aware that Springinsfeld, the man of war, exists at best on the fringe of the world of warmth — and light.

That Springinsfeld is a wanderer does not in itself distinguish him radically from the main figures of the other novels, but there is a special edge to his vagrancy. Well before his entry into military service, his mother has explicitly crossed the Rubicon from the settled to the unsettled state: "Also wurde meine Mutter aus einer seßhaften vornehmen Damen eine umherschweiffende Comoediantin" (And so, from being a settled young lady of aristocratic family, my mother became a wandering player: 56). Springinsfeld is the issue of her marriage to an itinerant Albanian juggler and rope-dancer, and so he belongs from birth to the travelling fraternity made up of vagrants of various kinds, which he rejoins, on his return as a cripple from Crete in chapter 26, in the hope of finding his wife, the Leirerin, again (124–5). We know from his reply to Simplicius's enquiry in chapter 9 that he has no family and no resting-place ("kein bleibende Statt": 53) on earth. In a way, his has always been an existence on the fringe; even in the one occupation (as landlord of an inn) that seems capable of drawing him into honourable ("ehrlich"; here, respectable middle-class) society, and in which he might, with time, have become rich, he is being "ridden by misfortune in a different direction" ("wann mich das Unglück...": 106) and as soon as difficulties arise, gravitates back to the world of war.

When a soldier is incapacitated, there is nothing left for him but to beg, as appears as early as in chapter 12 ("dann ich muste mich mit betteln behelffen...: 66) and after his return from the Turkish Wars in Hungary (chapter 22), he finds this the best and most congenial profession or trade ("Handwerck": 109) that he can adopt. He has no thoughts of entering civil society in an honourable capacity (110), and soon takes up with a beggar family presided over by a blind man, and falls in love with the blind man's daughter, who is a hurdy-gurdy player ("Leirerin"). The main conditions laid on him when he asks to marry her are worth considering. He must "never settle down in a home anywhere, nor quit the free estate of the beggar and allow myself to be seduced into accepting service under some master or other. Secondly, I should henceforth take no part in war, and thirdly, I should on every occasion that the blind man issued the order, betake myself from one happy and peaceful land into the next."(110–11)

That the beggar's life is often less than pleasant goes without saying, and Springinsfeld's appearance at the very outset has made this clear. That Springinsfeld has sunk low, lower, indeed, than the status of the soldier, is apparent. Even the soldier, though circumstances can sometimes place him in a state of war with society, has some kind of social status. As we have said, this book is a kind of crossroads, and we are moving, in terms of the cycle, towards a phase in which war, if still a possibility (it recurs in chapter 25 of this book, and as late as part 2 of the *Vogelnest*) is beginning to fade into the background, and in which man's continued fragility and potential isolation in time of peace will be a central issue. For the moment, we wish to return to an aspect of the theme of beggardom that is explicitly evoked in the blind man's conditions and which we have not yet considered, namely its element of freedom. This too is treated with Simplician polarity.

The theme of freedom arises in the early conversations between Springinsfeld and Simplicius. Simplicius, who is concerned principally about Springinsfeld's spiritual condition, seeing him as being almost as much under threat as Courage (39), wants to draw his former comrade (who is old, but not yet wise) into the social and spiritual fold, into a state of rest ("in einen geruhigen Stand": 46) which will enable him to contemplate the world from the eternal perspective. To continue to wallow in sin "like a sow in a swamp" and neglect one's immortal soul he sees (as no doubt did Grimmelshausen) as the height of folly. Springinsfeld though, without being in any way devilish, as Courage might be seen to be, nevertheless has a little of the character of the wolf about him,[14] in morally negative connotations, certainly, but also in his stubbornly independent suspicion of attempts to include him, to rescue him from his isolated peripheral situation:

> Närrisch thät ich / antwortet Springinsfeld / wann ich mein Geld daß ich mit grosser Müh und Arbeit zusammen gebracht / in ein Kloster oder Spital steckte / solches zu belohnen / damit es mich meiner Freyheit beraubte. (47)

> [I really would be a fool, replied Springinsfeld, if I were to put the money it took me so much trouble and labour to gather together into a monastery or hospital, as a reward to them for robbing me of my freedom.]

Springinsfeld is no longer under the obligation that he contracted towards the blind beggar, but he has taken on board the idea of the freedom of the beggar's condition, and when Simplicius, as one might expect, points out that this freedom of his is illusory and that he is in fact "a slave of the Devil" (47), he speaks as an old soldier whose mind is still rooted in the old days (in Soest perhaps?): "lasse die Pfaffen Predigen / denen die ihnen gern zuhören" (Let the preachers preach to those who like to listen to them: 47). The thread of this argument is taken up again at the end of Springinsfeld's autobiographical narrative, and the pattern is very much the same. Springinsfeld still rests content with a life in which he can enjoy a sufficiency "in aller Freyheit"; Simplicius, with a certain ecclesiastical unction, urges him "so to live his life in this world that he may not lose eternal life in the next," to which Springinsfeld retorts: "Münchspossen!" (Pious claptrap). He then, harking back yet again to the Soest days, expresses the belief that his old comrade must since then have been lurking in a monastery, "to come out with such stupid nonsense, completely different from the way you used to talk" (130). Of course, Simplicius is "right," and we are told, in Philarchus's concluding remarks, that Springinsfeld saw the error of his ways before he died (132). But these facts do not by any means nullify the effect of Springinsfeld's dogged independence here. To parody Sellar and Yeatman, Simplicius is right and Springinsfeld wrong; but the former does indeed seem to us to preach a little like a Roundhead at times, and the latter, if hardly a romantic Cavalier, does reflect, as Courage does too, Grimmelshausen's predilection for the vitality of even a disreputable life. Motion (and proneness to error) must give way to rest and wisdom eventually, but part of Grimmelshausen has not aged as much as has his principal hero, and regrets the loss of vitality and excitement that has occurred over time. Simplicius is not allowed to win every argument. When he (whose marital experience and achievement leave much to be desired) pontificates about the love and care of a good woman, and remarks that Springinsfeld has never yet known such a being, it is the latter who is given the last word: "Wahrhafftig *Simplice*... du kanst bey deinen Biren wol mercken wann andere zeitigen" (Sure enough, Simplex: you can tell by your own pears when others are ripe [That is — ironically — "You, of course, are an expert."]: 55).

Springinsfeld in Simplician Context

Though a detailed examination of the question of the existence and nature of a Simplician cycle must be reserved for our final chapter, we have touched on it before, and should do so again here. By locating a life story that belongs to the wartime past within a concretely realised peacetime present, each with its clearly defined narrator and main protagonists, Grimmelshausen has placed his readers, for the first time, on a platform of firm ground, from which they can gain some sense of the interrelation of all the individual details within a greater whole. Simplicissimus, Courage, and Springinsfeld are, if not united, at least gathered together in a loose grouping, to which the Leirerin, with her magic bird's nest, is later added. This does not, of course, generate an action or plot in the sense of a novel conceived in a modern mould, but it suggests possibilities beyond the merely linear structure of the classic picaresque form. Irrespective, to some extent, of time and place, we see these main figures existing in simultaneous relationship one to the other within a connecting network of philosophical and social attitudes. Especially in the opening sequence (where discussion dominates), but also within the narrative part of the book, our attention is drawn from time to time to certain polar relationships, or pairings.

Simplicius and Springinsfeld are a pair, linked to some extent by a former comradeship which has not entirely died (and which has been emphasized by Courage for her own purposes), but also by clear polar opposition (warpeace, settled-unsettled, pious-foulmouthed and so on). Springinsfeld and Courage are also a pair. Their two novels could well have been conceived as such and written "together," with the protagonists as distinctly different examples of the outsider theme. The Leirerin (herself an explicit variant on the Courage-figure) forms a narrative link with the theme of magic and of peacetime civil society with its own moral and satirical possibilities, and thus points strongly forward to the world of the *Vogelnest* novels, where the figure of the Young Simplicius, barely sketched in this book, is developed a little further.

Springinsfeld's particular attribute, according to the title, is his "Seltzamkeit."[15] This oddness, in that it reminds us of his peripheral situation vis-a-vis everyday reality, can have negative connotations, but it also contains much that is positive, as far as reader appeal is concerned: the interest of the unusual (but still real) and the liveliness and comic potential that comes of escaping from the thrall of the ordinary and respectable. Simplicius himself was, of course, described as "abentheurlich" and "seltzam" on the title page of the *Simplicissimus,* and he has retained a little of that quality even in the present work. His appearance, as we have seen, is odd. The wine-changing episode in chapter 2, where he uses an "art" (Kunst) picked up on his travels in Armenia, is more *seltzam* than symbolic. Streller sees this as an allegory of purified Christian doctrine, based on an analogy with the Communion.[16] But if the wine in the Communion is "the blood of Christ" (not the doctrine!), how can we talk of "purifying" it? At this stage, the "elixir" from Armenia remains an exotic oddity.

Soon after this, Springinsfeld appears and the aura of *Seltzamkeit* is transferred mainly to him. Though the marketplace scene in chapter 7 still has a great deal of vitality, its purpose remains primarily to reveal the wine-changing art as a patent allegory of Simplicius's "satyrisch" method in his own writings.[17] But even before that point, he has become less and less odd, and more and more serious and moral, indeed positively pious. He has come back from the desert isle almost aggressively Christian, but the salt has lost something of its savour. When in chapter 3, seeing the steward of the vineyard, who misunderstands the word for hoe, he laughs so hard that it makes him bounce up and down ("daß er hotzelte": 18), we see that the sense of humour of the Simplicissimus of old has not been entirely squeezed out of him, but this is a momentary lapse of what must be an iron control: "the first and last time I saw or heard him laugh," says Philarchus. And when he then goes on, with a *brio* which recalls the Simplicissimus of former days, to tell the story of the "Secret" in a way calculated to extract the maximum of laughter, he can even be said to be acting out of character, or more accurately, to be acting as a conduit for another current in the Simplician stream and therefore temporarily contradicting the character he has displayed but a few moments before in his almost ascetic diatribe against the laughing philosophy.[18]

Simplicius is now the almost conventional voice of the settled citizen, and the mantle of *Seltzamkeit* has fallen on the shoulders of the soldier-beggar Springinsfeld, who is "elend" (56) not only — perhaps not even primarily — in the sense of "misery," but also in the older meaning of "homelessness." The dialectic between Springinsfeld and Simplicius, explicit in the first nine chapters, remains largely implicit during the autobiographical section, in which our reactions to him seem to oscillate between attraction and repulsion. There is bleakness, but there is also humour (as in the sorcery episode in chapter 12, meanness (as at Nördlingen), but also a kind of heroism of endurance (for instance the Cretan episode), the spirit of the footslogging soldier who simply keeps going. And always, there is a vitality emanating from the language Springinsfeld uses, whether it be his colourful expletives (of which Simplicius thoroughly disapproves, but which Grimmelshausen is loth to delete), or the rueful, pithy and even humorous way in which he refers to his own misfortunes. It is Springinsfeld rather than Simplicius who is the vehicle for Grimmelshausen's colourful proverbial phrases such as "wer kein Glück hat / der fällt die Nas ab / wann er gleich auf den Rücken zu ligen kommt" (When your luck's out, your nose'll drop off, even if you're lying flat on your back: 86). It is he who lends an expressive edge to the picture of misery ("ellender Zustand") that ensues when he falls into the hands of a band of marauders, and so lifts the scene out of dreariness to the level of an interesting *Seltzamkeit*. Stripped of his own clothes, he is given a few rags to protect him against the cold:

> welches aber nicht vil mehrers that / als wann wir uns in zerrissene Fischergarn bekleidet gehabt hätten; weil gleichsam Stein und Bein zusamen gefroren war. . . . (80)

> [But this was hardly any more help to us than it would have been if we had dressed ourselves in torn fishing nets, because it was cold enough to freeze your insides together. . . .]

The Springinsfeld who is recalling this in itself depressing episode does so in anything but a mood of self-pity. He may, in Simplicius's words, be a "grober GEsell" (a stupid foulmouthed lout: 32), but we cannot deny him all respect. Nor is the language in which he narrates devoid of interest and intelligence; neither, indeed, of wit. Springinsfeld, like Simplicissimus, has borne a musket, and here, perhaps, the authorial persona of the ex-musketeer, rough, but not devoid of a ready wit, which Grimmelshausen first used in the prefatory skirmishes of the *Satyrischer Pilgram*, comes to the fore. We have seen how he manages to shape his confrontation with the wolf in military terms. When, on the battlefield at Nördlingen, he is forced by the return of the cavalry to drop to the ground and play dead, he phrases his account with an antithetical elegance of which any baroque author might have been proud: "mich den jenigen gleich zustellen / die ich zu berauben im Sinn hatte" (to bring myself down to the same level as those whom I had come to rob: 82). In commenting on the sexual laxity of the Leirerin, the beggar's daughter, he shows a nice irony in saying that this was conduct unbecoming of "eine fromme Leirerin" (a well-behaved hurdy-gurdy girl: 112).

Springinsfeld and Courage form a pair in that they both stand in relation to Simplicius as outsiders, with both the drawbacks that this entails and the advantages. The theme of freedom, for example, which we touched on in the case of Springinsfeld, arises also in the case of Courage. Not only does she herself insist on the "free life" (34) of the gypsies (as the Blind Man does in the case of the beggars); Philarchus himself tells us that they live "in ihrer Freyheit" (34) like the martens and foxes. But as this simile indicates, their freedom is that of the wild and predatory animal. They fox ("füchseln") domestic animals away from the villages and wolf ("wölfeln") them away from the herds (33). They are outsiders also in the moral and spiritual sense. This theme, with a typically Simplician dualism, Grimmelshausen pursues apart from and alongside the gypsy episode proper, where Courage is shown in action, as a leader,[19] and playfully ironic in her treatment of the greenhorn Philarchus. Even he, indeed, cannot stifle an expression of admiration now and then. As soon as this narrative is complete, and the three men are, so to speak, free of her presence, she becomes the object of reflection and criticism and we see the other side of her outsiderhood: she is "der Verdamnus nahe / bis über die Ohren im Sündenschlamm" (close to damnation, up to her ears in the filthy morass of sin: 38), and above all, a fool, because she is totally unable to see her predicament. Springinsfeld is also, potentially, such a fool, but he, it transpires, is capable of achieving salvation.

Here, we have to return to the idea that not only the characters, but also the novels can be seen as a pair, and were quite possibly conceived as such. The *Courasche* ends abruptly, with only a brief sketch of Courage's life as a gypsy: perhaps Grimmelshausen already had it in mind to develop this theme in *Springinsfeld*, where the question of the nomadic existence and the need to settle comes to a head. On the other hand, an important period in Springinsfeld's life, which underlies his attitude to and eventual judgement on her, is treated at some length in the central section of *Courasche*, and it is hard to resist the conclusion that we, the readers, are expected to know that description. The fact that Courage's life history has not yet appeared but soon will helps to strengthen our sense of an overlap between the two books and to make her a real presence in the second one. Both were published in 1670 and they were surely written, the *Springinsfeld* possibly in haste,[20] with the plan that they should come out close together.

Courage's importance as a point of reference for Springinsfeld is twofold. Firstly, as we have said, she acts as a moral foil, despite the parallels between them. Already, in the first of the two novels, in the campfire episode which we analysed earlier,[21] we have seen in Springinsfeld's dream that some instinct has warned him of a deeper threat in Courage. He is no saint, even at this point, but certainly no devil. Although he does not meet her again in the second book, and even though we may discount some of the curses he mouths against her — as we could Philarchus's abuse — as originating in shame and resentment, Springinsfeld's remarks upon her last appearance in the Simplician novels proper (and even then the spell of her remembered beauty has not yet worn off!) do strike home and recall her own account of her character, experienced by him in a way of which she would not have been capable:

> sie war in den Begierden nach Gelt so ersoffen: in allerley Schelmstücken und Diebsgriffen / solches zu erobern / so abgeführt und fertig: und in Vergnügung ihrer brünstigen Geilheit so gar *insationabilis*, daß ich gäntzlich davor halte / es hätte niemand keine Sünde daran gethan / wann er ihr zu Ersparung Holtzes einen halben Mühlstein an Hals gehencket: und sie ohne Urtheil und Recht in ein Wasser geworffen hätte.(74)

> [She was so thoroughly steeped in the love of money, such a complete mistress of all the skills of roguery and thievery which are used to acquire it and so incontinently obsessed with the gratification of the desires of her lustful flesh that I am utterly convinced that any man could, without sin, have hung a half-millstone round her neck (to save himself the cost of wood) and pitched her into a lake without benefit of trial or judgement.]

This solemn and formal condemnation of her as a witch (contrast the petulantly abusive "Zugab" in the *Courasche*!) has more of the ring of a genuine perception of demonic qualities than has the simple word "Hexe" flung at her in a fit of anger. The Leirerin, as I shall attempt to show, is a kind of successor-figure to Courage, and it is significant not only that Springinsfeld falls under the spell of her feminine charms as well, but also that when she has taken possession of the bird's nest, he distances himself from her proposed nefarious use of it: mainly, theft.

This woman, Springinsfeld's "andere und vil ärgere Courage" (second, and much worse Courage: 119), is, in a pattern we also meet elsewhere in the cycle, a reprise with variations of that first "Unholde" (monster). The terms of abuse flung at her (for instance, "Raben-Aas" [carrion, crow-bait], or "leichtfertig" [116: essentially, immoral]), recall, in many cases, those used to describe Courage, and she is, like Courage, promiscuous, a deceiving and vengeful person and a thief.[22] But Grimmelshausen knows better than to attempt a simple imitation of an inimitable figure. The Leirerin does serve as a vehicle for the continuation in Springinsfeld's life of many of the motifs that Courage had represented — for example, he becomes her "Knecht" (servant: 112), as he was formerly Courage's — but she has new functions as well. She does not have Courage's semi-aristocratic origin, and there is no indication that she is capable, as Courage is, of speaking in a "Manier / die ihren klugen Verstand . . . zu verstehen gab" (a way which showed that she had a good mind: 31). She is something of a scold, with "a tongue like a two-edged sword," (120) as Springinsfeld (who may well have had a harder time with her than with Courage), feelingly acknowledges, and a gift for vulgar, if vigorous repartee. She is altogether a meaner figure, mentally as well as socially, than Courage, who can still command the reluctant admiration of the men she has deceived and tormented, and who may have become a gypsy, but is still a queen.

Malice, in the Leirerin's case, frequently amounts to mischief, a spirit of disorder with both comic and serious moral and social connotations. She delights in disruption and uses the invisibility conferred by the magic bird's nest she has found to indulge in a number of pranks (especially in chapter 24), which Grimmelshausen of course exploits for comic and "odd" effect, but which at the same time have a moral and social dimension. Here, if anywhere in the cycle, it might have been possible to introduce the idea of the "carnevalesque," which Anne Leblans has discussed in connection with Simplicissimus. The contrast between rich and poor, privileged and deprived, and the sense of a "verkehrte Welt" run through this series of incidents, and the sympathy with the poor and hungry and disapproval of wasteful extravagance that Grimmelshausen showed in his juxtaposition of a banquet with the Lazarus figure in *Simplicissimus* (I: 30) is discernible here too. But while he wishes to raise these issues, he does not side with the Leirerin. Her random redistribution of the money she has stolen is meant not to do good, but to sow confusion and allow her to enjoy a frivolous "Spaß." Those who keep the money include not only the poor, but also those with no conscience (118). The chaos she causes at the rich man's wedding feast gives rise not only to an animated and comic scene, but also to comments on the extravagant squandering of "the sweat of the poor." But then again, these are comments made by "lücke Klügling" (empty-headed, frivolous wits: 119). The deflation of the well-meaning but somewhat pompous abbess, who treats her as a fallen woman (119–20), through some pointed criticism of the idle life of the well-off nuns, would no doubt have appealed to Grimmelshausen, but an attitude that questioned the whole order of society would not have. Courage herself does not directly challenge the latter, though she chooses eventually to live outside it.

As far as the sexual aspect of her relationship with Springinsfeld is concerned, we must remember that the perspective is his, and that she is the young "wife" (Springinsfeld calls her "das junge Raben-Aas": 117) of an old man who in this respect is also the classic comic figure, the "alter Geck" (old fool: 110). She is, we are told at the outset of the relationship, "ein junges geiles ding" (a wanton young thing: 112) and is allowed to "go and graze where she wants to." There is nothing very admirable here, but nothing of great dramatic import. Eventually, though, after she has taken possession of the bird's nest (or it of her?), this side of her nature asserts itself in a more questionable form. She dupes a baker's apprentice into believing she is a water-sprite from a folk tale (there is an undeniable comic element here as well) and he enters into an illicit sexual relationship with her, which ends in lurid catastrophe. She murders her "consort" and another man, is herself ripped open by a halberd and her body is consigned to the flames as befits a "sorceress" (chapter 26). This outcome is attributed by Springinsfeld, who hears the story from an innkeeper, and whom we have no reason not to believe on this occasion, to the potentially malign influence of the bird's nest on the mind of its holder.

The rather sombre ending of the cycle itself is prefigured here. The nest is a strange and wonderful thing ("wunderbarlich": 130) and a source of odd and amazing effects ("seltzam," "verwunderlich": 114) but also, as Springinsfeld instinctively recognized when he refused to make use of it, "mislich und gefährlich" (dodgy and dangerous: 15). It seems to contain, then, the characteristic Simplician polarity and the power (in the absence of war) to act as a force which drives the characters forward. With the story of the Leirerin, the foundation has been laid for the next stage.

Notes

[1] Cf. Menhennet, "Simplician Emblematics? The Title-Sequence of Grimmelshausen's *Springinsfeld*," *The Seventeenth Century* 9 (1994), especially 81 and 86.

[2] E.g. Klaus Haberkamm, in his "Nachwort" to *Springinsfeld*, (Stuttgart: Reclam, 1976), 190: "Die Rahmenhandlung des Springinsfeld."

[3] *Springinsfeld*, 16: "daß dich der Hagel erschlag" (May Old Nick strike you dead). Springinsfeld is expressing surprise (*Verwunderung*) rather than anger.

[4] *Springinsfeld*, 22. "du alter Geck..."

[5] For the motif of coldness in *Springinsfeld*, see chapter 1 passim; chapter 2: 12, 15 ("die eingenommene Kälte"), 39 (the market-place scene); 53, 80, 88, 111 (the "kalte Scheuer"); 132 (the ice on the Rhine).

[6] Haberkamm, "Nachwort" to *Springinsfeld*, 206

[7] The mutiny referred to was an actual one, which took place in Bavaria and was in all probability witnessed by Grimmelshausen himself, who was at the time acting as

Secretarius of von Elter's regiment (Cf. Könnecke, *Quellen und Forschungen zur Lebensgeschichte Grimmelshausens,* vol.1, 81–7.)

[8] For instance, (all references to *Springinsfeld*) 72: "die ehrlichen Soldaten"; 78: "wie ein rechtschaffener Soldat"; 122: "was einem redlichen Soldaten zustehet," and "mit ihren arbeitsamen und ritterlichen Fäusten."

[9] Meid, *Grimmelshausen,* 165.

[10] *Rathstübel Plutonis,* 64: "Ich bin jetzt nicht mehr so alber und unbesonnen / wie ich da war / da ich . . . alles vom Glück und Unglück annahme wie es kam."

[11] Meid, *Grimmelshausen,* 164; Streller, *Grimmelshausens Simplicianische Schriften,* 57. Streller speculates that this style may be meant to reflect the moral poverty of the hero's character . . . but is the "official" war narrative any "richer" in *Simplicissimus* or *Courasche*?

[12] See Arthur Bechtold, *Johann Jakob Christoffel von Grimmelshausen und seine Zeit,* (Heidelberg, 1914), 118.

[13] Streller, on the basis of a parallel passage in the *Vogelnest* (I, 137–8), sees the gathering of wolves as "probably" representing evil spirits conspiring against man (57). For all that a parallel does exist (the bearer of the nest is "encircled" by wolves that surround the area "Battalien weis" and is forced to climb a tree), there is a significant difference of atmosphere. This is no "Poß," but a conjuration scene, and it is specifically stated that such an assembly of wolves "could not happen naturally." It is confirmed in part 2 that these are "Geister in der Wölff Gestalt" (165).

[14] Philarchus is reminded by him in chapter 4 of an "old wolf" pricking up its ears. Friedrich Gaede, for whom Springinsfeld is a totally "negative example," sees the wolf image as representative of Springinsfeld's (Hobbesian) "natural state." Springinsfeld and Simplicissimus stand at opposite ends of a dichotomy between sensual and spiritual reality, with absolute priority being given to the latter. My argument is that, as always in Grimmelshausen, it is more accurate to talk of polarity, and that the vitality of nature has not been completely devalued. Indeed, the "denaturalised" (252) Simplicius has lost a certain amount of his savour. (See F. Gaede, "Homo homini lupus et ludius est," *Deutsche Vierteljahrsschrift* 57 [1983], 240–58).

[15] Cf. Menhennet, "Simplician Emblematics," 82.

[16] See Streller, *Grimmelshausens Simplicianische Schriften,* 59–60.

[17] On the allegory of satire in *Springinsfeld,* see P. Heßelmann, *Gaukelpredigt, Simplicianische Poetologie und Didaxe. Zu allegorischen und emblematischen Strukturen in Grimmelshausens Zehn-Bücher-Zyklus* (Frankfurt/Berne/New York/Paris, 1988). Grimmelshausen is seen as using "hermeneutic hints" rather than "explicative allegory" (52–65).

[18] Andreas Solbach ("Erzählskepsis bei Grimmelshausen im *Seltzamen Springinsfeld,*" *Simpliciana* 12 [1990], 337–8), argues that Grimmelshausen is being very serious here, in emphasising the moral satirist's need for "Kommunikationsfähigkeit" if he is to make his point. This is an allegory of the difficulty the allegorist has in making himself understood. The argument seems to depend too much on the assumption of Derrida-esque attitudes to be convincing: surely, one has only to read the passage to be convinced of the author's intention to amuse. Valentin ("Du

rire...," 107) discusses at length the theoretical debate that precedes the narration of the story and sees the problem of "reconciling" seriousness and "Schwank." He accepts as Grimmelshausen's theoretical basis what he agrees is the banal formulation of the "lesson" to be learned from a story ("édifier par la littérature," 110), but does not analyse the "Secret" story in this light. It is, we repeat, practice, not theory that should be decisive.

[19] Cf. *Courasche*, 30: "Courage... stellte die Ordre und theilet das Lumpen-Gesindel in underschiedliche Troppen aus..."

[20] It is well-known that one must be cautious in speculating about Grimmelshausen's texts, but the state of the *Springinsfeld* text does suggest a measure of haste. Editors find themselves embarrassed by some forms, such as "Fachtung" (8) for "Verachtung": Sieveke ventures the suggestion that the word is "vermutlich absichtlich verdreht oder entstellt," though without stating why. Haberkamm thinks it may be either a misprint or a "spielerische Angleichung an 'Achtung.'" ("'Fußpfad,' oder 'Fahrweg'? Zur Allegorese der Wegwahl bei Grimmelshausen," in *Festschrift Weydt*, ed. W. Rasch, et al., 134 fn. 20): There seems to be no obvious reason for the feminine form of the relative pronoun in: "Wer kein Glück hat / der fällt die Nas ab" (*Springinsfeld* 86). The omission of umlauts "ein Charakteristikum der Erstedition" (Haberkamm, 118) is perhaps the most likely indication that proper checks were not possible.

[21] Cf. above, chapter 2.

[22] The word is used to indicate not just frivolity in the usual sense, but an absence of moral awareness, of conscience. Thus Courage is described by Springinsfeld in the following terms: "Es ist kein leichtfertigere Bestia seit Erschaffung der Welt von der lieben Sonnen niemahl beschienen worden" (since the world was created, the sun has shone on no more immoral creature than that one: 24).

7: Peace and War:
Das wunderbarliche Vogelnest

WITH THE DEPARTURE of Springinsfeld from the scene, peace descends on the cycle; the recurrence of his name in the song heard by the merchant is a fitting "omen" of war's eventual return (*VN* 218). In fact, the polarity of peace and war is a constant throughout the ten books. Peace is always implicit as the narrator's present, the location from which he operates, but the fact that the fields of physical battle have fallen silent does not mean that there is not a war going on. Indeed, the war against man's old adversary, the devil, the war in which the prizes are human souls and the issue that of damnation or salvation, seems to become intensified, once reminders of God's presence and power, and of His just wrath against sin, become less frequent. For now, man feels less insecurity, is less aware of his own and the world's inconstancy, and the visibility of God is correspondingly reduced. That visibility depends on the keenness of man's spiritual vision and of his vigilance, his ability to fight off the "Müdigkeit / Der wir ergeben allezeit" (fatigue to which we are always prone) of which the Einsiedel sang in book 1 of *Simplicissimus*. Sloth ("der schädliche Müssiggang") and luxury, the besetting sin of the "sleepy soul," sins fostered by peaceful conditions (*VN* 282), strengthen the human tendency to spiritual blindness. It is entirely appropriate that the central motif of this bipartite novel, which deals essentially with the war for the soul in time of peace, should be the bird's nest, which confers invisibility and with it a false sense of security. As early as the third page of part 1, the nest-holder feels himself "versichert" (made secure: 7) and the nest eventually makes him a "sicherer Narr" (secure fool: 133), or, in the more intense form which is characteristic of the second part, "sicher und tollkühn" (secure and foolhardy: 299). This is a psychological and moral equivalent of the "Festigkeit" (physical invulnerability) that the merchant in part 2 obtains by other — but related — magical means, and it comes as no surprise that it is only in war that he can be jolted back into moral awareness, by a wound that is no misfortune, but "an act of God's grace" (300).

This may help us to understand why, in a work which is more firmly rooted than its predecessors (however unsettled the central figure may be) in settled existence, in a world of houses and households,[1] the balance within the Simplician duality has swung pronouncedly away from the temporal, towards the eternal, why Grimmelshausen has moved away from, rather than towards Sorel, and why we seem to hear more echoes of the asceticism of the *Continuatio* and of Ägidius Albertinus. It was in the *Continuatio*, indeed, that the theme of the moral instability of peace was first enunciated, in the hellish conclave in chapter 2, which is echoed in the "Gericht" scene in the "Spectacul" section of *Vogelnest* (chapter 21) and developed in the story of Julus and Avarus, and there, as we have already indicated, that the idea of an all-embracing Simplician unity may have begun to take shape in the author's mind. Grimmelshausen was capable, as the *Courasche* shows, of penetrating into the mind of a figure for whom the reality of the moment was what mattered, and ideas of heaven and hell were little more than conventional pieces of ideological scenery. But he did so without abandoning his own basis of belief. He always took the question of salvation more seriously than Sorel seems to have done, and the cycle has now entered a phase in which the storyteller's impulse to follow the thread of life wherever it leads is becoming progressively more inhibited by the moralist's desire to reach a conclusion that crowns the work in a spiritual sense. He will conclude on the idea of a Christian soul at peace with God and looking forward to eternal bliss, a state arising out of a thoroughgoing process of confrontation with sin and spiritual purification, such as we have not been given in the case of Springinsfeld, or even in that of Simplicissimus.

The two parts of *Das wunderbarliche Vogelnest* can be and deserve to be examined as separate books, but they are also parts of a whole single novel. The principal differences between them, in tone and structure, could be seen as arising out of the character of what binds them together, that is the strange and wondrous bird's nest, which is as much the master as it is the servant of the person who holds it, drawing him into indulgence of his particular sinful desires by offering opportunity and removing essential moral inhibitions.[2] The bearers of the nest are still responsible for their actions, but there is a certain passivity about them as well, which is reflected in their essential anonymity.[3] The nest leads them into temptation, and they succumb. The central figures of the earlier novels were running hard, prone to error and frequently tripped up by Fortune, but they were coping as best they could out of their own resources. When they fell, they would get up and start again. The halberdier who picks up the nest when the dying Leirerin drops it[4] and the merchant who acquires it as a by-product of a conjuration designed to restore the money she stole from him both seem to be in charge of events, but can also be said to be drifting on the tide of their passions and appetites.

Springinsfeld has, as we saw, expressed the belief that it was the malign influence of the nest that drove the "itch of the lascivious flesh" ("der Kützel ihres geylen Fleisches") in the Leirerin to the point where her body was consigned to the flames. She casts her shadow over the *Vogelnest* books as well. In part 1, not only is the nest linked with her on the title page, but the halberdier (who is in direct line of succession from her) also recalls at a crucial moment that she, as the previous possessor, suffered a miserable death and was burned as a sorceress (135). In part 2, she is a posthumous presence in the opening chapters. She is the thief who propels the merchant towards black magic, and it is in the forest in which she lived — where the stolen money is hidden — that the ants reassemble the magical components of the nest (136), which the sorcerer then retrieves (165–6). The first of the two men who carry the nest has, it would seem, healthier moral reactions to events than did the Leirerin, and shows a tendency to intervene against sin and on the side of virtue, most notably in his rescue of the Young Simplicissimus. But he is very much a reactive rather than a positive personality, a man prone to idleness, who is prodded —rather than driven — primarily by the desire to satisfy his curiosity on the one hand, and to fill his stomach on the other. (His "Appetit zum Essen und Trincken" is mentioned almost immediately after he is assured of his invisibility [7]). The merchant in part 2 is subject to fits of dark depression and is more strongly driven by fleshly lust — as was the Leirerin in her role of Melusina in the forest — which his invisibility enables him to gratify. The nest itself is in a way the most active agent in the work, and the most Simplician. It is more than a physical object; it works in the minds of those who bear it with a variety of effects that reflect the multifarious and variegated vision of reality, now serious and religious, now comic, curious and realistic, that we have come to expect of the Simplician manner.

We have touched on, and shall have to return to the question of the nest's effect on the moral character of its bearer, but we turn, for the moment, to the relation of that bearer to the world in which he moves, as an invisible presence, capable both of clear satirical vision (as is symbolised in the emblematic engraving to part 1, in which this element is particularly strong) and of intervention, to comic or disturbing effect. As a narrative element, the nest is "wunderbarlich" not only in the sense of wondrousness or magicality, but also in that of strangeness, which can be comic or frightening, and often comic to the knowing observer precisely because it is frightening to the uninitiated. It produces this effect of alienation on each of the occasions on which it acquires an owner. Springinsfeld (chapter 23) finds it "verwunderlich" and "seltzam," the halberdier "seltzam und verwunderlich" (*VN* 139) and the merchant "überauß verwunderlich und entsetzlich" (extremely strange and frightening: 166), and it continues to function in this way, even in what might be seen as straightforward satirical passages. The satirist does not, after all, really need invisibility; or rather, he confers it upon himself and his reader, as he does the power of stripping off the masks (the "Schambärt" of the title page engraving) which might fool the naïve observer. But the nest is more than simply an emblem of the satirist's privileged ability to observe. It integrates that ability into the reality of the story itself, adding to a satirical scene what is essentially an ironic twist with both comic and moral implications. The burden of the phrase "Der Wahn betreügt" (in essence, the appearance — what we think we see — is self-deception) which, as the halberdier recalls (72) was used in the illustrations to the so-called *Barocksimplicissimus* of 1671,[5] becomes not just commentary, but an active reality: the constant presence within the action of one who knows the true state of the affairs of the other figures (though not of his own!) heightens our sense of their ignorance, and eventually, through the motif of God's all-seeing eye (107, 123) of our own.

It is important to remember, since the balance in this work swings undeniably towards the moral and didactic, that the comedy is not totally assimilated or integrated. Hypocrites and deceivers are themselves deceived, and we are privy both to their exposure and their deception, since they are unwittingly performing as comic characters before an observer who is having to restrain his laughter, which is of course a signal and a spur to us. Herr von Drffgkt" (that is, "Dürfftigkeit": Milord Impecunious, so to speak) is, as the speaking name suggests, conceived satirically, but when he arrives, *sans* wig and with freshly shorn pate, on his servant's horse at the castle where he hopes to find a rich bride, he is already identified as a comic figure, the victim of a "Bossen" (prank) for whom one can feel that kind of amused sympathy expressed in the phrase "der gute Juncker" (the poor [gentle-]man: 9) which is a spontaneous response to the phenomenon of the ridiculous. It is the nest that has brought about this comic mischief. He is chasing his own horse, which has been ridden off by the invisible halberdier, and we enjoy with the latter the lurid threats ("Halß und Bein brechen") hurled at the innocent animal. This is a *comic* irony: we can hardly exercise satirical criticism of the man for his failure to understand on this occasion (unless, of course, with an exegete's eye, we seek — and, inevitably, find — an allegory). The enjoyment of the invisible observer (the halberdier) who has to bite back his laughter to remain unobserved adds another dimension to the reader's enjoyment of the comic irony of this and subsequent scenes, particularly when the nobleman's servant, grimacing horribly, swallows some nasty and totally unnecessary medicine in order to back up his master's story.

When the young lady reveals (by her anxiety about the soiling of borrowed sheets) that she is as poor as her suitor, the "seltsam" quality of the nest asserts itself. The mother's anger causes their invisible guest (who has already stolen a sausage from the dinner table and brought the dog into undeserved disrepute), to laugh out loud: "causing such a terrible fright that old and young, woman and maiden, in sum, everything capable of running, ran out through the doorway" (18), causing us, in our turn, to laugh. Here, the nest causes a comic disruption of the order of familiar reality. We are reminded of the stampede caused by the sudden laughter of the prank-playing Leirerin at the wedding feast in *Springinsfeld* (chapter 24), though in that case, our awareness of the nest-holder's malicious love of disorder tinges the inherent comedy of the situation with a darker note. In some circumstances, the dualism and disruption of reality can bring about at least a temporary moral upheaval. The nest is indeed the main agent in the novel of the Simplician awareness of a dual reality, not least because the bearer himself exemplifies the rule that he sees exemplified in others: "Der Wahn betreügt."

The nest is a powerful force, but it is also parasitic: it feeds on the moral character and intentions of those who use it. In the story in part 1 of the man who sells a landowner his own cow and later attempts a burglary in the full consciousness that it might involve murder we have an interesting example of the moral ambivalence of the nest itself and of the author's ability to switch between the humorous and the moralistic perspectives. The trickster is tolerated in the case of the first escapade; indeed, there is a note of amused admiration in the characterisation of the whole as "meisterlich" (masterly: 74). The behaviour of the nest-holder corresponds to this tone : he takes "what is due to him" of the wine that is given in part-payment for the cow, "because I had been party to [present at] the sale" (73). There is no moralising here, merely a light humorous aside. It is only later, when dark deeds are afoot, that he sees himself as a thief (76). Knight, among others, argues that Grimmelshausen has "bridged the gap" between narration and moral edification, thanks to his use of the retrospective narrator. But what we have just seen is coexistence, not integration.[6]

In a later episode in part 1, the comic and the moralistic come closer to being mixed together, though they in fact remain distinct. The halberdier needs to replenish his store of food. He goes into an inn and filches a ham from the pot in which it has been put to boil, replacing it with an old shoe "so that I should not get my food without paying anything at all for it" (84). One does not know quite what to make of this phrase. It is hard to see the placing of the shoe in the pot as anything else but an impulse caused by the working of the nest-principle — the teasing and disruptive intervention of the invisible in the visible world — in his mind. True, conscience seems to have awoken in the narrator to the extent that he has resolved at least not to steal from Christians (83). But can we assign any moral motivation to this idea of payment? The likely outcome — an old shoe fished out of a pot which should have contained a ham — is odd ("wunderbarlich"), but comically, rather than edifyingly so. Yet it effects a conversion. When he discovers the shoe, the landlord is so frightened by this "Wunder" that he takes the alteration ("Veränderung") as a sign from heaven that he and his family should desist from cheating their customers with alterations of their own. He solemnly places the "miraculously" transmogrified piece of footwear on the table and with much weeping and heavy sighing, prays for mercy and forgiveness for all his misdeeds. Up to this point, the effect is predominantly a comic one: true, the landlord's immoral behaviour has been exposed, but our awareness of his error, with the shoe staring us in the face, so to speak, makes it hard for us to take all this breast-beating quite seriously.

The tone then changes. The banal and rather ridiculous cause of the situation fades into the background and we find ourselves confronted with the language of the catechism:

> . . . ja er und die seinige bezeugten eine solche Reu / und ihr leidwesen war
> so groß / daß es mich gleichsam zum Mitleyden zwang; Ich gedachte /

ach! wie wird sich die grundlose Barmhertzigkeit GOttes hierüber bewegen? Ich erfreuete mich / daß er durch meinen Diebsgriff zu solcher Reu und seiner selbst Erkantnus kommen war. (85)

[Indeed, he and his family showed such repentance and their anguish was so great that I was moved, as it were, to pity. "Ah," I thought, "how deeply the boundless mercy of God will be stirred by this." I rejoiced that by my thieving trick, he had been brought to such repentance and self-knowledge.]

The observer's use of phrases like "God's boundless mercy" and "self-knowledge" introduce a note of genuine seriousness, a foretaste of part 2. The merchant, too, is brought "durch GOttes Gnad zu [seiner] Selbst-Erkandtnus" (to self-knowledge through God's grace: 308) and to the resolve to amend his life. We do not know, in this case, whether the landlord's resolve turns out to be constant (86). The suspicion must be that it will not. Sudden conversions in a state of inner turmoil are suspect to Grimmelshausen, as we saw in the case of Simplicissimus at Einsiedeln (book V, chapter 2). Lasting conversion occurs, as we learn in part 2, "selten einsmahls"(rarely all at once: 251). There is a haphazard aspect to this intervention — as indeed to all the halberdier's interventions, even when the impulse is a morally good one — that makes us feel that the dynamic variations and vicissitudes of life have not yet been suspended. The solution is not final, just as the temporary relief afforded to the poor man, the Lazarus figure who stands in a polar relationship to the rich man, as in Luke 16 (64), leaves him, as Grimmelshausen himself shows, essentially no better off than he had been before (70–1). The halberdier himself, initially made "Gottsdächtig" (mindful of God) by this episode, is soon prowling the corridors and rooms of a monastery, seeking shoes that he may purloin.

Even in part 2, the comic potential of the nest is not left unexploited, the outstanding example being an episode on which we have already drawn in an earlier chapter in commenting on the Simplician duality, and to which it now seems appropriate to return.[7] To punish his wife for her planned adultery with the doctor, the merchant has made use of the nest to assume his rival's identity in bed and subject her (in the doctor's name) to coarse and brutal treatment, which, it has to be said, Grimmelshausen seems to regard as a source of comedy ("Spaß": 191). He then lures her into a meeting with the unsuspecting medical man at dinner, behaving, of course, with great courtesy and tender conjugal concern, and savouring, as does the reader, the irony of the situation. The magic property of the nest is no longer needed, but it is the root cause of a misunderstanding that underlies a scene in which Grimmelshausen deploys all his comic and narrative skills. Firstly, the aggrieved woman is described in a paragraph full of graphic and racy language, yet framed, for greater comic effect, in a rhetorically sophisticated form: an accumulation of phrases, rising to a climax:

> Dann gleich darauff setzte es bey ihr erschröckliche Minen / sie sahe auß wie eine höllische furi, und blitzte mit den Augen / als wann sie hätte Feuer darauß speyen wollen: sie ruckte mit dem Arß hin und wieder / als wann sie Wespen drinn gehabt / sie trilte den Deller herumb / und wieder hinumb / wie Hans Wurst seinen Hut / so wolte ihr auch Messer / Gabel und Löffel niemal nach ihrem Sinn recht ligen / sie liesse das Maul hangen wie ein Lait-Hund / kein Wort kam herauß / und weder Speiß noch Tranck hinein: anfänglich schiene sie wie ein stumm / und auffs letzte gar wie ein geschnitzelt Bild. (194–5)

[And then her face immediately assumed a terrifying expression. She looked like a Fury from Hell and her eyes flashed as if she would have liked to spit fire from them. She shifted her backside to and fro as if she had wasps in it, she twirled her plate round this way and then that way as Hans Wurst does his hat in the comedy; she could never seem to get her knife, fork and spoon into a position that pleased her. Her mouth drooped like a hunting-dog's: not a word came out of it and not a scrap of food or a drop of drink went into it. To begin with, she looked like a dumb woman and finally, like a carved wooden statue.]

As we noted in chapter 2, Grimmelshausen can step sideways, within the loose-knit Simplician structure, to leave transcendental and moralistic thoughts behind and immerse himself in the rough-and-tumble of life. The penitential context in which the merchant is writing his life history is forgotten in chapter 8, from which we have just quoted.[8] The merchant's appeal to the doctor's "Christlichs Mitleyden" (Christian sympathy: 197) is of course heavily ironic and could even be said to contain an irreligious bravado. Not until the next chapter do thoughts of his own folly and adulterous nature return.

Nor do we detect a deep sense of guilt in the (to modern eyes sometimes distasteful) narration of the deception by which the merchant exploits "foolish" and "superstitious" Jewish messianism in order to enjoy the beautiful but silly Esther. It is true that when he makes the sideways step onto the parallel path of moralistic reflection, the narrator avers that what may seem merely an amusing prank was in fact a step further into the mire of sin ("Aber ach Nein . . .": 239). But the episode itself is designated and narrated as a "Spaß," a "masterly deception" like that of the cow thief in part 1. Esther is a comic fool-figure who is mockingly patronised: "die gute Esther" (244), "die Tröpffin" (fool: 245), and in the outcome (the birth of a girl when the Messiah had been expected), the whole pious Jewish community is made to look ridiculous (246). The reflective element, which specifically engages the reader's "auffrichtige christliche Seele" (upright Christian soul: 239) and is transparent enough, carries significant weight, but does not undermine, or even perhaps directly affect the comic and realistic content, which is interesting for its own sake. True, Grimmelshausen felt the need, in the preface to part 2, to defend his "lustige[n] Stylu[m]" by adducing the traditional shell and kernel and sugared pill images (149). But the close proximity (on the same page) of his reference to the envy and malice of those (above all Christian Weise) who attack him for "Salbaderey" make it likely that this "Rezeptionskorrektur," to use Heßelmann's term,[9] is polemic rather than a critical key to his technique, to be used retrospectively. Neither he nor we can rewrite what has been written: the books must make their point themselves and they do this by the way in which they are written. But does it really require a "preacher trained in exegesis" like Prokop von Templin,[10] who, as a Capuchin "Volksprediger,"[11] is conditioned to look in popular sources for meanings he can use for his own purposes, to see the allegorical kernel in Grimmelshausen's stories? If so, there is little he could have done, if he genuinely wished to be better understood (and not simply to wrap himself in the satirist's mantle), but make concessions to the theological style. His storytelling is, as we saw in chapter 2, markedly different from even Schupp's. If his tales really were meant to convey moral meaning, he had to check the vitality of the sheer story, and foreground the abstract meaning. On the contrary, his tone is aggressively defiant: he will continue as he has begun, even if "hardly one in seventeen" will understand him. He entertains, we must assume, because he wants to entertain, and scorns the dry and humourless souls who apparently see little merit in the vitality of life itself. The novel does seek to instruct and improve, but its didacticism is patent and in no need of allegorical elucidation. To attempt to strip off the reality of the storytelling to reveal a "Lehre" would be counterproductive. The former will always assert its validity.

A fine example of the ability of the real to assert its own independent validity in a context of avowed moralistic abstraction occurs in the sequence in part 1 in which the nest-bearer (echoing the Simplicius of the *Continuatio*) is drawing moral lessons from observation of "the book of nature." In the example of the horse attacked by bees, an episode whose emblematic character Haberkamm brings out very well,[12] the incident itself acquires a vivid individuality and a comic quality that are foreign to emblematic practice.[13] A butcher hitches his horse to a post on which a beehive is resting:

> Ich kam eben darzu als ein Immlein diesen fremden Gast umb die Ohren schnurret / welches das Pferd nicht leyden wolte / sondern mit dem Kopff zurück schnellet / und den Stützen woran es gebunden unten am Boden / da er zimlich faul und versporrt war / entzwey brach; Pordutz lag der Bienstock auff dem Boden! welches die Honigmacher dermassen erzornte / daß sie umb solcher ihrer Reichs-Zerstörung willen an dem armen Pferd grausame Rache zu üben Armee-weis mit ihren Stacheln gleichsam wie mit eingelegten Lantzen darauff loß flogen; Ich fande mich zu allem Unstern / wie oben gemeldet / eben bey dieser Rencontre / und vermeinte vor den zornigen Immen eben so sicher als unsichtbar zu seyn; aber weit gefehlet / dann in dem mich selbige nicht sahen / sondern durch meinen Leib wie durch den andern freyen Lufft zu fahren vermeinten / fienge ich in einem

huy ein par hundert Angel auff / die mehrentheils mir beydes durch Hemd und Haut giengen / weil ich der grossen Hitz wegen mein Wams außgezogen und uber den Buckel gehengt hatte. . . . (132–3)

[Just as I arrived on the scene, a bee was buzzing about the ears of this foreign intruder. The horse was not going to put up with that, and jerked its head suddenly backwards, breaking off the post to which it had been tied, and which was pretty thoroughly rotted through at the bottom. Wham! There was the beehive lying on the ground. A fact that so incensed the honey-makers that in order to inflict a cruel revenge on the poor horse for having destroyed their empire, they formed up in squadrons and swooped upon it with their stings levelled like lances. As bad luck would have it, I chanced, as I have said, to be present at this encounter and thought I would be as safe from the irate bees as I was invisible. But I was well wide of the mark, for since they could not see me and thought they could fly through me as freely as through all the other empty air, I was pierced on the instant by a hundred hooks, most of which went through both my shirt and my skin since, it being a very hot day, I had taken off my doublet and hung it over my back . . .]

The nest, then, embodies on the one hand the principle of the all-seeing eye and eventually, when the holder sees through (so to speak) the illusion of his own invisibility, that of the ever-present eye of God, "die göttliche Gegenwart," first enunciated by the peasant-lad (107) and reiterated in the preface to part 2 (148). On the other hand, in accordance with the operation of the Simplician polarity, it allows the holder to function as a vehicle for appreciative and often ironic observation, from within rather than without, of the practical realities and the comedy of human life. Grimmelshausen himself has aged, as has Simplicissimus (who makes a guest appearance in part 1), and it could be argued that metaphorically speaking, each of the *Vogelnest* books goes through an ageing process, as vitality gives way to piety. But it is worth noting that both of the nest-bearers experience the events they relate as relatively young men, and are thus more susceptible to the temptations and stimuli of life and are more fitting protagonists of a tale told "auff Simplicianische Art" (in the Simplician way) as the title page of part 1 proclaims, and the preface to part 2 reaffirms. This is the logic of the statement, made in that preface, which seems to imply that both books have been written by the same person, who is also the author of the *Simplicissimus*. From the literal viewpoint, this is manifestly not the case. But both "narrators" belong to the general category of Simplician "author" in the sense that their work can be contained within the idea of a composite *Gesamtwerk* that is consistently Simplician, whichever persona seems to hold the pen at a given moment, and hence constitutes an overarching "Lebens-Beschreibung . . . deß Abentheurlichen Simplicissimi." This is claimed in the preface, which one can think of as perhaps written by Grimmelshausen himself, intervening in the authorship-game as an editor, as he did previously at the end of the *Continuatio* (150).

This, as we have said, is a novel of peacetime, and as might be expected, the social aspect bulks larger in it than in its predecessors. The nest itself may be an antisocial phenomenon, insulating the bearer to a considerable extent from the society around him, its requirements and constraints. But that society itself is a relatively solid and real presence, such as we have seen before only in the Julus-Avarus episode in the *Continuatio*. It is a world ordered by God, in which men must work to earn their living, form and maintain relationships, and above all, to save their souls, the rich through humility and benevolence and the poor through patience and contentment (71). It is the same world in both cases, but the two parts of the novel present it differently. In each case, the invisibility conferred by the nest detaches its holder from the physical and moral disciplines of the society within which he lives, and offers, apparently, freedom from the requirement to work. Each part ends with renunciation of that false freedom, the realisation of the need to reform, and the return to full participation in society. The structure and perspective adopted differs, however, from part 1 to part 2. Like Fortunatus, to whose story specific reference is made (6), the halberdier receives the nest as a gift of Fortune and accepts it unthinkingly. For the first, and much the longest of the book's three phases, he leads a vagrant existence, with no real aim apart from the idea of seeking some vague "Fortun" (8). This part of the book presents us with a series of narrative and satirical vignettes that also affords a panoramic view of society, from the very rich to the very poor, noblemen to beggars. It is a world just as much infested with vice (and folly) as was that of wartime.

The sequence (87–106) in which the younger and the old Simplicissimus appear, is perhaps best seen as having a transitional function. On the surface, this interlude seems something of a mixed bag: the young Simplex has an appealing German honesty (his "Teutsches Maul" [mouth] is referred to: 91) and his willingness to help others, but his innocent simplicity (an echo, perhaps, of his father's in Hanau?) makes him a potential victim of deception in a society where human frailty, both in moral terms and in terms of the penchant for judging by deceptive appearances, is rife. He suffers loss of favour and expulsion from the monastery where his father has placed him, and, while at an inn, comes under grave suspicion of adultery for having carried a sack of flour for the jealous landlord's wife, from which he is rescued by the nest-bearer, who has seen all and can reveal the truth. Simplicissimus himself, waiting for his son at another inn — the latter having gone to the wrong one by mistake — comes upon a copy of Philipp von Zesen's *Assenat* (1670), which covers much the same ground as did his (and Grimmelshausen's) own *Keuscher Joseph*.[14] He anatomizes the annotations, defending his own treatment of the story and use of sources, and attacking Zesen for having stolen from him on the one hand and embroidered (in essence, turning the story into a courtly novel) on the other.

There is a thread running through this disparate mixture, namely the theme of probity and social self-sufficiency, brought out particularly strongly at the end, where Simplicissimus and his son are shown as able to find their way in a society in which patient, honest German merit suffers the spurns of the unworthy, just as Grimmelshausen the honest German author has failed to gain acceptance among the educated literati.[15] Learning that, on the basis of a false report from the monastery, his son has now been rejected by an aristocratic household in which he had hoped to place him, Simplicissimus concludes:

> Wer mein Herr nicht seyn will / dem darff ich auch nicht dienen; die gantze Welt steht uns offen . . . und ist mein Sohn nicht zum Mönchen praedestinirt, so werde er ein Soldat; der ist ein Narr der sich drumb henckt / wenn man ihn nicht in ein Gefängniß setzt / denen sich beydes das Hof und Closterleben vergleicht. (106)

> [If a man does not wish to be my lord, I do not need to become his servant; the whole world is open to us . . . and if my son is not destined to become a monk, let him become a soldier. Only a fool is going to hang himself because they won't put him in prison, with which you could compare life in a monastery or at a court.]

The honest man will survive, and truth will prevail: salutary lessons for the halberdier as well. The phase that follows is one of self-examination, repentance, and renunciation of the life he has led, still punctuated occasionally by episodes of narrative and comic interest, culminating in a series of lessons learned from the contemplation of nature, after which the nest is torn up and thrown away and the halberdier vows to seek out a girl whom he has ravished while in a state of drunkenness, and to make an honest woman of her. Whether or not he remains constant in his resolve we never learn, but before the book ends, we see the nest material reassembled by the very ants from whom he has learned the lesson of industry, and acquired under sinister circumstances by a second owner. We are not unduly surprised to see the foundation laid for a sequel here, for although he makes copious use of the language of contrition, we do not feel that through the halberdier, the potential of the nest for moral destructiveness has been, or could be fully examined.

The war against sin, adumbrated in the final phase of part 1, needs to be followed through in a different context; the second, darker and more devilish part of the heritage of the Leirerin. The world of magic is still to be fully investigated, and there is in addition another war in the domain of human reality that Grimmelshausen wishes to bring into play. This is the Dutch campaign of Louis XIV, whose armies invaded Holland in 1672: among the victims on the Dutch side, as we shall see in due course, is the second holder of the magic bird's nest. Grimmelshausen himself will have felt some of the effects of this martial activity in his capacity as mayor of Renchen, and it would be interesting and profitable in this context to look briefly at another, non-Simplician, work in which he dealt with this theme, namely *Der stolze Melcher*.

Published in 1672 as a political tract against French recruitment for the Dutch Wars, this little work also has considerable merit as a narrative, and pursues the civil/military and insider/outsider dualities, which we have already touched on, in an interesting way. Melcher (Melchior), a peasant farmer's son, runs away to gain fame and fortune with the French army and returns chastened in body and mind. The prodigal is eventually received by his irate parent, after a great deal of pleading that he has learned his lesson: "Jetzt weiß ich den Unterschied zwischen dem Leben der Soldaten im Krieg und der Bürgers-Leuthe in dem Frieden" (Now I know the difference between the life of the soldier in war and the civilians during peacetime).[16] He now wishes to be reintegrated into the fabric of civil society and to "remain within the bounds of honourable and proper behaviour."[17] One of his companions, a Swiss craftsman, vows to resist all temptation to rejoin the army; he would rather, he says, work his fingers to the bone ("das mir die Schwarte kracht").[18] The same expression is used by the halberdier in part 1 of the *Vogelnest* (also 1672); considering the "cheerful industry" of the ants, he resolves to: "arbeiten daß mir die Schwarte krachen mögte /umb mich ehrlich zu ernähren und niemand beschwerlich zu seyn" (to work my fingers to the bone to earn my bread honestly and be a burden to no one: 137). Under the influence of the nest, he has drifted into sloth and outsiderhood, and it is as a working member of society that he will work out his salvation, as Simplicissimus is doing and as the repentant merchant of part 2 will no doubt also do. The "free" life of the outsider can have its attractions as well as its drawbacks, but the time eventually arrives to come in from the cold. The hermit's estate is an honourable one, and can serve as an ideal and a beacon to sinful man, but it is not the final solution. One has to strive to scale the moral heights and conquer the "World" while remaining in the world, within the continuous flow of life which brings a new beginning after every "end," however spectacular the latter may have been.

It is now time to turn to part 2 of our novel. The central figure is a man of means, a merchant from whom Springinsfeld's Leirerin has stolen a large sum of money. He has not been ruined, but the loss has thrown him into a melancholia, a deep and obsessive depression, in which state he turns to the black arts in the hope of recovering his money. This is a more explicit turning away from God than occurs in part 1. As Harsdörffer says in the anecdote *Der Alraun* (The Mandrake), which Grimmelshausen may have known, the man who trusts such devices has "turned his trust away from God and placed it in the devil."[19] In a powerful conjuration scene, the merchant acquires the bird's nest, or rather the fragments of it, which have been brought together by the ants and which he is able to carry with him in a handkerchief. He finds out that his wife (whom he has neglected) is planning infidelity. As in the case of Courage, Grimmelshausen can feel his way into her situation too, and shows that she has a grievance, but this does not excuse such behaviour in his eyes. He allows the merchant to take his revenge in a sequence that is essentially comic, and in which, as we have seen, the penitence of the retrospective autobiographical narrator is thrust into the background by the Simplician author's enjoyment of a lively and comic story. This phase of part 2 corresponds roughly to the first phase of part 1, where comedy and satire predominate.

The second is set in Amsterdam, and is dominated by the merchant's lustful desire for the beautiful Jewess Esther, which he manages to gratify by a trick in which he employs the nest to exploit what is called foolish Jewish superstition about the Messiah. Esther is then lured away from Judaism and married off to the converted Jew Erasmus. This sequence contains the elements of a comedy, which are certainly not neglected, but the balance within the Simplician polarity seems to be moving from the temporal to the eternal perspective. As in his portrayals of women, so in the case of the Jews, it is not freedom from prejudice, but his responsiveness to the vitality of individual reality that enables Grimmelshausen, on occasion, to go beyond the stereotype and endow his figures with their own vigour and validity. Aaron the Jew in the *Rathstübel Plutonis* is hardly evidence of Grimmelshausen's ability to rise above anti-Semitism, but by comparison with those Jews who appear here, who are comic or satirical lay figures, he has genuine life and interest. And in the handling of what is an inherently comic action, the general tone is darker and more serious, reflecting the thickening cloud of sin gathering round the nest-bearer. He has continued his association with practitioners of magic, and when he discovers, too late, that his wife has died and he might have had Esther for himself, his mood becomes one of desperation (273–4), and his involvement with the black arts becomes deeper still.

Grimmelshausen uses this situation to introduce a magic "spectacle" in which the gods discuss the sinfulness of men rendered forgetful and blind by the security and prosperity of peace, and Jupiter decides that another taste of war, a "punishment from God" ("Straff von Gott": 283) is necessary to awaken their sleepy souls. Confident that his invisibility and the art of making himself "fest" (invulnerable) by magic means will keep him safe, the merchant enlists against the French, but is wounded in the thigh, trampled by horses, and left in desperate straits on the battlefield. This apparent misfortune, however, is an act of divine grace, for it begins the third phase, a gradual and thoroughgoing process of moral rehabilitation under the supervision of a Catholic "Pater." This is a preparation for his reintegration as a cleansed, penitent and truly Christian being, into the human society within which he has been living, but from which he has been separated by what one might call an armour of darkness, which he has now cast off and whose last vestiges disappear into the Rhine when the Pater destroys the nest for good and all.

That this novel is planned as the rounding-off of a cycle suggests one further topic for consideration before we turn to examine the Simplician corpus as a whole; namely, its effectiveness as a conclusion. We have already had occasion to comment on Grimmelshausen's ambivalent use of the word *Ende*, and his natural tendency, as one who is fascinated by the process of life, to open-endedness. That there is a potential future for the central character is guaranteed by the fact that he is also the narrator, that this is a "Lebens-Beschreibung" in the picaresque tradition, and it is striking that in the preface to part 2, not just the book in question, but the whole cycle is described as such. Life as a phenomenon cannot end: there is always another generation, and as we have seen in Simplicius's comment on his son's potential future, "the whole world stands open to us" (106). In a way, then, this book cannot be brought to a final conclusion; the aim must be a formal conclusion with an extra degree of finality, albeit within a context that is essentially open-ended. Grimmelshausen now seems (perhaps even with a sense of his own end in mind) definitively to wish to call a halt, and the penitential theme that dominates part 2, in particular the later stages, repeating the pattern of part 1 at a higher level of intensity, may well be the principal method by which he aims to achieve the desired effect.

The destruction of the magic nest, almost a formal and final exorcism, contributes also to the sense of conclusiveness. The Pater, the chaplain with the French army into whose hands the merchant gave himself as he lay wounded on the battlefield and to whom he has at last yielded the nest, has designated the Rhine as its final resting-place. This second dismissal (the same word, "cassiren," is used on both occasions) seems to rule out all hope of survival for the stubborn principle that inhabits the nest. Whereas in part 1 (135–6.) it is torn up and thrown away at a place where the unceasing life force of nature, through the ants, can give it a continued existence, the nest is here "drowned," as a witch might be, in an element that is particularly effective against magic: water.[20] One wonders (and we have no means of knowing) whether the depth of the halberdier's repentance and of the self-knowledge he has gained from reading the "book of nature" will be enough to prevent him from future backsliding. We have no guarantee in the case of the merchant either, but at least, he has been through a more formal and thorough process of purification. Indeed, the penitential perspective is present from the very beginning in part 2, as is the theme of potential damnation and of the battle against Satan, the infinitely cunning archenemy ("der Seelen Untergang und ewige[m] Verderben der tausendlistige Ertzfeind": 154), whereas this mode is entered only in the last quarter of part 1.

Part 2 could be said to build on its predecessor by repeating its general pattern, but at a point higher up the scale of moral intensity. The halberdier comes to his conversion by contemplating the world around him, both human behaviour and the "book of nature" (128–32) and "learning" from them, even learning, he says, from contemplation of the devil himself (130).

He does all this without benefit of clergy; the words that first make him enter into inward self-examination are spoken by a peasant lad and work "viel besser als wann sie ein Prediger außgesprochen" (much better than if they had been spoken by a preacher: 107). This is the formula that seems to correspond to a rejection, or at least a questioning, of the theological style, and it is true that in this book, in which comedy, satire, and the vitality of life in general have the stronger hold, the clergy function rather more as social types than as representatives of God, and do not always appear in an especially good light.[21] In spite of the harsh words he sometimes uses of himself in this section, even though he speaks of himself as under threat from the devil and (in a direct echo of the *Courasche*) as being sunk "in diesem Sünden-Schlamm biß uber die Ohren" (up to the ears in this slime of sin: 125), we cannot feel that the halberdier has plumbed the depths of sin. It is possible that Grimmelshausen originally thought that he might be able to call a halt at this point, for the title page gives no hint of a bipartite structure, and he does indeed conduct his hero through a penitential process. But he clearly came to feel that this was not a figure through whom the devil could be formally cast out, and so the end, as far as the cycle is concerned, is not yet.

The preface to part 2, which can be seen as the axis of the whole novel, endorses the halberdier's message, namely that one should always be aware of God's presence, but the preface-writer, intervening for the first time, feels the need to add a warning against direct dealings with the Prince of Darkness. There have been hints of such behaviour before — in the case of Olivier and the provost sergeant, for example — but now the subject is to be taken up in all proper form. The title sequence (significantly, there is no separate title page) confirms this new emphasis, and its style is much less overtly Simplician. The merchant involves himself in black magic from the start, and complements the "Sicherheit" conferred by the nest with a magically-acquired "Festigkeit" in the war sequence. We should not underestimate the seriousness with which Grimmelshausen took such dabblings, but the psychological and moral aspects are perhaps more important than the hocus-pocus. The merchant's social and economic situation, in which money and status bulk larger, make it harder for him to achieve the relative freedom and simplicity of spirit that are already latent in the halberdier's approach to life and to the vicissitudes of Fortune. The merchant is much more susceptible to black, introspective depression, and to temptations, including those of the flesh. The halberdier's venture into *luxuria* occurs under the influence of alcohol, and impulsively, and is immediately regretted. The merchant's seduction of Esther is an adultery planned in cold blood, and it is clear that, had he known his wife had died, he would have wished to continue the relationship. Far from wishing to make amends, he plunges into even deeper levels of sin. This is indeed material for a serious sermon and we can adopt the phrase used by Eberhard Mannack, in registering the general trend in this direction in the *Vogelnest*, and speak of a "radicalisation of [a theme] that has already been adumbrated in the novel."[22]

Both parts raise the issue of the danger of damnation and the need for salvation, but it is only in the second that the actual (practical and theoretical) process of salvation eventually takes centre stage. Devotional texts may well be reflected in part 1, but in part 2, the sinner is put through what amounts to a formal course of penitence that recalls, though not with an exact correspondence, the "contritio-confessio-satisfactio" sequence that Grimmelshausen could have found in Ägidius Albertinus's supplement to *Gusman*, or possibly material from the *Beicht- und Communion-Büchlein* of Pater Canisius, adduced by Valentin as having perhaps been parodied in the opening chapter of the *Courasche*.[23] Grimmelshausen seems to want to check the forward progress of his "Lebensbeschreibung" and bring it to a halt by sheer weight of ecclesiastical ballast. The full panoply of the church's painstaking theological analysis of sin is brought to bear: the hardness of man's heart, the need to drive the devil out of every cranny in which he can take refuge, the need for Divine Grace and the redemptive role of Christ.[24] There is even a reappearance of the eschatological theme announced at the beginning of *Simplicissimus*, though this time with a much heavier rhetorical weight behind it:

> ... die unbehutsame Menschen... vor demjenigen treulich zu warnen / was sie / wie gemeldt / gar leicht vom höchsten Gut absondern / hingegen in deß leidigen Teufels Gewalt und... in die ewige Verdamnus bringen mag / worzu er vornemlich bewogen worden / als er gesehen / wie unzehlbar viele sich in jetzigen elenden / vielleicht letzten Zeiten mit allerhand liederlichen Künsten schleppen... (149)

> [... faithfully to warn incautious man against that which (as has been said) can very easily cut him off from the Highest Good and deliver him instead into the power of the accursed Devil and eternal damnation. To which course he has been moved by seeing how immeasurably great is the number of those who, in these wretched days, which may perhaps be the Last Days, are dabbling in all kinds of dubious arts...].

The halberdier acquires the nest by chance, the merchant through deliberate involvement with the black arts. He has to be prised out of the devil's clutches by heavy pressure and close argument (see especially chapters 25 and 26). He argues that he too acquired the nest "by accident, not by my own seeking and striving" (300) but the Pater makes it clear that he should have recognized its nature by its origin. After his confession, he is told that now that he has been raised out of "the deepest mire and most sinful pit of the most abominable vice," he will still need to strive with all his might to avoid falling into it again (294–5). There is "hardness of heart" in him that makes him seek excuses and must be overcome before full repentance is possible (299). He must empty himself before God (symbolised, perhaps, by the final surrender of the nest). In language that has the solemn and stylised quality (so different from the Simplician style to which we have become accustomed) of a devotional book, the Pater works to give the sinner full conviction of sin and break the "eygene[n] verkehrte[n] Wille[n]" (stubborn self-will)[25] that still separates him from God and from the benefits of Christ's sacrificial death on the cross (306).

Nowhere else in the whole cycle does Grimmelshausen bring such a concentration of solemnity, such a weight of heavy ecclesiastical artillery to bear. Nowhere, one is tempted to say, is he less Simplician in manner; he is trying, after all, to find a conclusive conclusion, something to which the Simplician manner is inherently resistant. Negus complains that the process of penitence and regeneration is "tediously depicted"[26] and he is surely right. But it can be argued that Grimmelshausen is showing his understanding of the artistic needs of his work, taken as a whole, by here resisting the temptation to entertain. Indeed, we can see that the temptation subsists when two anecdotes — which the good father himself admits are "lächerliche Sachen und kurtzweilige Possen" — occur like alien outcrops in the long discourse on "Festigkeit" (305). But by comparison with the liveliness of the description of the emblematic horse tormented by the bees, this is the merest ripple of vitality. As we have said, a concentration on the quality of life as a value in its own right means that a story can have no true end. The fact that this quality is ruthlessly squeezed out of the concluding chapters, to be replaced with an earnest homily, may well be attributable to the fact, not that Grimmelshausen's arm has lost its cunning, but that he now wishes to rise to a climax of true finality on the concept of a "seliges ENDE."

Notes

[1] In this novel, we are taken much more often into an interior, and shown the working of a household, in which, incidentally, women play an important role that Grimmelshausen acknowledges, though without giving them the respect they deserve.

[2] In part 1, there is a retrospective reflection on the ambivalent and dubious nature of such "verwunderliche Stück" (6); in part 2, the Pater tells the nest-bearer that it has "caused him to fall into the most horrible of sins" ("da dich deine Unsichtbarkeit . . ." 301).

[3] The merchant of part 2 has no name; the appellation "Michael Rechulin von Sehmsdorff" appears only on the title page of part 1, and seems alien to the character and status of the halberdier.

[4] Cf. *Springinsfeld*, chapter 27.

[5] So dubbed by J. H. Scholte. See Manfred Sestendrup, "Die Illustrationen des 'Barocksimplicissimus,'" *Simplicius Simplicissimus. Grimmelshausen und seine Zeit*, 103–7, and M. Koschlig, *Das Ingenium Grimmelshausens*, 193.

[6] K. G. Knight, "Die 'strafende' und die 'scherzhafte' Satire bei Grimmelshausen und Christian Weise," *Simpliciana* 15 (1993), 52. On integration, cf. also E. Mannack, "Grimmelshausen und das Monströse," ibid., 155: "Der Verfasser des Simplicissimus verschmolz Fabel und Unterweisung zu einer Einheit...." A "successful integration" is claimed, but not demonstrated from the text.

[7] Above, chapter 2.

[8] There is a parallel case in part 1 in the Münchhausenesque "Poß" (119) of the man in the barrel who catches a wolf by the tail, which is followed by a rather lame moral against boasting (120). In essence, this is a comic interlude along the road to repentance. The halberdier has already decided (110) "to become a totally different person."

[9] P. Heßelmann, *Simplicius Redivivus. Eine kommentierte Dokumentation der Rezeptionsgeschichte Grimmelshausens im 17. und 18. Jahrhundert* (Frankfurt am Main, 1992), 50.

[10] For Prokop, see ibid., 23.

[11] Cf. W. Barner, *Barockrhetorik. Untersuchungen zu ihren Grundlagen*, (Tübingen, 1970), 326.

[12] Cf. K. Haberkamm, "'Fußpfad' oder 'Fahrweg'?...," 287: the writer demonstrates "... die Konsequenzen für denjenigen, der seinen Trieben nachgibt."

[13] Cf. Menhennet, "Simplician Emblematics," 83.

[14] For details see Volker Meid's "Nachwort" to Philipp von Zesen, *Assenat*, (Tübingen 1967), 23–8.

[15] Cf. the references to Christian Weise's attack on his "Salbaderey" (in Weise's *Die drei ärgsten Ertznarren*), *VN*, 149. That this rejection by the member of the literary establishment to whom, as a fellow-satirist, he perhaps felt particularly close, really hurt Grimmelshausen is instanced by the fact that he also takes up the matter at some length in the *Teutscher Michel*.

[16] Grimmelshausen, *Kleinere Schriften*, 39.

[17] Ibid., 40 ("mich selbst in den Schrancken der ehrbaren gebühr zuenthalten.")

[18] Ibid., 45–6.

[19] Cf. *Jämmerliche Mordgeschichte*, 151: "... sein vertrauen von Gott ab- und zu dem Teuffel gesetzt." It may be of interest that Hedwig, the younger daughter in this story, who covets and acquires the mandrake, marries a baker's lad ("Beckenknecht," 152): this was also the trade of the young man ensnared by the Leirerin!

[20] Springinsfeld, as we have seen, suggests drowning Courage as a witch. The dying Magdalon, in Harsdörffer's *Der Alraun*, commands that the mandrake be thrown into "ein fliessendes Wasser" (flowing water: 152).

[21] E.g. the Susanna episode (44–9) and the case of the priest who comes home late from a banquet "sternvoll gesoffen" (blind drunk; 126).

[22] E. Mannack, "Grimmelshausen und das Monströse," 158 ("Radikalisierung des schon im Roman Angelegten.")

[23] Cf. Ägidius Albertinus, *Gusman*, 507 ff., and Valentin, "Théologie," 283 ff. (especially 286–8). Canisius's manual is cited on 287–8. The modern Catholic catechism still sets out the sequence: "Gewissensforschung / Reue / Vorsatz / Sündenbekenntnis / Genugtuung." (Cf. *Katholischer Katechismus der Bistümer Deutschlands*, Ausgabe für das Erzbistum Köln, [Düsseldorf 1962], 173.) I am indebted to Dr. Gaby Wright for help in following up this point.

[24] E.g. 295: "the blood of the Lamb"; 306; and 314, in the very last sentence: "der Verdienste des Erlösers theilhafftig zu werden."

[25] One is reminded of the tenour of the Ash Wednesday service and of the sentence from Psalm 51 (which occurs there): "The sacrifice of God is a troubled spirite, a broken and contrite herte, (O God) shalt thou not despise." (Quoted from the "First Prayer Book" in *The First and Second Prayer Books of Edward VI*, [1910; reprint, London/New York: Everyman, 1957], 284.) The line belongs in the context of "vollkommene Reue" in Catholic tradition: cf. *Katechismus*, 169: "Ein Herz, das zerknirscht und gedemütigt ist, Gott, verschmähest Du nicht."

[26] Negus, *Grimmelshausen*, 141.

8: Squaring the Circle: Simplician Structure

FROM TIME TO time, we have found ourselves having to juggle with complications, even apparent contradictions, in attempting to define the Simplician principles of movement, variegation, and coexistence. The latter stages of the foregoing chapter presented us with a prime example of this problem: the search for an ending that, without ever achieving total stillness, nevertheless reaches a point of rest. What was being ended, we have argued, was not just a single book, but a whole sequence of novels. Grimmelshausen himself, acting as editor for his "Simplician author," raised the issue in the preface to part 2 of the *Vogelnest*. It behoves us now to wrestle with the problem of the Simplician cycle, its unity and structural integrity.

We will not be able to avoid the kind of complexity we have referred to, for if we are to find a Simplician integrity, it cannot be one that truly integrates. And our discussion must remain speculative, for Grimmelshausen has given us no positive evidence. Obviously, in a series of books emanating from the same pen, a constant set of ideas and attitudes will periodically make its presence felt, but it seems a little excessive to think of this as a structural scaffolding ("Gerüst")[1] indicative of planning on the grand scale. The Simplician novels are, it is true, loosely linked together in that each develops the narrative potential of a figure or motif introduced episodically in its predecessor, but this linkage is relatively slight as a narrative structure, and insufficient, as Meid has said, to justify the claim made in the *Vogelnest* preface.[2]

This claim is the only instance in the corpus of an explicit reference to the cycle. But there is an interesting passage in the *Continuatio* that could be said to prepare for it. As in the *Vogelnest* preface, Grimmelshausen steps back from his Simplician authorial *personae*. He introduces a third ending, a *Beschluß* (conclusion, dated 1668) to which he appends his own initials and in which he announces that he is editing this manuscript from the posthumous papers of Samuel Greifnson von Hirschfeld, deceased. This gentleman (whose name is an anagram of Grimmelshausen's own) has, we learn, earlier brought out the *Satyrischer Pilgram* and *Der abentheurliche Simplicissimus* (also 1668). His death gives him and his work a concrete place in the reader's present world, and this impression is strengthened by the fact that he has left behind other "feine satyrische Schriften," which have yet to appear. These are in all probability the *Courasche* and *Springinsfeld*, which are described as forthcoming in the "Zuruff" appended to *Dietwalt und Amelinde* (early 1670). They did indeed follow close after the other novels, and the second of them provides a stable platform in present time from which a panoramic view of the whole corpus, from the Balkans to Westphalia and from 1600 to 1670, can be obtained. The period from 1668 to 1670 is explicitly established by Grimmelshausen as the nodal point of a network of potential references between characters and events — a process to which, as we shall see in due course, the *Ewig Währender Kalender* also makes its contribution. The fictional line is carried into the factual present, and the fictional action takes place within a framework of actual time, the framework within which the disparate phenomena of real earthly life coexist. Something like a palpable framework for all the variations and wanderings of the Simplician world seems to be emerging.

The relation between Greifnson and Simplicissimus as characters created by Grimmelshausen and in particular as "author" figures is worth examining, since it seems to open a perspective on a set of relationships that is at least analogous to the one we shall be pursuing in this chapter. Grimmelshausen himself, after all, raises the question, partly in the *Beschluß* to the *Continuatio* (which he signs with his own initials), partly by references to authorship in various works. Thus the name Greifnson appears on the title page of the *Keuscher Joseph* (though there is no reference to this work in the *Satyrischer Pilgram*), yet Simplicissimus himself claims, as we have seen, to be its author in part 1 of *Das wunderbarliche Vogelnest* (as indeed he also does in *Der abentheurliche Simplicissimus*).[3] Are Greifnson, Simplicissimus and the ex-musketeer of the *Pilgram* one and the same? It would certainly seem as if Grimmelshausen wishes to encourage cross-reference and speculation on the subject among his readers. But if he has in mind a simple identification, why the added mystification of the names given on the title pages of *Simplicissimus* and *Continuatio*? Both are new anagrams of Grimmelshausen, as indeed is the full name of the "author" of the *Courasche* and *Springinsfeld*, Philarchus (who is of Swiss origin and who cannot be identified with Greifnson, as he and Simplicius do not meet until late in 1669). "H.I.C.V.G." (that is, Grimmelshausen) dates his *Beschluß* to the *Continuatio* from "Rheinnec" (that is, Renchen), the location from which the "Vorrede" provided by Simplicissimus himself for the preface, dated 1669, of the so-called *Kalendersimplicissimus* is said to emanate. And as we know, Grimmelshausen, in *Dietwalt und Amelinde*, uses a fictitious friend ("Urban von Wurmsknick") to congratulate himself on his achievement as the "maker" of Simplicissimus, Courage, and Springinsfeld.

What can we make of all this? Clearly, Grimmelshausen is aware of what he is doing, and his purpose can hardly be to conceal his own identity. He is playing a transparent game with his reader, whom he is, as it were, drawing into a Simplician world. Is this some baroque "Vexierspiel," aimed at undermining the sense of reality, or a denial of a unitary meaning (as would seem to be the implication of the views of Zeller and Schmitt to be discussed later), in a kind of anticipation of modern deconstructive techniques that bury the idea of coherence under an avalanche of contradictions and *apo-*

rias?[4] We should exhaust explanations more congenial to the seventeenth century before venturing into this territory in dealing with a man like Grimmelshausen, who, like Goethe, would probably have found theory for its own sake grey and sterile. Certainly, he is playing a game around the idea of authorship, but it could well be a game with a practical purpose, namely to harmonise it with the nature of the Simplician world, which in its turn attempts to reflect the combination of variety and unity in human life itself. Convention demands that every individual book shall have its individual author, but Grimmelshausen seems to be creating a fictional literary world in which authorship is a facet of a larger entity, what we might perhaps call Simplician character, a character that is variable and transferable. The mantle of Simplicissimus himself can descend, if we are to believe the dedication provided by the Young Simplicius for the *Ewigwährender Kalender,* on the congenial reader. The two books that make up *Das wunderbarliche Vogelnest* have discrete first-person narrators, yet Grimmelshausen sees no contradiction in attributing both books, in the preface to part 2, to a single Simplician author.

We are being schooled towards flexibility. A quality of multi-faceted plurality is being introduced into the concept of authorship. We can certainly read each text and take each figure as an entity in itself, but they exist also within a kind of authorial network that contains a multiplicity of *personae,* who can manifest themselves at many different points. That of the uneducated "Ignorant," for example, is ironically assumed by Greifnson in the *Satyrischer Pilgram* (6) and by "Signeur Meßmahl" (the anagram is transparent) in what is avowedly "The World-famous Simplicissimus's *Teutscher Michel,*"[5] taken up almost as a battle-cry by the unnamed narrator of *Der erste Beernhäuter,* and adopted by the narrator of part 1 of the *Vogelnest.*[6]

As to the 1668 *Beschluß,* in which, for the first time, a promontory of solid present fact seems to jut out into the swirling and shifting sea of the story, we need to examine implications for the relationships between the Simplician books a little further. As we stand beside the real person whose initials it bears, we look forward as well as back. To be sure, the books which are to come are not designated as continuations of *Simplicissimus.* Indeed, the *Beschluß* refers to the *Continuatio* as itself a conclusion. But it does prepare the ground for the statement in the *Vogelnest* preface that asserts that all the Simplician works are in some way "integrated."[7] The work published so far is seen as consisting of six parts: "diesen Schluß hab ich nicht hinderhalten mögen / weil er [Greifnson] die erste fünf Teil bereits bey seinen Lebzeiten in Druck gegeben" (I could not hold back this conclusion because he had already brought out the first five parts in his own lifetime). This, then, specifically designates the *Continuatio* as a sixth part or book, and lays the foundation for the later description of the *Courasche* as the seventh, *Springinsfeld* as the eighth, and *Vogelnest* 1 and 2 as the ninth and tenth of a greater himself. And while conclusive proof is not available, he has given us at least some indicators to help us.

The notion of "War and Peace" as a structural principle that lends stability to an epic novel has a familiar ring, and although Grimmelshausen is no Tolstoy, the handling of time and space that enables the Russian writer to incorporate into his work not just the dramatic action centred on the Rostov and Bolkonsky families, but whole nations and a whole continent, suggests points of departure that could be fruitful for our purpose. All the individual occurrences in Tolstoy's book are contained in a wide framework of time and space, viewed from the vantage point of the post-Napoleonic era. We have already seen something of the alternation of war and peace in Grimmelshausen's cycle, and if we conceive these two as structural poles (including the lives of the narrators as well as the narrated matter), then the necessity of the *Vogelnest* books becomes all the more clear. And that theme in itself suggests a framework, and that in turn presupposes a vantage point of the kind we have been discussing. From a ridge extending as far forward in time as the later 1660s and the earlier 1670s (the period in which the books are written and read), we have a perspective stretching from the present back to the beginning of the Thirty Years' War and indeed beyond. Similarly, while we are securely anchored in and near Strasbourg, we can see from this high ground over the whole German empire and beyond.

In the opening section of the *Springinsfeld* we become fully aware of the ground on which we stand, together with the figures who have come through the war and its aftermath, but the *Ewigwährender Kalender* has helped to mark it out and made a substantial contribution towards fixing it in time. Among the works that exist on the periphery of the cycle proper, but are identified as Simplician, it occupies a special position. A possible reference to it as being currently in composition occurs in the *Satyrischer Pilgram*,[10] the work in which Greifnson makes his debut as a potential "Simplician author." A knowledge of the *Kalender* is presupposed by the *Springinsfeld*: Philarchus recognizes the members of Simplicius's family from its title engraving (39). Its involvement of the Young Simplicius, and its peculiar compositional principles are points to be considered separately, but it also provides useful material towards the establishment of the framework with which we are at present concerned. It represents Simplicissimus the farmer and family man, before the final excursion from which he has not yet returned. Its composition (within the scheme of the cycle, that is, as a work by Simplicissimus) predates the *Continuatio*.[11] The *Kalender*'s publication date (1670) is explicable by the unusual and Simplician circumstances of its discovery by Christian Brandsteller, the purported editor, who has the title of "Stattschreiber zu Schnackenhausen," which suggests, perhaps, the "Satyric" Mayor of Renchen: a *Schnack* is a triviality, or *Posse*. This locks it into a precise time and place. "Als ich im verwichenen Julio dieses 1669 Jahrs..." begins Brandsteller, "... die Saurbrunnen Chur brauchte..."

(When I was taking the cure in the spa [Griesbach] in July of this year of grace 1669 . . .).[12] In this significantly Simplician location, he meets a peasant woman who turns out to be Simplicius's "Meuder" (foster mother), from whom he buys butter wrapped in pages from the "Calender" of a writer known "for some six months now" as "den offendürlichen [abentheurlichen] Simplicissimus." The first novel in the cycle, then, has already appeared. Simplicissimus is now "in the new world" and not expected to return.[13]

This section most obviously, and the work as a whole as a reflection of Simplicissimus's reading and interaction with others, is a part of his life history. What is of particular importance for our present purpose is the precise dating by Grimmelshausen of Brandstetter's encounter with Simplicius's "Meuder," and of his final signature, at the end of the anecdotes appended to the narrative section headed "Auffschneyderey" (boasting, bragging): "Dat. Grießbach den 29 Jul. 1669."[14] This fits precisely enough with the 1670 publication date, and slots into the time scheme of the appearance of the Simplician works between the *Continuatio* and the framework section of *Springinsfeld* (winter 1669–70), where it is established that Simplicius has returned from the new world "erst vor einem halben Jahr."[15] So much precise detail must be for the benefit of the contemporary reader. The present world of the Simplician figures and narrators is endowed with an actuality that is cognate with that of the reader's own present.

Present and past in interrelation are an integral part of the first eight books of the cycle, due to the format of retrospective narration. The difference between "then" and "now" is not infrequently alluded to. The theme of the passage of time is brought out where appropriate through the motif of ageing, which becomes more prominent as the cycle progresses. All the narrators who have noticeably aged show an awareness that the events they describe belong to the realm of "then" (damals) rather than now. Courage feels her beauty fading with the years,[16] and the theme comes really to the fore in the *Springinsfeld*, not only in the figure of the principal narrator, but also in the appearance of Simplicissimus himself, who is then shown in part 1 of the *Vogelnest* as an ageing man, whose son is about to start his career. The interrelation of war and peace is similarly an integral part of the format. And this too emerges fully in the *Springinsfeld*, which acts as a kind of axis for the whole cycle — even though its position is not precisely central — by virtue of the fact that it is a point not only of convergence for threads that have previously run separately (and will separate again), but also, through the appearance of the magic bird's nest, of prospect into the future.

The mention of Soest in this novel is a clear example of the possibilities it offers the reader for cross-reference and Simplician *Zusammenfügung* (combination). Springinsfeld has appeared in the *Simplicissimus* as the enterprising henchman of the Jäger von Soest (books II-III) and in the *Courasche* as a naïve youngster, the slave and assistant of the arch-deceiver. Now, he limps into our present time as a decrepit but unregenerate old soldier, still violent and foulmouthed. Simplicissimus reproves his comrade, who has aged, but not learned:

> ... du alter Geck / es ist nit mehr um die Zeit die wir zu Soest belebten und unserm Muthwillen nach gleichsam über das gantze Land herrschten; du must ietzt mit deiner Steltzen nach einer andern Pfeiffen tantzen.(22)

> [... you old fool, the times are gone when we were at Soest and could command the whole country, so to speak, as the fancy took us; now, you and your peg-leg must dance to a different tune.]

This passage is a direct evocation of the lapse of time, and also one of the relatively rare explicit examples of cross-reference by the characters themselves within the framework of the cycle: from Westphalia in the mid-1630s (wartime) to the Upper Rhine in 1670 (peace). The three major figures have roamed far and wide over a period of some seventy years (Springinsfeld is approaching the end of his natural span) and occasionally, their paths have crossed. Another example of such cross-reference occurs when Courage (who appears via Philarchus's account of their meeting) refers to her encounter with Simplicissimus at the spa and Simplicius caps her story of deception, emphasizing again the difference between then and now (*Springinsfeld* 28–9; cf. *Courasche* 128–9, *ST* 391–2). The whole cycle takes place within a network of time and space — often precisely indicated — that could indeed be indicated in the form of maps,[17] though to superimpose the three itineraries one on the other would produce a hopeless confusion graphically. The question here is whether the consciousness of this time-space network will operate in the reader's mind to produce, sometimes explicit cross-reference, sometimes just an awareness of a greater whole within which the vivid individual events occur.

The reader, an ideal reader of course, has all the novels available for perusal, re-perusal, and comparison. One passage need not necessarily cancel out another. Time passes, and things and people change, and from the perspective of Eternity, to which Grimmelshausen can also refer, such phenomena evoke universal concepts, such as that of *vanitas*. But within the temporal framework of the cycle, each individual moment still stands, valid in its own right. The sprightly younger Springinsfeld, for example, beside the raddled old soldier. The main point is that they can be envisaged one beside the other and in the awareness of the context (above all that of ever-moving, actual time) in which they live. We know that Springinsfeld has been in thrall to and trained in the arts of deception by Courage — and indeed, in case we have momentarily forgotten, our memory is jogged in the *Springinsfeld* (31–2). We know how he and Simplicissimus worked together at Soest: the passage we have quoted is clearly written in the expectation that the reader will be able to refer independently to the relevant parts of *Simplicissimus*. If reference back is possible here, reference forward in time (that is, "back" to

Simplicissimus) will have been equally possible in the case of the relevant chapters in the *Courasche*, as Courage herself hints, in her jeering way, to Simplicissimus, whom she imagines reading her book. She, of course, has read his.

The passage quoted from *Springinsfeld* is clearly written in the expectation that the reader will come to this book with a knowledge of *Simplicissimus* (which Springinsfeld, of course, does not have, so that he cannot make cross-references in his own narrative), and be able to place the Soest sequence from that novel alongside the present situation where the older men are reunited in a Strasbourg inn. This latter encounter is precisely timed by the opening words of the book: "verwichne Weyhnacht-Mes" (last Christmas-tide, that is, towards the end of 1669). Simplicius himself gives a reasonably close timing of the Soest episode ("over thirty years ago": 15) and cross-checking, we find that this fits well enough: Simplicissimus comes to Soest (*ST,* book II, chapter 30) fairly soon after the Battle of Wittstock in 1636 (described in chapter 26). The men themselves have aged, but Germany has moved on as well: from the order of wartime, when might was right, to the social and moral order of peace. Springinsfeld, alas! has not made the psychological and moral transition with it. He has, in fact, not been able to settle and has left Germany for foreign wars; otherwise he has existed (as has Courage) on the fringe of society.

This theme (the polarity of wartime and peacetime existence) is a constant through the cycle and is articulated as early as chapter 4 of the first book (*ST* 17) by means of a direct address to the reader, who is addressed as a "lover of peace," but must be taken into a scene of pillage because the story demands that "die liebe posterität" (dear posterity) be shown "was vor Grausamkeiten in diesem unserm Teutschen Krieg verübet worden" (what atrocities were perpetrated in this German war of ours). The reader is part of the posterity referred to: he knows about the war, but has not experienced it. He knows the world of peace, whereas "damals," as the narrator puts it a little later, "[stunde] gantz Teutschland in völligen Kriegsflammen" (then, all Germany was totally enveloped in the flames of war). Coming to the Soest passage in *Springinsfeld*, he will no doubt recall with some enjoyment the escapades of Simplicissimus and Springinsfeld there, but also the fact that when the soldiers ruled, so to speak, no man's property was safe. There was a breakdown of the social order which the present day reader may find hard to relate to his own experience. Springinsfeld as narrator makes a similar point in the chapter 16 following the description of the Battle of Nördlingen, in which he tells of the siege he has to endure in a deserted village, pinned down by a pack of wolves. He feels he has to tell the story, he says, "ohnangesehen ihrer viel / denen der damalige elende Stand des ruinirten Teutschlandes unbekant / mir solches nicht glauben werden" (although many of those, to whom the depth of wretchedness a ruined Germany was reduced to at that time is unknown, will not believe me: 87). At such moments, the potentiality of a time-framework that can enable the reader to envisage the cycle as a whole seems to be realized.

The reader cannot know the circumstances of the past from personal experience, but he is clearly expected to have a conception of the principal events and battles of the war. It is part of his history. He will know the dates and locations of the more important battles, such as Nördlingen (1634), which decisively halted the tide of Protestant victory, and even when he does not do so with the precision that Grimmelshausen, who has the *Teutscher Florus* and *Theatrum Europaeum* to hand, can achieve, the details dispensed with such liberality will add up to a framework of solid historical and geographical reality that is common to the life histories of the various characters and enables the reader to relate them to each other. Occasionally, as we have seen, the state of a character's knowledge permits cross-reference within the text. The *Courasche*, in which the narrator is constantly looking over her shoulder at the enemy whom she wishes to "show up," is naturally the book in which explicit cross-reference most often occurs. We know that Courage is older than Simplicissimus, as he was born after the Battle of Höchst (1622: another reference point).[18] She was already a lively young thing at the outbreak of the war itself, and just as others have preceded him in enjoying her favours (*Courasche*, 25), so she takes pleasure in revealing that she trained Springinsfeld in the roguish arts in which he later showed his "dexterität" in Soest, during the Italian campaign of 1629 (*Courasche*, 103, 107). As we can work out for ourselves, Simplicissimus was at that time no more than a "Bub," capable at best of tending his Dad's pigs in the Spessart. The three very disparate figures are consciously related together within the framework of time and space.

Discussing the aftermath of Nördlingen, Courage draws a parallel between the stages of life that she and Simplicius reached in that year (1634, when he was about twelve, and she approximately twenty-seven years of age): "dergestalt sein wir meiner Rechnung und deiner Lebens-Beschreibung nach / zu einer Zeit zu Narren worden" (So that according to my reckoning and what you say in your life history, we were made fools of at one and the same time: 126). When Springinsfeld, traversing the same ground, appears as a scavenger on the battlefield of Nördlingen (chapter 15), there can of course be no explicit cross-reference (he does not know the other two novels), but it would be quite natural for the reader (who does) to see the three figures momentarily side by side in time, and in their different stages and places in life. And, of course, in the context of war. They are widely separated, individual and distinct, but all encompassed within the same framework.

In times of peace, or of detachment from war, the sense of precise actual time and concrete reality is noticeably weaker, and the reflective, even allegorical tendency correspondingly stronger. Between the sieges of Breisach (1638), which precipitates the reunion with Herzbruder, and of Offenburg

(1645), which sends Simplicissimus off on his travels to Russia and elsewhere, the most prominent sequence is the strongly satirical Mummelsee episode, in which Grimmelshausen's realist vein manifests itself mainly in the curious nature of the sights and beings his hero experiences. When Simplicissimus returns to his farm, the Thirty Years' War is at an end and as far as he is concerned, a period of indeterminacy ensues, one which encompasses the most transcendentally oriented part of the whole corpus, the *Continuatio*. In this book, which we have described as a phase of "reaction," the incipient sense of a cycle that could possibly have been generated in Grimmelshausen's mind by the idea of a retrospective narrative corpus, extending from the early seventeenth century to the present, fades into the background. It is renewed at the very end, however, by the *Beschluß*, where it begins to take firm shape for the first time. The *Courasche* then fills in detail from the earlier years of the war and Springinsfeld's story casts the net wider still, so that on the platform (as we have called it) finally established by the latter novel, a cyclical perspective is finally and definitively possible. War has, in fact, been the constitutive and moving principle, and while it is replaced by the bird's nest at the point when the narrated time has more or less caught up with that of the narrator, its constitutive function is finally reasserted with a reference to the beginning of the Dutch Wars, a more or less contemporary event. When Grimmelshausen points to the future — and in effect to the resumption of the flow of time — as he does through the figure of the Young Simplicius, he envisages for the young man a career as a soldier (*VN* I, 106).

We have not, of course, forgotten the duality of time for Grimmelshausen, as for any truly baroque writer. Time has its transcendental as well as its earthly aspect; eternal, as well as temporal welfare needs to be considered. As Simplicissimus, in penitential mood, says (as indeed the young Simplex had been taught by the hermit), "die edle Zeit" is "noble" because it is given to man so that he may use the moment to ensure his eternal bliss ("zu meiner Seeligkeit anlegen": *ST* 456). And it is to this perspective that we return at the end of the cycle. The eternal is, to use our earlier phrase, the parallel path that runs alongside the temporal. The eternal perspective can also provide a kind of unity for the whole, in that each single event is related to it as all the points on the circumference are to the centre of a circle, and the sequence of events can therefore be interrelated by constant reference back to that centre. This is of particular importance for the *Vogelnest*, whose orientation becomes progressively more theological, and correspondingly less Simplician as the cycle gradually inclines towards a conclusion. But just as the Simplician manner eschews the "Theologische[r] stylus" (*Continuatio* 472), so the life that is described in the cyclical *Lebensbeschreibung* itself (that is, the life *within* the circle) is preponderantly the temporal, not the eternal one. An attempt to derive the structure of the cycle from the transcendental perspective would lead to distortion and obscure much of what makes Grimmelshausen particularly remarkable and valuable as a writer. There are, then, two types of coherence, and they operate simultaneously, but the one that enables the reader to truly link the various books is surely that of actual time. The transcendental, for Grimmelshausen, is not (as we can see from his handling of the hermit motif) a matter of withdrawal from life, but a perspective from within it. And our human life is not a perfect circle, but a conglomeration of points in time.

And this is important, since the eternal perspective is essentially reductive; it tends to rob the detail of its living individuality, whereas the temporal leaves room still for the variety of life. The one has the stillness of the perfect circle; the other (which we know is bounded by the perfect circle, as the snake with its tail in its mouth surrounds the contents of the *Ewigwährender Kalender:* see figure 2, page 196), allows for the dynamic quality and the inclusiveness and variety without which the Simplician corpus would not be Simplician. One knows that the series cannot go on for ever, but there is still a sense of violence in the way in which Grimmelshausen tears himself away from it in part 2 of the *Vogelnest.* One feels that we have here a loose structure which could contain so much more, or, to quote the verse on the S-shaped strip inside the circle in the *Kalender* engraving, "Ich fasse der selben je lenger je mehr" (The more of it [I am given], the more I can hold).

The figures on the outer circle in that engraving represent, after all, the four seasons, and suggest a process that is constantly renewing and repeating itself. The engraving does not itself stem from Simplicissimus, but his "Vorred und Erinnerung" is included, and this contains a commentary on the principle of composition, namely an "ordentliche Unordnung," (ordered disorder) in which material is intermingled "mit Fleiß" (deliberately). Rosmarie Zeller sees in this concept a realisation by Grimmelshausen of the mutually "contradictory" nature of the material assembled, leading in turn to a "deep insecurity."[19] But Simplicius does not, surely, despair of coherence, even in an apparently wilful confusion. Paradoxically, it seems as if the first step towards understanding is to accept confusion, to be willing to read horizontally as well as vertically (splitting the material into separate "matters"). The vertical "ordentliche Folg" (normal order) will not lead the reader to understanding, but if he "repeats the reading" (as the "disorderly order" is designed to make him do), he will be able to more truly grasp ("eigentlicher fassen") the work's coherence.[20] It is the coherence of earthly life. Out of an impression of disorderly variegation there arises the principle of coexistence.

This is not the first time that Grimmelshausen has seemed to flaunt a principle of disorder. In the *Satyrischer Pilgram*, the carping critic Momus objects that the musketeer/Greifnson has created a work that lacks all "Ordnung" and likens him to the pilgrim who was driven out by a satyr because he blew hot, then cold. The author accepts the title of pilgrim in deliberate defiance of the criticism, and Greifnson, in his postscript to the foreword, explains that this is being done to reflect the essentially mixed nature of all earthly things.[21] Both the author of the tract and the author of the calendar assert the principle of variegation, and claim that it is compatible with unity; a coherence of variety and multiplicity which can surely only be contained within the infinitely flexible context of life itself.

Can we carry something of this compositional principle over to the idea of the Simplician novels as a complementary group, and in particular the concept of a reader who is able and willing to read again, to interlink and cross-refer, to grasp the unity of the network? Both the calendar and the *Vogelnest* preface, after all, use the phrase "eigentlich fassen." Does Grimmelshausen perhaps intend (or sense), that by scanning and re-scanning the lives, indeed the Life he has given us, with its infinite breadth and variety within a common progressive framework of time, we would see that the human condition is to be both temporal (and therefore changing, inconstant) and eternal (still and constant) — and simultaneously so? It is clear that he cannot have meant the reference to "Simplicissimus's life history" literally. The figure of Simplicissimus, it is true, remains alive throughout, but after the *Continuatio*, he stays, at most, on the sidelines, and in part 2 of the *Vogelnest*, not even that. The books concerned are "Simplicianisch" by virtue of the manner of their narration. The word "life" here has to be a concept capable of expanding to include all that happens within a particular sphere, something akin to the "vision of life itself" which Dorothy van Ghent has seen as the unifying structural principle of *Don Quixote*.[22] While the term "Lebensbeschreibung" itself seems to be associated with the biographical/autobiographical tradition of the picaresque, Grimmelshausen (who undoubtedly learned from this tradition, with its relatively loose and episodic form), is here developing it for his own purposes.[23] He doubtless wishes to retain the quality of flexibility, but at the same time to indicate a unity which he has come to see in his own work, as a reflection, perhaps, of the nature of life itself: unity without loss of vitality or variety.

But "Lebensbeschreibung" cannot be "Life"-description unless it is open-ended. We have to return once more to the idea of a structure based on circularity, the representation of eternity and the life whose end is in its beginning, as is alleged by Rosemary T. Morewedge in the case of the *Simplicissimus*.[24] Here, the theological perspective seems to assert itself. A. A. Parker has argued strongly that the Spanish picaresque biography is informed by a religious principle, influenced by the *vitae* of the saints,[25] which suggests a circular progress: a departure from God and a return to God, an eventual conversion. Parker points out that Ägidius Albertinus introduced such an ending, a "religious direction," independently in his rendering of Alemán's *Guzmán de Alfarache*,[26] a work which of course influenced Grimmelshausen. But while we know that Grimmelshausen was strongly interested in the vitae of the saints,[27] and, more important, that he concluded not just the *Simplicissimus*, but also the whole sequence of novels, with a conversion, we have to take account also of the Protean nature of Simplician reality.[28] As we have seen, if we focus on the phenomenon of life itself, we recognize that it never can and never will stop, for all the repetitions and revisitations that it contains, until the only final "Ende," which is not the end of any individual life, but the end of the world. True, Grimmelshausen's characters can grow old, even die — as in the case of Springinsfeld — but young ones appear to enter the struggle, and open a perspective into the future. The two bearers of the bird's nest are much younger than Simplicissimus (who may still be hovering in the background); they will outlive him, and while the nest itself is no more, they have unfinished business. And above all, there is the Young Simplicissimus to consider as an indication of the continuity of life, even if Grimmelshausen has, in all probability, no intention of writing that *Lebensbeschreibung*.[29]

These are loose ends, the Young Simplicissimus, who has not even begun a career, patently so: a denial of the motionlessness of a final conclusion. Time, in the Simplician world, has a dual nature. As "eternity," it has shape (the circle) and constancy. Man has access to it through the mind and spirit, but this is not the element within which he lives. This latter, time as temporality, cannot be pictured. It is finite, but indefinite in extent and full of movement and change, an unbounded space, stretching further than the eye can see in any direction. In its latter aspect, as a constitutive structural principle, it requires the extension of the Simplician sequence to include the *Vogelnest* novels, an extension that might even be said to be prefigured in the Young Simplicius's preface to the *Kalender*. It would not have been impossible to end tidily with the *Springinsfeld*. Just as the *spiritus familiaris* and the Leirerin are consumed in fire in that book, so the nest could have met its end in either fire or water, and Springinsfeld's conversion could have been incorporated into the action proper. But Grimmelshausen felt the need to carry the theme of human life and of the war for man's soul into present and future time, and magic, hitherto less prominent, now becomes the major motive force that enables him to do so, acting as a channel both for temporal and eternal concerns and disrupting the normal course of events in both comic and serious ways.

We can essay a provisional, and inevitably, speculative answer to the question of the kind of integration and comprehension implied in the *Vogelnest* preface. In fact, the word "integration" has proved a false friend, in that it seems to imply harmonisation, and, indeed, meaning (which in turn places a question-mark behind the word "comprehension"). It is hard to see how life can have a clear unitary meaning: unless, of course, one detaches oneself from it, which Grimmelshausen will not, or cannot do. But that does not mean that life within a structure of temporality is necessarily totally lacking in coherence. One can see how, if the object is to find an over-arching "meaning" based on transcendental points of reference, Gaede can come to speak of "Substanzverlust," or Axel Schmitt of a structural principle of "wechselseitige Suspendierung, ja Ent-deutung der einzelnen Bedeutungselemente" (mutual suspension, indeed de-signification of the individual significatory elements).³⁰ While Grimmelshausen does not deny the authority of eternity and eternal values, and eschews any kind of moral relativism, he will not subordinate his description of life to a structural framework derived from "eternal" and universal sources. This, it could be argued, would involve the reduction of individual reality to general terms, and in consequence, to the loss of that vitality which endows even a reprobate like Courage with a certain existential validity. A framework based on temporality — the coexistence in time of a wide variety of figures and events — might offer the best chance of a coherent — yet Simplician — cycle. We can grasp ("eigentlich fassen," as the *Vogelnest* preface has it) that the merriment of the prank played by Simplicissimus on the miserly notary of Cologne (*ST* book III) and the spiritual insights of Simplicissimus on the Island of the Crosses are different but coexistent parts of one whole. This is not "menschliches Leben selbst vor aller bewußten Formung" (raw life, unformed by artistic hand), as Leo Domagalla calls it³¹ but a cunning and flexible format which enables us to understand life in its spiritual context, from the perspective of eternity, without destroying or indeed truly interrupting the flow of its material vitality. The ideal and the "real" perspectives need not be mutually exclusive, as long as neither seeks to impose its absolute authority over the other. This, surely, is cognate with the essential tolerance that is the hallmark of the comic vision. Grimmelshausen the thinker can be reconciled with Grimmelshausen the serious, but essentially comic, storyteller.

Notes

[1] Cf. Streller, *Grimmelshausens Simplicianische Schriften*, 133 and ff.

[2] Meid, *Grimmelshausen: Epoche-Werk-Wirkung*, 155 ("reicht nicht aus . . .").

[3] *Simplicissimus*, book III, chapter 19, 265: " . . . als er eben in meinem Joseph lase."

[4] Cf. S. H. Olsen, *The End of Literary Theory* (Cambridge: Cambridge U.P., 1987), 205–6.

[5] *Teutscher Michel*, title page.

[6] *Vogelnest* I, 157: "Ich als ein ungelehrter Idiot."

[7] Ibid., 150.

[8] Meid, 155.

[9] Rohrbach, *Figur und Character*, 35 (thematic links or connections).

[10] Cf. "Vorred oder Momi placat," *Satyrischer Pilgram*, 7: "ein Werck . . . das sich ad infinitum hinein erstreckt," and W. Bender, introduction to Grimmelshausen, *Satyrischer Pilgram*, ix. Koschlig (*Das Ingenium Grimmelshausens*, 144) considers the "ad infinitum" reference to be a hint at a calendar project inspired by Colerus, and sees the *Ewigwährender Kalender* as a "Vorstufe" of the Simplician works.

[11] Haberkamm gives the date of completion as August 1669; publication was in 1670: cf. "Beiheft" to Grimmelshausen, *Ewigwährender Kalender*, ed. K. Haberkamm (Konstanz 1967), 3–4.

[12] *Ewigwährender Kalender*, 96.

[13] Ibid., 92 (Dritte Materia).

[14] Ibid., 204.

[15] *Springinsfeld*, 13. According to the preface to the so-called "Calender-Simplicissimus" (1670), rushed out by Felßecker to counter a pirated edition and claiming (falsely) to contain the *Ewigwährender Kalender*, the precise date is 7 September 1669: cf. *Springinsfeld*, x.

[16] E.g. 124: "Ich war damahl noch zimlich glatt und annemlich . . ."

[17] Cf. *Simplicius Simplicissimus. Grimmelshausen und seine Zeit.* (Münster, 1976), 89 (Simplicissimus), 118 (Courage), and 119 (Springinsfeld).

[18] Courage makes a capture at Höchst, and Springinsfeld is also present at this battle. As Aylett points out, the characters are "moving around simultaneously in a real world" (*The Nature of Realism*, 142). It is, however, the "plausibility" of Grimmelshausen's work (146) that interests Aylett, not, as in our case, the simultaneity, which helps to underpin our sense of a framework of time and space.

[19] R. Zeller, "Die ordentliche Unordnung als poetologisches Prinzip in Grimmelshausens *Ewig-währender Kalender*," *Simpliciana* 16 (1994), 131.

[20] "Das Lesen zu wiederholen / auf daß du alles desto eigentlicher fassen möchtest," *EWK*, 3.

[21] *Satyrischer Pilgram*, 6–7, 10, and 13.

[22] Cf. Menhennet, "Baggy Monster," 113

[23] For the theme of freedom in relation to the picaresque, see A. A. Parker, *Literature and the Delinquent* (Edinburgh, Edinburgh U.P., 1967). On looseness of structure and the "vision of life," cf. Menhennet, "Baggy Monster."

[24] See Rosemary T. Morewedge, "The Circle and the Labyrinth in Grimmelshausen's 'Simplicissimus,'" *Argenis* 1 (1977), 373–409. On the subject of circularity, cf. also W. Müller-Seidel, "Die Allegorie des Paradieses in Grimmelshausens Simplicissimus," in *Medium Aevum. Festschrift für Walter Bulst*, ed. H. R. Jauss/ D. Schaller, (Heidelberg 1960), 253–78.

[25] Parker, *Literature and the Delinquent*, 21.

[26] Ibid., 79.

[27] Cf. Ilse-Lore Konopatzki, *Grimmelshausens Legendenvorlagen*.

[28] For the Protean aspect, cf. also B. L. Spahr, "Protean Stability in the Baroque Novel," *Germanic Review* 40 (1965) and F. Gaede, "Das Beschreiben bei Grimmelshausen," *Simpliciana* 12 (1990), especially 180.

[29] Though it is true that in his dedication to the *Ewigwährender Kalender*, the Young Simplicius expresses his willingness to "serve [the reading public] further."

[30] Cf. A. Schmitt, "Intertextuelles Verwirrspiel. Grimmelshausens Simplicianische Schriften im Labyrinth der Sinnkonstitution," *Simpliciana* 15 (1993), 71.

[31] L. Domagalla, *Der Kalendermann Grimmelshausen und sein Simplicissimus* (Würzburg 1942), 141.

Figure 2: Title engraving from the Ewig-währender Kalender

Works Consulted

Primary Sources

Ägidius Albertinus. *Der Landstörtzer Gusman van Alfarche* (1615). Reprint, ed. J. Mayer, Hildesheim: Olms, 1975.

——. *Hirnschleiffer*. (1618) Ed. L. Larsen, Stuttgart: Hiersemann, 1977.

Beer, Johann. *Die teutschen Winter-Nächte. Die kurtzweiligen Sommer-Täge*. Ed. R. Alewyn. Frankfurt am Main: Insel, 1963.

Buchner, August. *Anleitung zur deutschen Poterey*. Ed. M. Szyrocki. Tübingen: Niemeyer, 1966.

Greflinger, Georg. *Der Deutschen Dreyßig-Jähriger Krieg* (1657). Reprint, ed. P. M. Ehrle. Munich: Fink, 1963.

Gryphius, Andreas. *Gesamtausgabe der deutschsprachigen Werke*. Vol. 1. Ed. M. Szyrocki. Tübingen: Niemeyer, 1963.

Harsdörffer, Georg Philipp. *Frauenzimmer Gesprächspiele* (1641-42). Reprint, ed. I. Böttcher, 8 vols. Tübingen: Niemeyer, 1968–.

——. *Poetischer Trichter* (1660–1663). Reprint in 1 vol., Darmstadt: Wissenschaftliche Buchgesellschaft, 1969.

——. *Der große Schau-platz jämmerlicher Mordgeschichte[n]*. (1656) Reprint. Hildesheim: Olms, 1975.

Höck, Theobald. *Schönes Blumenfeld* (1601). Ed. K. Hanson. Bonn: Bouvier, 1975.

Hoffmannswaldau, Christian Hoffmann von. *Herrn von Hoffmannswaldau und anderer Deutschen auserlesener und bisher ungedruckter Gedichte erster Teil*. Ed. A. G. de Capua and E. A. Phillipson. Tübingen: Niemeyer, 1961.

Moscherosch, Johann Michael. *Wunderliche und wahrhafftige Gesichte Philanders von Sittewalt* (1642). Ed. W. Harms. Stuttgart: Reclam, 1986.

Opitz, Martin. *Buch von der deutschen Poeterey* (1624). Ed. R. Alewyn. Tübingen: Niemeyer, 1963.

——. *Gesammelte Werke*. Ed. G. Schulz-Behrend. Vol. 1. Stuttgart: Hiersemann, 1968.

Rist, Johann. *Sämtliche Werke*. Ed. E. Mannack. Vol. 2. Berlin: de Gruyter, 1972.

Schupp, Johann Balthasar. *Streitschriften I*. and *Streitschriften II*. Ed. C. Vogt. Halle: Niemeyer(?), 1910 and 1911 respectively.

Sorel, Charles. *Histoire Comique de Francion*. Ed. E. Roy. Paris, 1924. (First German translation, 1662).

Spee, Friedrich von. *Güldenes Tugendbuch* (1649). Ed. T. M. van Oorschot. Munich: Kösel, 1968.

Vondel, Joost van den. *De Werken van Vondel*. Ed. J. M. Sterck. 5 vols. Amsterdam: Maatschappij voor Goede en Goedkoope Lectuur, 1931.

Weise, Christian. *Die drey ärgsten Ertz-Narren von der gantzen Welt* (1672). Ed. W. Braune. Halle, 1898.

Ziegler und Kliphausen, Heinrich Anselm von. *Asiatische Banise* (1689). Reprint, Munich: Winckler, 1965.

Secondary Sources

Alewyn, R. "Realismus und Naturalismus." In *Deutsche Barockforschung*, ed. R. Alewyn, 358–71. Cologne/Berlin: Kiepenheuer und Witsch, 1965.

Allott, Miriam. *Novelists on the Novel*. 1959; reprint, London: Methuen, 1965.

Arnold, H. A. "Die Rollen der Courasche." In *Die Frau von der Reformation zur Romantik*, ed. B. Becker-Cantarino. Bonn: Bouvier, 1980.

———. "Moralisch-didaktische Elemente und ihre Darstellung in Grimmelshausens Roman 'Courasche.'" *Zeitschrift für Deutsche Philologie* 88 (1969): 521–60.

Ashcroft, J. "Emblems and Imagery in Grimmelshausen's 'Simplicissimus.'" *MLR* 68 (1973): 853–61.

Aylett, R. P. T. *The Nature of Realism in Grimmelshausen's "Simplicissimus" Cycle of Novels*. Berne/Frankfurt: P. Lang, 1982.

Barner, W. *Barockrhetorik. Untersuchungen zu ihren Grundlagen*. Tübingen: Niemeyer, 1970.

Battafarano, I. M. "Hexenwahn und Teufelsglaube im *Simplicissimus*," *Argenis* 1 (1977), 301–72.

Bechtold, A. *Johann Jakob Christoffel von Grimmelshausen und seine Zeit*. Heidelberg: Winter, 1914.

Benjamin, W. *Ursprung des deutschen Trauerspiels*. Ed. R. Tiedemann. Frankfurt: Suhrkamp, 1963.

Blühm, E. "Neues über Greflinger," *Euphorion* 58 (1964), 74–97.

Breuer, D. "Der sinnreiche Poet und sein ungewöhnlicher neuer Stil. Grimmelshausen und die europäische Argutia-Bewegung," *Simpliciana* 15 (1993), 89–103.

Clark, G. N. *Early Modern Europe*. London: Oxford U. P., 1966 (Opus 4).

Cysarz, H. *Deutsches Barock in der Lyrik*. Leipzig 1936.

Dallett, J. B. "Grimmelshausen und die neue Welt." *Argenis* 1 (1977), 141–227.

Domagalla, L. *Der Kalendermann Grimmelshausen und sein "Simplicissimus."* Würzburg 1942.

Enzensberger, H. M. *Nachwort* (afterword) to *Courasche,* by Grimmelshausen. Munich: DTV, 1963.

Ermatinger, E. *Barock und Rokoko in der Lyrik.* Leipzig 1926.

Feldges, M. *Grimmelshausens "Landstörtzerin Courasche." Eine Interpretation nach der Methode des vierfachen Schriftsinnes.* Berne: Francke, 1969.

Frye, N. *Anatomy of Criticism.* Princeton: Princeton U. P., 1957.

Gaede, F. "Das Beschreiben bei Grimmelshausen." *Simpliciana* 12 (1990), 179–93.

———. "Homo homini lupus et ludius est." *Deutsche Vierteljahrsschrift* 57 (1983), 240–58.

———. *Humanismus, Barock, Aufklärung.* Berne/Munich: Francke, 1971.

———. *Poetik und Logik. Zu den Grundlagen der literarischen Entwicklung im 17. und 18. Jahrhundert.* Berne/Munich: Francke, 1978.

———. *Substanzverlust. Grimmelshausens Kritik der Moderne.* Tübingen 1989.

Gebauer, H. D. *Grimmelshausens Bauerndarstellung.* Marburg: Elwert, 1977.

Gersch, H. *Geheimpoetik. Die "Continuatio des abentheurlichen Simplicissimi" als Grimmelshausens verschlüsselter Kommentar zu seinem Roman.* Tübingen: Niemeyer, 1973.

———. "Ein Sonderfall im Zeitalter der Vorreden-Poetik des Romans. Grimmelshausens vorwortloser *Simplicissimus.*" In *Festschrift Weydt,* ed. W. Rasch et al., 267–84. Berne/Munich: Francke, 1972.

Geulen, H. "Wirklichkeitsbegriff und Realismus in Grimmelshausens *Simplicissimus Teutsch." Argenis* 1 (1977), 31–40.

Gutzwiller, P. *Der Narr bei Grimmelshausen.* Berne 1959.

Haberkamm, K. "'Fußpfad' oder 'Fahrweg'? Zur Allegorese der Wegwahl bei Grimmelshausen." In *Festschrift Weydt,* ed. W. Rasch et al., 285–317. Berne/Munich 1972.

———. "Johann Michael Moscherosch." In *Deutsche Dichter des 17. Jahrhunderts,* ed. H. Steinhagen and B. von Wiese. Berlin: E. Schmidt, 1984.

———. *Nachwort* (afterword) to *Springinsfeld,* by Grimmelshausen. Stuttgart: Reclam, 1976.

Harms, W. "Emblem. Emblematik." In *Theologische Realenzyklopädie.* Berlin: de Gruyter, 1982.

———. "Hic et nunc. Satirische Funktionen lokalisierter Handlung in Moscheroschs 'Philander' und Grimmelshausens 'Simplicissimus.'" *Études Germaniques* 46 (1991), 79–94.

Harper, A. *David Schirmer: A Poet of the German Baroque.* Stuttgart: H. D. Heinz, 1977.

Hayens, K. *Grimmelshausen*. Oxford: Oxford U. P. 1932.

Herzog, U. "Barmherzigkeit — Die im Roman 'verborgene Theologie.' Zu Grimmelshausens *Simplicissimus*." *Argenis* 1 (1977), 257–77.

Heßelmann, P. "'Dessen Schwall mache Jesuiten verstummen.' Grimmelshausen und die Rhetorik." *Simpliciana* 15 (1993), 105–22.

———. *Gaukelpredigt, Simplicianische Poetologie und Didaxe. Zu allegorischen und emblematischen Strukturen in Grimmelshausens Zehn-Bücher-Zyklus*. Frankfurt: Lang, 1988.

———. *Simplicius Redivivus. Eine kommentierte Dokumentation der Rezeptionsgeschichte Grimmelshausens im 17. und 18. Jahrhundert*. Frankfurt am Main: Klostermann, 1992.

Hillen, G. "Allegorie und Wirklichkeit. Untersuchungen zu Prosatexten von Moscherosch und Grimmelshausen." *Daphnis* 19 (1990), 67–80.

Hübscher, A. "Barock als Gestaltung antithetischen Lebensgefühls." *Euphorion* 24 (1922)

James, Henry. *The Art of the Novel*. Ed. R. P. Blackmur. London 1935.

Jöns, D. W. *Das Sinnen-Bild. Studien zur allegorischen Bildlichkeit bei Andreas Gryphius*. Stuttgart: Metzler, 1966.

———. "Emblematisches bei Grimmelshausen." *Euphorion* 62 (1968), 385–91.

Kernan, A. B. *The Plot of Satire*. New Haven/London, 1965.

Kleinschmidt, E. "Die Wirklichkeit des literarischen Fiktionsbewußtseins und das Problem der ästhetischen Realität von Dichtung in der frühen Neuzeit." *Deutsche Vierteljahrsschrift* 56 (1982), 174–97.

Knight, K. G. "Die 'strafende' und die 'scherzhafte' Satire bei Grimmelshausen und Christian Weise." *Simpliciana* 15 (1993), 45–53.

Knopf, J. *Frühzeit des Bürgers. Erfahren und verleugnete Realität in den Romanen Wickrams, Grimmelshausens, Schnabels*. Stuttgart: Metzler, 1978.

Könnecke, G. *Quellen und Forschungen zur Lebensgeschichte Grimmelshausens*. Ed. J. H. Scholte. Weimar and Leipzig, 1926–8, 2 vols. Reprint in 1 vol., Hildesheim: Olms, 1977.

Konopatzki, I.-L. *Grimmelshausens Legendenvorlagen*. Berlin: E. Schmidt, 1965.

Koschlig, M. *Das Ingenium Grimmelshausens und das "Kollektiv."* Munich: Beck, 1977.

Kremer, M. "Wirklichkeitsnähe in der barocken Literatur. Zur Gestaltung der Realität bei Grimmelshausen und Beer." *Simpliciana* 13 (1991), 143–56.

Lämmert, E. *Bauformen des Erzählens*. 3rd. ed. Stuttgart: Metzler, 1968.

Leblans, A. "Grimmelshausen and the Carnevalesque. The Polarisation of Courtly and Popular Carnival in *Der abentheurliche Simplicissimus*." *Modern Language Notes* 105 (1990), 494–511.

Lugowski, C. "Literarische Formen und lebendiger Gehalt im 'Simplicissimus.'" In *Der Simplicissimusdichter und sein Werk*, ed. G. Weydt, 161–78. Darmstadt Wissenschaftliche Buchgesellschaft, 1969.

Mannack, E. "Grimmelshausen und das Monströse." *Simpliciana* 15 (1993), 149–62.

Mayer, G. "Die Personalität des Simplicius Simplicissimus." *Zeitschrift für Deutsche Philologie* 88 (1969), 497–521.

Meid, V. *Grimmelshausen. Epoche-Werk-Wirkung.* Munich: Beck, 1984.

———. *Nachwort* (afterword) to *Assenat*, by P. von Zesen. Tübingen 1967.

Mendilow, A. A. *Time and the Novel.* New York 1965.

Menhennet, A. "Cutting Linguistic Capers: The Title-Sequence of Grimmelshausen's *Teutscher Michel*." *German Life and Letters* 48 (1995), 277–91.

———. "Grimmelshausen, The Picaresque and the Large Loose Baggy Monster." *The Seventeenth Century* 1 (1986), 111–26.

———. "Narrative and Satire in Grimmelshausen and Beer." *MLR* 70 (1975), 808–19.

———. "Simplician Emblematics? The Title-Sequence of Grimmelshausen's *Springinsfeld*." *The Seventeenth Century* 9 (1994), 77–91.

———. "The 'Simplicianische Manier' in a Satirical Context: Grimmelshausen's *Teutscher Michel*." *MLR* 81 (1986), 646–54.

———. "The Three Functions of Hugo Peter in Gryphius's *Carolus Stuardus*." *MLR* 68 (1973), 839–42.

Morewedge, R. T. "The Circle and the Labyrinth in Grimmelshausen's 'Simplicissimus.'" *Argenis* 1 (1977), 373–409.

Müller-Seidel, W. "Die Allegorie des Paradieses in Grimmelshausens *Simplicissimus*." In *Medium Aevum Vivum. Festschrift für Walther Bulst*, ed. H. R. Jauss and D. Schaller. Heidelberg, 1960. 253–78

Negus, K. *Grimmelshausen.* New York; Twayne, 1974.

Noehles, G. "Das Titelkupfer zum *Simplicissimus Teutsch*." *Simplicius Simplicissimus. Grimmelshausen und seine Zeit.* Münster, 1976. 109–14.

Olsen, S. H. *The End of Literary Theory.* Cambridge: Cambridge U. P., 1987.

Parker, A. A. *Literature and the Delinquent.* Edinburgh: Edinburgh U. P., 1967.

Penkert, S. "Grimmelshausens Titelkupfer-Fiktionen." In *Internationaler Arbeitskreis für deutsche Barockliteratur. Erstes Jahrestreffen. Vorträge und Berichte.* Wolfenbüttel, 1973.

Petersen, Jürgen H. "Formen der Icherzählung in Grimmelshausens Simplicianischen Schriften." *Zeitschrift für Deutsche Philologie* 93 (1974), 481–507.

Praz, M. *Studies in Seventeenth-Century Imagery.* 2nd. ed. Rome 1964.

W. Rasch, H. Geulen, and K. Haberkamm, eds. *Rezeption und Produktion zwischen 1570 und 1730. Festschrift für Günther Weydt zum 65 Geburtstag.* Berne/Munich: Francke, 1972.

Robbins, B. "Death and Vocation: Narratizing Narrative." *PMLA* 107 (1992), 38–50.

Rohrbach, G. *Figur und Charakter. Strukturuntersuchungen an Grimmelshausens Simplicissimus.* Bonn: Bouvier, 1959.

Schäfer, W. E. "Laster und Lastersystem bei Grimmelshausen." *Germanisch-Romanische Monatsschrift*, n.s., 12 (1962), 233–43.

———. "Der Satyr und die Satire. Zu Titelkupfern Grimmelshausens und Moscheroschs." In *Festschrift Weydt*, ed. W. Rasch et al., 183–232. Berne/Munich, 1972.

Schmitt, A. "Intertextuelles Verwirrspiel. Grimmelshausens Simplicianische Schriften im Labyrinth der Sinnkonstitution." *Simpliciana* 15 (1993), 69–81.

Scholte, J. H. *Zonagri Discurs von Waarsagern.* 1921. Reprint, Wiesbaden: M. Sändig, 1968.

Schöne, A. *Emblematik und Drama im Zeitalter des Barock.* Munich: Beck, 1964.

Schönert, J. *Roman und Satire im achtzehnten Jahrhundert.* Stuttgart: Metzler, 1969.

Sestendrup, M. "Die Illustrationen des 'Barocksimplicissimus.'" *Simplicius Simplicissimus. Grimmelshausen und seine Zeit.* Catalogue of exhibition at Westfälisches Landesmuseum für Kunst- und Kulturgeschichte, Munster Landesverband Westfalen, 1976. 103–7.

Simplicius Simplicissimus. Grimmelshausen und seine Zeit. Catalogue of exhibition at Westfälisches Landesmusuem für Kunst- und Kulturgeschichte, Munster Landesverband Westfalen, 1976.

Skrine, P. *The Baroque.* London: Methuen, 1978.

Solbach, A. "Erzählskepsis bei Grimmelshausen im *Seltzamen Springinsfeld*." *Simpliciana* 12 (1990), 323–56.

———. "Macht und Sexualität der Hexenfigur in Grimmelshausens *Courasche*." *Simpliciana* 13 (1986), 71–87.

Spahr, B. L. "Protean Stability in the Baroque Novel." *The Germanic Review* 40 (1965).

———. "Grimmelshausen's Simplicissimus: Astrological Structure?" *Argenis* 1 (1977), 7–29.

Spellerberg, G. *Verhängnis und Geschichte. Untersuchungen zu den Trauerspielen und dem "Arminius"-Roman Daniel Caspers von Lohenstein.* Bad Homburg: Gehlen, 1970.

Stopp, F. J. "Reformation Satire in Germany." *Oxford German Studies* 3 (1968), 53–68.

Streller, S. *Grimmelshausens Simplicianische Schriften. Allegorie, Zahl und Wirklichkeitsdarstellung.* Berlin: Rütten & Loening, 1957.

——. "'Ob gienge ich zuviel Satyricè drein.' Traditionslinien und Wandlungen in Grimmelshausens Satireauffassung." *Simpliciana* 15 (1993), 35–44.

Tapié, V.-L. *The Age of Grandeur.* 1957. Reprint, London: Weidenfeld, 1969.

Tarot, R.: "Grimmelshausens Realismus." In *Festschrift Weydt*, ed. W. Rasch et al., 233–65. Berne/Munich: Francke, 1972.

——. "Grimmelshausens *Simplicissimus* und die Form autobiographischen Erzählens." *Études Germaniques* 46 (1991), 55–77.

——. "Simplicissimus und Baldanders. Zur Deutung zweier Episoden in Grimmelshausens Simplicissimus Teutsch." *Argenis* 1 (1977), 107–29.

Trieffenbach, P. *Der Lebenslauf des Simplicius Simplicissimus. Figur-Initiation-Satire.* Stuttgart: Klett-Cotta, 1979.

Valentin, J.-M. "Du rire au plus haut savoir. Sur les écrits poétologiques de Sorel et Grimmelshausen," *Études Germaniques* 46 (1991), 95–111.

——. "Grimmelshausen zwischen Albertinus und Sorel." *Simpliciana* 12 (1990), 135–57.

——. "Théologie et esthétique. Sur le chapitre premier de la *Landstörtzerin Courasche.*" *Études Germaniques* 42 (1987), 278–90.

Van Ingen, F. "Krieg und Frieden bei Grimmelshausen." *Études Germaniques* 46 (1991), 35–53.

Vosskamp, W. *Romantheorie in Deutschland. Von Martin Opitz bis Friedrich von Blanckenburg.* Stuttgart: Metzler, 1973.

Weydt, G. *Der Simplicissimusdichter und sein Werk.* Darmstadt: Wissenschaftliche Buchgesellschaft, 1969.

——. "Grimmelshausen und Homer." *Simpliciana* 8 (1986), 2–17.

——. *Nachahmung und Schöpfung im Barock.* Berne/Munich: Francke, 1968.

——. *Nachwort* (afterword) to *Courasche*, by Grimmelshausen. Stuttgart: Reclam, 1971.

Wiedemann, C. "Barockdichtung in Deutschland." In *Deutsche Literatur in Humanismus und Barock*, ed. B. Könnecke and C. Wiedemann. Frankfurt am Main: Athenaion, 1973.

Wiethölter, W. "'Baldanderst Lehr und Kunst.' Zur Allegorie des Allegorischen in Grimmelshausens *Simplicissimus Teutsch.*" *Deutsche Vierteljahrsschrift* 68 (1994), 45–65.

Windfuhr, M. *Die barocke Bildlichkeit und ihre Kritiker.* Stuttgart: Metzler 1966.

Zeller, R. "Die 'ordentliche Unordnung' als poetologisches Prinzip in Grimmelshausens *Ewig-währender Calender.*" *Simpliciana* 16 (1994), 117–36.

Index

The first part of the index aims to reflect the nature of the Simplician Cycle by singling out in discrete sections the names of the fictional figures (with the exception of the most common) and geographical locations which help to constitute its structural network. An index of other names follows, and this is followed by an index of topics.

Simplician Figures

Baldanders 71, 96–7, 100–02, 107, 116 (n. 15), 141
"Einsiedel" 9, 17, 30–32, 36, 38, 56, 83, 91, 105–6, 114, 133, 160
Greifnson von Hirschfeld, Samuel 97, 111–12, 135, 141, 179–80, 181, 190
Herzbruder, elder 75, 93 (n. 15)
Herzbruder, younger 8, 36, 72, 75, 83–4, 86, 104, 107, 145, 188
"Jupiter" 70, 86
"Knan" 18, 67, 141
"Leirerin" 129, 143, 144, 146, 149, 150, 152, 154, 155–7, 161–2, 163, 170, 171
Lumpus ("Colonel") 50, 146–7
"Meuder" 9, 67, 141, 143, 185
Musai 71, 110
Olivier 8, 72–4, 79, 89, 174, 182
"Schermesser" 41–5
Young Simplicius 141, 142, 152, 162, 169, 173, 184, 189, 192; as author 181

Geographical Names

Albania 149
Antilles 96
Amsterdam 172
Armenia 152
Balkans 180
Bavaria 4, 157 (n.7)
Black Forest 136
Bohemia 124, 125, 128
Breisach 4, 188

Cairo 102
Cologne 79, 89, 90
Crete 145, 149, 153

Danube River 46

Egypt 97
Europe 108, 110, 111

Gaisbach 4
Gelnhausen 3
Glogau 9
Griesbach 104, 132, 185

Hamburg 52
Hanau 3, 56, 67, 71, 79–80, 169
Herbsthausen 135, 137
Höchst 92 (n.9), 188
Holy Land 97
Hungary 149, 183

Italy 183, 188

Kassel 4
Kinzig River 4

Lippstadt 68, 76–7
Lützen 144

Magdeburg 4, 72, 75
Mummelsee 69, 75, 78, 141, 189

Nördlingen 3, 67, 92 (n.9), 144, 153, 154, 187, 188
Nuremberg 10, 67

Offenburg 4, 134, 188

Paris 37, 38, 68, 76, 78, 89, 106
Philippsburg 32
Pomerania 72
Prague 22, 124

Rench River 4
Renchen 5, 115, 148, 171, 180, 184
Rhine River 4, 172, 173, 186
Russia 189

"Sauerbrunnen" (spa): see Griesbach
Soest 72, 75, 76, 89, 143, 151, 185–7
Spessart 3, 17, 188
Strasbourg 4, 141, 184, 187
Switzerland 83, 97, 103, 171, 180

Venice 145
Vienna 125

Westphalia 4, 180, 186
Wimpfen 134
Wittstock 4, 89, 134, 183

Other Names

Aesop
Albertinus, Ägidius 33, 82, 88, 94 (n. 42), 119, 121–2, 131, 160, 175, 191
Aleman, Mateo 51, 121, 191
St. Alexius 97
Amadis of Gaul 40
St. Antony 31

St. Augustine 42

Bakhtin, Mikhail 87
Ballantyne, Robert Michael 32
Beer, Johann 34–5, 42, 51, 116 (n. 7)
Belvedere Palace 10
Birken, Sigmund von 42
Bossuet, Jacques Bénigne 10
Brant, Sebastian 55
Bruegel, Pieter, the Elder 49, 183
Buchner, August 11
Bunyan, John 45, 149
Busch, Wilhelm 79

Canisius 175
Capuchins 167
Cervantes Saavedra, Miguel de 40, 43–4, 70, 84–5, 103, 191
Charles I, King of England 9
Circe 99, 100
Colerus (Christian Köler) 194 (n.10)
Cologne, Elector of 58
Compton Burnett, Ivy 95 (n. 45)
Cromwell, Oliver 9

Democritus 16
Derrida, Jacques 158 (n. 18)
Dickens, Charles 87

Eichendorff, Joseph, Freiherr von 31, 65
Elter, Johann Burkhard von 4
Erasmus, Desiderius 14
Eugene, Prince, of Savoy
Eulenspiegel, Till 16, 66, 125

Faust chapbook 11, 66
Ferdinand III, Holy Roman Emperor 9
Fielding, Henry 120
Finckelthaus, Gottfried 14
Fischart, Johann 70
Fortunatus 11, 66, 169

Garzoni, Tomasso 22, 99, 137
Gifford, William 71
Goethe, Johann Wolfgang von 181
Götz, Johann Wenzel von 4
Greflinger, Georg 8, 14
Grimmelshausen, Johann Jakob
Christoffel von: Life 3–6
Works by:
Barocksimplicissimus 162
Bart-Krieg 58
Continuatio des abentheurlichen Simplicissimi 5, 14–15, 41–5, 52, 57, 65, 72, 80, 96–118, 141, 160, 167, 169, 180, 181, 183, 184, 185, 189,191
Das wunderbarliche Vogelnest 5, 8, 9, 15, 16, 33, 37–8, 39–40, 43, 92 (n. 12), 100, 107, 110, 111, 123, 150, 152, 158 (n. 13), 160–78, 179, 180, 181, 182, 183, 184, 185, 189, 190, 191, 192, 193
Der abentheurliche Simplicissimus 5, 6, 8, 16, 17,20, 21, 22–4, 29–34, 37, 38–9, 39–40, 43, 48–50, 55–7, 58, 65–95, 96, 99–100, 104, 105, 107, 109, 110, 111–12, 113, 114, 129, 141, 148, 152, 156, 160, 165, 168, 175, 179, 180, 181, 182, 185, 186, 187, 191
Der erste Beernhäuter 16, 181
Der seltzame Springinsfeld 5, 6, 8, 9, 15, 16, 18, 32, 35, 42, 48, 50, 54–5, 55–6, 80, 84, 87, 102, 110, 112, 114, 124, 137–8, 141–59, 161, 179, 180, 181, 184, 185, 186, 187, 192
Der stoltze Melcher 53–4, 171
Dietwalt und Amelinde 5, 14, 15, 16, 32, 35, 112, 113, 115, 179, 180

Ewigwährender Kalender 5, 180, 181, 184–5, 190, 192, 194 (n. 10)
Gauckel-Tasche 109
Kalendersimplicissimus 180, 194 (n.15)
Keuscher Joseph 5, 9, 71, 90, 93 (n. 13), 110, 112, 169–70, 180
Lebensbeschreibung der Ertzbetrügerin . . . Courasche 5, 6, 19, 46–8, 87, 110, 112, 119–140, 141, 144, 146, 152, 154, 155, 156, 161, 172, 174, 175, 179, 180, 181, 182, 185, 186, 187, 188, 189
Proximus und Lympida 5, 14, 32, 35–6
Rathstübel Plutonis 5, 18–20, 84, 110, 128, 146, 172
Satyrischer Pilgram 5, 16, 18, 78, 84, 86, 97, 154, 179, 180, 184, 190
Simplicianischer Zweyköpffiger Ratio Status 110, 112, 115
Teutscher Michel 5, 16, 17–18, 20, 21–24, 88, 181
Verkehrte Welt 86
Grimmelshausen, Melchior Christoph 3
Gryphius, Andreas 7, 9, 10, 28–9, 101, 133
Guevara, Antonio de 30, 88, 112
Gustavus Adolphus, King of Sweden 144

Habsburg Dynasty 6
Harsdörffer, Georg Philipp 7, 11, 12, 23, 51, 67, 124, 146, 171
Henniger, Catharina 4
Heraclitus 52
Hobbes, Thomas 158 (n. 14)
Höck, Theobald 10–11
Hoffmann, Ernst Theodor Amadeus 37

Hoffmannswaldau, Christian
    Hoffmann von 29
Hogg, James 119, 121
Holy Roman Empire 5, 6, 7
Homer 17
Horace 16, 39, 51, 113

James, Henry 87
Juvenal 71

King Arthur 92 (n. 12)
Kueffer, Johannes 4
Kuhlmann, Quirinus 70

Lauremberg, Johann 14
Lazarillo de Tormes 51
Lazarus (the beggar) 79, 156, 165
Leibniz, Gottfried Wilhelm 15, 85
Lipsius, Justus 28
Lohenstein, Daniel Casper von 8–9,
    29, 35, 89
Louis XIV, King of France 5, 53,
    170–1
Lucian 14, 17

Machiavelli 74
Meistersinger 10–11
Melander, General Peter 145
Mercy, General Franz von 145
Milton, John 15, 102
Molière, Jean-Baptiste Poquelin de
    16
Moscherosch, Johann Michael 12–
    14, 15, 18, 20, 45, 55, 57, 69, 89
Moscherosch, Quirin 15

Nebuchadnezzar 109
Neville, Henry 96
Nicolai, Philipp 31

Opitz, Martin 8, 10, 11, 51
Ovid 35

Pappenheim, Gottfried Heinrich,
    Graf von 144

Paracelsus 105
Perez, Andrea 51, 129
Picara Justina see Perez
Pliny 43
Prokop von Templin 167
Pythagoras 16

Rachel, Joachim 55
Ramsay, James 3, 36
Rist, Johann 7, 9–10, 14
Rochefort, César de 96, 98
Rosweyde, Heribert 31

Sachs, Hans 9, 10, 11, 96, 100–01
Schauenburg, Carl Bernhard von 4
Schauenburg, Hans Reichard von 4
Schirmer, David 11
Schupp, Johann Balthasar 12, 14,
    52–4, 57, 167
Schütz, Heinrich 7–8
Sellar, Walter Carruthers 151
Shakespeare, William 15, 33
"Silver Star" Inn 4–5
Sophocles 136
Sorel, Charles 13, 20, 35, 36, 57, 82,
    116 (n. 13), 120, 138 (n. 8), 160,
    161
Spee, Friedrich von 11–12
Spinola, Ambrogio 146
Strasbourg, Bishop of 5

Templin: see Prokop
Teutscher Florus 188
Theatrum Europaeum 188
Tolstoy, Lyev Nikolayevich 136, 184
Tscherning, Andreas 12, 13

Versailles, Palace of 10
Vittoria Colonna 99
Vondel, Jan van den 9

Wallenstein, Albrecht Wenzel
    Eusebius von 9, 25 (n. 14)
Weise, Christian 15, 16, 111, 167,
    177 (n. 15)

Wickram, Jörg 9, 11
Winter Palace 10
Witsch, Johannes 4

Yeatman, Robert Julian 151

Zesen, Philipp von 11, 16, 169–70
Ziegler und Kliphausen, Heinrich Anselm von 36

Index of Topics

abentheurlich 66, 69, 71, 81, 92 (n. 12), 97, 98, 152
absolutism 9–10
"alamode" 13–14, 19, 20, 57
allegory 6–7, 34, 40–50, 51, 70, 78–9, 80, 81, 96–105 *passim*, 106, 114, 119, 120, 123, 124, 125, 129, 135, 136, 144, 145, 147, 152, 163, 167, 188
anagram 18, 111, 112, 115, 117 (n. 34), 179, 180, 181
anecdote 24, 33, 80, 135, 146
anti-courtly style 12–14
aristocratism 9–10, 15, 23, 170
asceticism 31, 84, 107, 114, 153, 160
astrology 144
authorial principle 34, 37–8, 39–40, 72, 83, 84, 86, 107, 110–12, 114, 120, 127, 154, 168–9, 179, 180–1 (see also: Greifnson)
autobiographical narrator 65, 68, 72, 83, 91, 112, 119, 151, 164, 185, 189, 191
avarice 79, 96, 103, 106

baroque 8, 9–12, 14, 6, 17, 23, 28, 39, 51, 66, 75, 88, 89, 90, 100, 109, 122, 129, 130, 154, 180, 189
beggar motif 142, 143–51, 153
Bestia motif 32, 48, 67
"book of nature" 99, 108, 167, 173

capitalism 45
carnevalesque 87, 156
Catholicism 4, 6, 35, 121, 172
change (*Veränderung, Wechsel*) 35, 38–9, 66, 68, 71, 85, 96, 100–01, 147, 191
chiliasm 69–70
circularity principle (structure) 189–91
Classicism 50
clown-figure 15, 23, 45, 68, 113
coexistence principle 30–2, 34, 37–8, 40, 44, 51, 58, 75, 77–82, 119, 148, 164, 182, 183, 190, 193
cold (and warmth) symbolism 135–7, 141–2, 144, 147, 148
comic intention 10, 13, 19–20, 22, 23, 32, 35–40, 42, 43, 46, 47, 50, 57, 68, 70, 73, 76–7, 79, 83, 102, 103, 115, 128, 132, 135–7, 144, 145, 152–3, 156, 157, 163, 165, 172, 183, 193 (see also: *Posse, Schwank*)
Communion 152
conceit (baroque) 53, 54, 90, 122
conclusiveness 92 (n. 11), 108, 109–15, 173, 176
Confession 33, 121
conscience 121, 122, 164 (see also: *Leichtfertigkeit*)
constancy 7, 28, 35–40, 68, 71, 142, 170, 191
curiositas ("Fürwitz") 42, 133
cursing 153, 186
cycle 5, 34, 110, 113, 115, 142, 150, 151–7, 161, 173, 174, 179–95

deconstruction 180–1, 192–3
Devil 75–6, 79, 82, 97, 100, 125, 126–8, 129, 130, 137, 150, 155, 160, 170, 171, 173–6
devotional literature 108, 114, 164, 175
dialect 32, 89
"discourse" (narrative) 84

dream-visions 41, 75, 106
Dutch literature 11
Dutch Wars 5, 53, 170–1, 189

emblematics 28, 69–71, 96, 97, 99, 101, 116 (n. 6), 130, 145–6, 162, 167, 176
Enlightenment 12, 29
epigram 100
eschatology 69, 109, 112, 175
exegetics 41, 42, 48, 80, 163, 167
exemplum 81, 122, 136, 145, 146
extravagance 96, 103, 106

fantasy 42, 70, 78, 84, 102
farce 24, 47
fate 8, 33, 86, 121, 135, 146, 147
Fathers (of the Church) 30
folly 17–18, 32–3, 56–7, 69, 81, 83, 133, 147, 150, 154, 188; (ignorance) 32, 56–7, 68, 74
forest motif 32, 67, 74. 81, 83, 106, 133
fornication: see *luxuria*
Fortune 6, 8, 9, 36, 50, 68, 75, 82, 85, 121, 133, 145, 161, 169
Frau Welt 47–8, 128
frontispieces 41, 66, 68–72, 84, 146, 162, 190
freedom motif 35, 87, 106–7, 125, 132, 150–1, 154, 169, 170, 171
French fashion 19, 20 (see also: alamode)

gambling 75, 93 (n. 15)
"Gaukeltasche" 141
"Geistesgeschichte" 28
German (*Teutsch*) 12–14, 18, 19, 20, 23, 69, 80, 119; German patriotism 7; "German War" 6, 48, 146, 187
ghost story 103–5, 113
gluttony 79, 81, 99, 162
God (as agent, presence) 7–8, 9, 10, 37, 67, 74, 82, 86, 99, 100, 106, 107, 112, 121, 126, 128, 131, 133, 145, 160, 161, 163, 165, 168, 169, 171, 175–6, 191
grace (of God) 160, 165, 172, 175
gypsies 48, 87, 124, 125, 127, 134, 135, 141, 154

Hell 29, 72, 96, 101, 102–3, 149, 161
hermit motif 29–30, 36, 40, 69–72, 96, 97, 114, 171 (see also: "Einsiedel")
heroic novel 36, 76, 170
humanism 8, 10, 11
humility 43
hymn 11, 31

illusion 162–3, 168
imagination (in poetry) 100
individuality principle 50, 51, 55, 75, 79, 81, 82, 123, 132, 143, 144, 146, 167, 172, 183, 186, 190
irony 22, 23, 66, 72, 79, 91, 110, 119–138 *passim*, 151, 154, 162, 163, 165, 166, 168
invulnerability ("Festigkeit") 160, 172, 174, 176

Jewry 74, 166, 172
judgement motif 38, 45, 69, 112, 161

"Kipper und Wipper" 61 (n. 30)

language 17–18, 23
Latin 10
learning 15–16, 18, 70, 170
Lebensbeschreibung (narrative form) 65, 111, 142, 146, 148, 168, 173, 182, 185, 189, 191
Leichtfertigkeit (lack of conscience) 32, 76–7, 121, 122, 129, 133, 146, 155, 159 (n. 22)
libertinage 35, 36

"lustig" (entertainment) principle 23–4, 40, 45, 51, 58, 72, 78, 79–81, 84, 122, 166
luxuria (lust) 37, 46, 76–7, 78, 99, 123, 125, 129, 130, 160, 162
lyric 31

magic 8, 37, 72, 100, 128–9, 152, 153, 158 (n. 13), 160, 162, 165, 170, 171–5, 182–3, 192
manner (Simplician) 5, 20, 24, 30, 32, 34–5, 38, 41, 45, 57, 58, 71, 78, 81, 84, 85, 109, 111, 122, 123, 148, 162, 168, 176, 182, 189, 191
marriage 54–5, 87, 126–7, 130, 132, 134, 151, 165
medieval characteristics 37, 41, 42, 47, 99–100, 114
melancholia 171, 174
"Merodebrüder" 72, 87
Messianism 70
middle class 9, 10
moderation 107
money 106, 117 (n. 18), 146, 171
mons veneris 37, 68, 76
moralising 35, 36, 37–9, 50, 57, 69, 76, 79, 96, 105–9, 119, 161, 163, 167
musketeer motif 4, 16, 32, 37–9, 50, 52, 57, 58, 69, 76, 79, 96, 105–9, 119, 161, 163, 167
mysticism 99

narrative 33, 34, 38, 41–58 *passim*, 49–50, 51, 52–8, 65, 68, 72, 74, 77–91, 100, 103, 105, 119, 122, 130, 141, 154, 162, 165, 183 (see also: autobiographical narrator, *Schwank*, *Stücklein*)
Nativity 28
natural magic 102, 152
"nature" (as force) 120, 124, 129–30, 133, 173
negative example 121, 122, 145

neo-Aristotelian thought 28
network structure 142, 151–2, 181, 186, 191
niederer Roman: see picaresque
"nightingale" hymn 31, 83
novella 142, 146

oddness (*Seltzamkeit*) 45, 66, 71, 72, 74, 81, 83, 84, 93 (n. 12), 97, 98, 101, 102, 105, 128, 130, 136, 141, 152, 156, 162, 163 (see also: *abentheurlich*)
order, reversal of: see *verkehrte Welt*
outsider 16, 120, 124, 146, 152, 154, 171, 187 (see also: cold)

paradise motif 97, 101
parallel paths (structure) 34, 82–8, 121, 122, 148, 166, 189
parody 45, 88, 91, 121, 175
peace (and war) 96, 102, 108, 109–10, 141–2, 150, 152, 160–1, 171, 186, 187
peasantry 4, 13, 18, 67, 101, 122, 135–7, 171
Petrarchism 57, 129
phoenix image 68
picaresque 22, 36, 37, 39, 48, 50, 51, 65, 82, 86, 92 (n.6), 102, 119, 141, 152, 173, 182, 191
poet (concept) 11, 39
Posse, "possierlich" 38, 45, 51, 52, 56–7, 61 (n. 37), 66, 76, 79, 113, 135, 147, 163, 176, 184
preacher-figure 32–3, 46, 76, 121, 122, 151, 174
pride 17, 42, 75, 81, 122, 124
Prodigal Son 38, 53–4, 171
prosody 10
proverbial language 17, 74, 89, 90, 143, 153
Providence 9, 35–6, 48, 68, 86

reader (-awareness, -involvement) 39, 48, 80, 81, 86, 100, 105, 109,

125, 131, 141, 149, 152, 166, 180, 185, 186–9, 190, 191
reality, realism 3, 28–35, 40–58 *passim*, 61 (n. 30), 68, 68, 70, 84, 98–9, 101, 103, 104, 129, 133, 134–5, 146, 147, 162, 166, 167–8, 180, 188, 191
rebellion 9, 88, 131, 132, 144
Renaissance 8, 10, 11
repentance 121, 170, 171, 175–6
retrospective narration: see autobiographical narrator
rhetoric 9, 11, 12, 16, 39, 88–91, 92 (n. 11), 115, 149, 165, 175
Romanticism 31, 92 (n. 6)

salvation 108, 109, 112, 114, 120, 154, 160, 161, 171, 173–6
satire 12–14, 20, 21–4, 34, 39, 41, 42, 45–6, 50–8, 68, 69, 75, 78, 80, 86, 103, 115, 120, 122, 123, 132, 152, 162, 163, 167, 169, 172
Satyr 69, 190
Schwank 50, 104, 114, 127, 158 (n. 18)
self-knowledge 69, 165
sequel technique 110, 170, 179
sexuality: see *luxuria*
shell and kernel motif 42, 45, 51, 98, 113, 167
Simplician (quality) 5–6, 16, 17, 19, 21, 23, 24, 33, 34, 36, 37, 39, 50, 51, 58, 67, 81, 102, 148, 153, 162, 165, 168, 170, 174, 180–1, 189 (see also: Manner)
Simplicianisation 71, 110
Sin (condition) 75, 78, 103–5, 107, 119–22, 123, 150, 154, 160, 172, 174, 176
sixteenth century 9, 10
sloth 71, 109, 160, 162, 171
social dimension 15, 18–19, 23–4, 26 (n. 42), 75, 87–8, 120, 121,

124, 131, 141, 144, 147, 150, 169, 187
Socratic method 123
soldier 33, 72, 87, 128, 141–2, 143–51, 153, 170, 171, 187, 189
Spanish picaresque 51, 65, 191
Sprachgesellschaften 24
stoicism 8, 87
Stücklein 80, 135
structure 82–7, 112, 113, 142, 166, 179–95
sugared pill motif 39, 45, 113, 167

"theological style" 33–4, 39, 45, 52, 84, 109, 113, 115, 167, 174, 189
Thirty Years' War 3–4, 6–8, 10, 24 (n. 4), 48–50, 67, 86, 108, 128, 130, 133–6, 143, 146–8, 184, 189
time 69, 78, 185–7, 189–90, 192–3
tropes 11
Turkish Wars 149, 183

Utopia (Isle of Crosses) 109

vanitas 28–9, 30, 38, 66, 68, 75, 78, 82, 85, 92 (n. 3), 92 (n. 11), 101, 133, 137, 186
variegation 23, 27 (n. 43), 66, 70, 74–5, 84, 85, 90, 101, 162, 180, 190, 191
Verhängnis 8–9 (see also: fate)
verkehrte Welt 34, 50, 88, 126, 148, 156
vigil 31
vitality 6, 22, 23, 33, 34–5, 36, 40, 48, 50, 61 (n. 30), 66, 68, 71, 75, 78, 82, 91, 119, 120, 122, 124, 125, 128–9, 133, 134, 138, 151, 153, 167, 168, 172, 176, 183, 191, 193
Volksbuch 11, 16, 66
Volkslied 11, 91, 100, 123, 124, 154

wit 89, 91, 100, 123, 124, 154

witch(craft) 126, 129, 130, 155,
    157, 173, 177(n. 20)
women (in seventeenth century) 36,
    54–5, 76, 123, 124, 125–6, 129–
    32, 140 (n. 30),172, 176 n.1)
word-play 89, 91
World (of sin) 66, 67–8, 70, 75, 80,
    81, 83–4, 91, 96–7, 98, 112, 114,
    120, 171
wrath 122

OHIO UNIVERSITY LIBRARY

Please return this book as soon as you have finished with it. In order to avoid a fine it must be returned by the latest date stamped below. All books are subject to recall after two weeks or immediately if needed for reserve.

OCT 17 2010

RECEIVED
SEP 29 2010

CF